WHY NOT
SAY WHAT
HAPPENED

Frontispiece: The boy in the sailor suit, who could not save his grandmother from dying, 1942.

For information about permission to reproduce selections from this book,
write to Permissions, Liveright Publishing Corporation,
a division of W. W. Norton & Company, Inc.,
500 Fifth Avenue, New York, NY 10110

For information about special discounts for bulk purchases, please contact W. W. Norton
Special Sales at specialsales@wwnorton.com or 800-233-4830

Manufacturing by Courier Westford
Book design by Helene Berinsky
Production manager: Louise Parasmo

Library of Congress Cataloging-in-Publication Data
Dickstein, Morris, author.
Why not say what happened : a sentimental education / Morris Dickstein. — First
edition.
pages cm
ISBN 978-0-87140-431-2 (hardcover)
1. Dickstein, Morris. 2. Jews—New York (State—New York—Biography. I. Title.
F128.9.J5D539 2015
974.7′043092—dc23
[B]
2014037881

Liveright Publishing Corporation
500 Fifth Avenue, New York, N.Y. 10110
www.wwnorton.com

W. W. Norton & Company Ltd.
Castle House, 75/76 Wells Street, London W1T 3QT

1 2 3 4 5 6 7 8 9 0

WHY NOT SAY WHAT HAPPENED

A Sentimental Education

MORRIS DICKSTEIN

LIVERIGHT PUBLISHING CORPORATION
A Division of W. W. Norton & Company
New York   London

ALSO BY MORRIS DICKSTEIN

Dancing in the Dark:
A Cultural History of the Great Depression

A Mirror in the Roadway: Literature and the Real World

Leopards in the Temple:
The Transformation of American Fiction, 1945–1970

Double Agent: The Critic and Society

Gates of Eden: American Culture in the Sixties

Keats and His Poetry: A Study in Development

ALSO BY MORRIS DICKSTEIN

The Revival of Pragmatism: New Essays on Social
Thought, Law, and Culture

Great Film Directors: A Critical Anthology
(coedited with Leo Braudy)

For Lore

with love always

Contents

Foreword

THE PAST IS PROLOGUE

❦

To knock at the door of the past was in a word to see it open to me quite wide.
—HENRY JAMES, A Small Boy and Others

The past is a foreign country: they do things differently there.
—L. P. HARTLEY, The Go-Between

THIS IS a ghost story, though I don't believe in ghosts. These pages are haunted by people long gone, including earlier versions of myself. Sometimes they've come back unbidden, like uninvited guests. More often I conjured them up to fill out the story of who I was, where I had been, whom I had known. "Why not say what happened?" wrote Robert Lowell in one of his last poems, "Epilogue," appealing simply for the grace of accuracy. We ourselves are tissues of memory, our recollections interwoven with our hopes and fears, desires and disappointments. When I've actually revisited places I once lived, such as New York's Lower East Side, powerful feelings spontaneously welled up. I've found myself drawn with burning curiosity even to scenes I had been eager to escape. Or else I would shuffle my memories like a pack of cards, feeling tiny spasms of pleasure, regret, or astonishment. Was that really me in that little drama? Did I actually say that, do that? Was I ever that smart, that fresh, that obtuse, that unforeseeing? How did I survive *that* one? Yet I never wanted to break off these encounters, to shout warnings at the movie screen, like Delmore Schwartz in his story "In Dreams Begin Responsibilities" as he watches the reel unfold of his mismatched parents' courtship. He stands up to admonish them never to marry, never to bring him forth. What an ambition, never to have been born!

There was a moment in 1966 when I came to realize how much past experiences resonated for me. My wife and I, still newlyweds, were living in New Haven during my last year as a graduate student in English at Yale. We had a modest ground-floor apartment on Beers Street, half a block from St. Raphael's Hospital, not more than five or six blocks from where I lived when I first came to town five years earlier. In 1961 I'd left my native city but brought my native customs with me. I had grown up in an Orthodox Jewish family in New York, where keeping the faith was an easy matter since everyone around me did much the same. Though I had by then left much of my religious observance behind, I needed an apartment I could share with roommates who, like me, would keep a kosher kitchen. The freedom, even the impulse, to break with this commitment was well beyond me; the attachments of a lifetime kept me in the fold. Luckily, two advanced graduate students in chemistry, also Jewish, also lightly religious, advertised for a third to share the rent, and I moved in with them. They were good fellows both, Marcel and Eli, agreeable and easy to live with, though apart from religion we had little in common.

I spent the first two years after college in that furnished flat at 98 Sherman Avenue, wrestling with my courses, working at assignments that kept me as busy as I'd ever been in my life. It was hardly a garret, but it was nestled under the eaves of a typical three-story New Haven frame house: three bedrooms, sparsely furnished, with a long hall that connected them to a small dining room and an even smaller kitchen in the rear. It was the first apartment I'd ever had and, spare as it was, I was thrilled to be on my own. The house was an easy mile from the Yale campus and even closer to a synagogue that had recently established a kosher kitchen providing dinners for a small group of Yale students several evenings a week.

So long as I kept the faith, even minimally, my years on Sherman Avenue were like going away without really leaving home. Reading and writing under fierce academic pressure, a regimen I loathed, I managed to get a world-class education in English literature on top of the less professional one I'd enjoyed as an undergraduate. In this apartment I finally lost my virginity one hot night in October 1962, not in my own messy and cramped bedroom, piled high with books and papers, but on neutral ground, the neatly made bed of one of my absent roommates. I had fallen in love with a woman I had met a few months earlier on a boat ride to Bear Mountain to celebrate Eli's coming nuptials. Two and a half years later, after many complications, including a year abroad, I married her.

So here we were, for a time the only tenants in our house on Beers Street. The neighborhood, the block, was rapidly turning black, and our landlord, a Korean, at first refused to rent to black people. My new wife would bike to work at Yale's biology department while I dithered on my thesis, trying at once to write and not to write it. My old student digs on Sherman Avenue were not far away but out of my usual orbit, almost forgotten. One day in 1966 I was out for a walk and happened to pass the building, which I hadn't seen in years. To my surprise, my consternation, it looked altogether deserted. Neither the ground-floor flat nor the landlord's place above it looked inhabited. I was distressed to think the building was empty, as if part of my old life had been hollowed out, never to be recovered. Perhaps the house was to be torn down, a rarity in New Haven, an economically depressed town where little changed from decade to decade. The place had the sad look of an abandoned house but to me it offered an irresistible temptation. What was happening there? Where had those years gone? I was growing agitated; my limbs were trembling slightly. I had been close to miserable the years I lived there but for some reason I had to see the place again.

I walked up a flight of stairs that felt familiar yet strangely unfamiliar, like an uncanny apparition. I knocked on what had been the landlord's door though no name was posted on it, but there was no sign of life. I went up another ghostly flight and tapped on the door of the old flat, though I had no idea of what to say when someone opened it: I once lived here? I'm a graduate of this building? For reasons I can't explain, I desperately need to see this apartment again? None of this made the least sense. When there was no answer to my third knock, I tried the door and it swung open. Folks often did not lock their houses then—those were halcyon times—but they certainly locked their apartments. Without quite intending to, I hesitantly walked in, assuming the flat was deserted. Soon it was clear that people *were* living there, and this annoyed me no end. What were they doing in my

old haunts? A moment later it also offended me. What right did they have
to be there? I looked into Marcel's old room, immediately to my left, and
saw a huge pyramid of empty beer cans stacked up against the wall, like
junk sculpture—not at all the way three good Jewish boys had been living.
And the scale was off; the apartment seemed much smaller than the one
I remembered. It must have expanded in my mind as it receded in time,
though scarcely three years had passed since I had been living there.

Everything seemed subtly askew, a touch hallucinatory, like the stylized
sets in *The Cabinet of Dr. Caligari* reflecting the disoriented perceptions of
a madman. The room that had been mine looked even more alien. The fur-
nishings were the same but differently lived in, and it seemed tiny compared
with my recollection of it. The long hall had shrunken to a modest corridor,
but with my heart thumping wildly out of fear and curiosity, my breathing
shallow, I had to explore all of it. Some urgent, headstrong emotion was
driving me and I was not in control. I expected that any moment someone
would step out from Eli's old room with a gun or a baseball bat and nail me
as an intruder. It was not the apartment I was burning to reclaim but a lost
fragment of the past. Bursting with some overweening need, I'd become a
kind of voyeur, trespassing on my own life. I left with a tremendous feeling
of excitement followed by a deep calm, a mood of relief and satisfaction.
Did I learn anything from this escapade except that it mattered to me?

The emotions I brought and still bring to this peculiar incident remind
me of one of my favorite poems. In 1798 William Wordsworth and his
beloved sister, Dorothy, revisited a scene on the river Wye, near the border
of England and Wales, that he had last seen five years earlier. The poem he
wrote about it proved to be his breakthrough as a writer, the moment when
he discovered his vocation and his deepest subject. He was twenty-eight,
not much older than I was in my New Haven incursion. The landscape
was the same but seemed entirely altered for him. He realizes how much
he himself has changed in those five years: grown, moved on, experienced
losses and gains. In language of ecstatic remembrance and sober reflection, he thinks back to his childhood, his youth, the wild feeling for nature
he can no longer sustain. In his very bones he experiences the passage of
time. With anticipation he thinks of the years ahead, imagining the present
turning into the past yet nourishing the future. Darkly he anticipates one

last inexorable change, his own death, and hopes his sister will think back to this very moment for consolation. In writing the poem he makes it a moment of communion, of consecration. He shares his faith that memory can endure even where life cannot.

With touching English reserve, Wordsworth gave the poem a long but modest title stressing the time and place rather than his feelings; it begins, "Lines Composed a Few Miles above Tintern Abbey . . ." As a reader and teacher I return to the poem again and again, never tired of it, never disappointed. Like Wordsworth's Immortality ode and his other poems about time and memory, it took on a freight of personal meaning for me, threading itself into my own emotional life. I can grasp what Wordsworth learned in revisiting the past, but what do I learn? What draws me to ghostly scenes of recollection like the one in that unassuming student flat on Sherman Avenue? Writing this book about my shaping years and earliest memories provided me with some answers. It was only as I completed it that I grasped what it was about: an education of the feelings as well as the mind, a journey from one world to another, from an immigrant Jewish family to a secular, cosmopolitan society, a coming of age in a culture that was itself going through startling transitions that inevitably carried me along. Yet also I found that I'd never quite left those early influences behind, and probably never would.

WHY NOT
SAY WHAT
HAPPENED

One

SHERMAN AVENUE

Iᴀʟᴡᴀʏꜱ ꜰᴇʟᴛ that if I hadn't come to Yale with an indestructible love of literature, serving time as a graduate student would have deadened it for me. There was little of the real teaching I had come to expect in college. After four consuming years at Columbia, living with colorful characters who remain friends to this day, studying with teachers whose memories I still cherish, the numbing routines of my first years of graduate work chilled me like a cold bath.

I had landed at Yale by pure chance. Despite long years as a college English major, I knew little about literary scholarship and had no idea where to apply except on the basis of prestige and reputation. Drawing up a lazy list of preferences, I had applied to Yale and Harvard and, despite good grades, was turned down by both. This was a surprise and a shock to my ego. Only the intervention of the Columbia College dean, the scion of an old New England family, John Gorham Palfrey, whom I had gotten to know from interviewing him as a student journalist, persuaded Yale to change its mind and take me in.

I was a brash Jewish kid from New York, no real scholar, hence not an especially good candidate for graduate work, at least the way it was understood in those days at schools such as Yale. Like so many people who pursue careers to literature, I had been smitten by the written word at an early age, and it was that consuming early love that finally landed me at Yale. Living on the Lower East Side until the age of nine, I haunted the Seward Park branch of the New York Public Library, which still stands, isolated and dwarfed by later housing projects. I can recall some of my favorite books from those green years, especially the sports novels of John R. Tunis, such as the baseball classic *The Kid from Tomkinsville*, about a rookie pitcher from nowhere who makes it as a pitcher for the Brooklyn Dodgers. I too felt like a kid from nowhere, besides being an insatiable baseball fan. I was also hooked on an eight-volume Civil War series by Joseph Altsheler, beginning with *The Guns of Bull Run*, centering alternately on the adventures of two cousins on opposite sides of the bloody conflict. I loved the portraits of colorful generals like Stonewall Jackson and was intrigued by the fratricidal violence of the conflict. Sports and American history would remain my reading passions for years to come, partly because they were far outside the limits of the urban immigrant world in which I was growing up.

In high school I burrowed my way through the branch library in Flushing, Queens, little more than a storefront overlooking the Long Island Rail Road station. Hungry to know, I found myself devouring books subject by subject, starting with anthropology. My life felt confined, pinched, and reading gave me access to a wider world. I was fascinated by Margaret Mead's books on growing up in Samoa and New Guinea, which contained titillating discussions of strange puberty rites. To a sheltered adolescent in the 1950s, they conveyed a seemingly natural relation of boys and girls to their bodies and to each other that I certainly envied, though they were as foreign to me as Samoa itself.

I eyed the books on the librarian's locked shelf, from which I managed to retrieve Norman Mailer's *Deer Park*, though I somehow missed the brief scene of oral sex that got the book rejected by its first publisher. My attraction to genuine literature took off when I read *A Tale of Two Cities* and *The Scarlet Letter* as a sophomore in high school. I was transported by Dickens's re-creation of the atmosphere of the French Revolution, even more by the architecture of his sentences and the intricacy of his plot, which tied every thread together with wondrous symmetry by the end. This diabolically inventive way of telling a story struck me so dramatically that I wanted to read the book again immediately to figure out how it was put together.

In Hawthorne too I could see the historical imagination at work, this time on the American past, but bolstered by an awesome symbolism that opened up the story's meaning. Hawthorne's austere, finger-pointing Puritans must have reminded me of some of the Orthodox Jews I'd grown up with, some lax, some strict, some joyous, but many of them prescriptive and forbidding, with long lists of dos and don'ts that weighed heavily on me. But I also was struck by Hester Prynne's sexual independence, her defiant refusal to feel ashamed. I could not imagine writing like Dickens or Hawthorne, but I could grasp their awesome themes and the precise carpentry that gave shape to their work. I found I loved language for its own sake, and this first glimmer of critical thinking lit up my reading experience.

The relish I took in the sheer craft of writing helped make me a painstaking reader, though some pedantic quality—a methodical cast of mind—must have played a part. I savored each sentence separately, remembered it, and had a visual recall of where on the page I had come upon it. But this plodding way of assimilating books—phrase by phrase—could not survive my freshman year at Columbia. In the core course in Humanities, a rapid succession of Western classics from Homer to Dostoevsky, we were expected to read a big book virtually every week, and I learned to keep up, though there were some books I couldn't finish. This galloping pace highlighted the big picture yet also demanded a fresh personal encounter with each work. Reading in translation tilted the course toward broad questions, so appealing to undergraduates—toward social and cultural history, not literary technique. It pressed students to reach for the human center of a writer's vision to see how it refracted the world around it. It spoke to us about the meaning of life itself and how it had been understood in starkly different times and places.

The benefit of faster reading, of taking books in with large gulps, had already struck me in my senior year of high school. In an English class we tortured *Macbeth* line by line for two months until I lost all sense of what was happening in it. On an impulse, after we were done, I read through the play in one sitting and was amazed at how it was transformed. The drama itself leapt out at me: the changes in the characters, the use of poetic language as speech, not as archaic phrases to be parsed and cast aside. This was what reading, what literary understanding, was all about—a human experience, wonderfully brought together, not a puzzle to be solved or a minefield to be carefully crossed.

Years later, in the required Anglo-Saxon course in my first year of graduate school, I had another bolt of recognition. In the hands of a venerable medieval scholar, John Pope, we studied the earliest English literature more as specimens of a foreign language than as poetry, patiently working through some forty lines of verse each day. One day the linguistic problems in a passage of *Beowulf* made this trudge especially tortuous, and as the class ended Professor Pope decided to go back and read the whole passage aloud. This he did in a remarkably gentle, mellifluous voice that softened the Anglo-Germanic gutturals into song. My ears perked up as if awakened by distant music, a rumble of poetic thunder, and I was awestruck. "That was beautiful," I said to him afterward. He stared at me, quizzically but benignly, as if I had borrowed an alien concept from some remote zone of language. The category of beauty, the ecstatic moment of personal transcendence, had little relevance to literary scholarship. He could feel it, could intuitively *perform* it, but somehow could not acknowledge it.

By 1961, when I arrived at Yale, the more ascetic forms of pure scholarship were already an anachronism. The spirit of modern criticism—the focus on the meaning and form of literary works—had by then made serious inroads into the university, not only for undergraduates but even in Ph.D. programs. Close reading had arrived in New Haven not long since, domesticated into a methodical rote, though there were still many gentleman scholars of the old school—some of them monastic bachelors, deeply closeted, who lived on campus, or wealthy eccentrics who took no salary. Their labors, sometimes Herculean, were bent to establishing facts and texts, not to appreciating beauty, form, or meaning.

For students the system seemed designed to promote facility rather than thinking. Most of the courses tied you to a rack, an inexorable cycle that made you produce a serious essay every third week. Class time was devoted not to teaching but mostly to hearing fellow inmates read their papers aloud, followed by perfunctory comment or discussion. It was imperative to synchronize your schedule so that your turn at writing came up in a different course each week. If you were that lucky, you had a day or two to research your essay, another day to write it, this on top of a mountain of reading.

To keep to this killing schedule it was important not to get caught up in any subject, simply to churn out eight or ten pages of serviceable prose on whatever was on tap that week. The result was coarse, invariably routine; it produced pedestrian stuff that dulled rather than sharpened your literary sense, if you still felt it. This industrial approach seemed designed to replace the vagaries of inspiration with professional versatility, sheer fluency. To my shame I became quite adept at it, though I strained to bring something of myself, some tincture of literary passion, to every assignment. For a journalist meeting the demands of deadlines this would have been valuable training; for a critic it constituted the slow death of the soul, bleeding from a hundred nicks and cuts. I watched some fellow students ground under; a few even dropped out by the end of the year.

One piece of good fortune: I had an unlikely but generous fellowship from the Danforth Foundation, which covered my expenses through all of graduate school—unlikely because this was a seriously Christian operation, funded by good people at the Ralston Purina cereal company. Starting a decade earlier, each year they had given a hundred fellowships to a hundred promising young Protestant gentlemen. After a few years this became a slight embarrassment, and by the late 1950s they had begun bestowing their munificence, typically, on ninety-seven Protestant gentlemen, two Catholics, and one Jew. Robert Alter, who would later make a fine career as a literary critic, translator, and biblical scholar, was the first of the tribe so honored, and I was, I suppose, the designated Hebe from the class of 1961.

I can guess how I came to receive this boon, which put bread on the table for the next five years. Besides one's academic record, College Board scores, and recommendations, it demanded evidence of serious religious affiliation, something I thought I could show. While at Columbia I had taken years of courses at the Jewish Theological Seminary, its neighbor on upper Broadway. I was always too busy to give them my full attention but one of my teachers, Dr. Ravid, was glad to testify on my behalf. He was a warm, amiable Israeli, fiercely devoted to the Hebrew language and its intricate grammar, but I suspect he was more impressed by my frequent articles for the *Columbia Spectator*, Columbia's undergraduate newspaper, than by my lackadaisical work in his Hebrew class.

The final hurdle for the fellowship was an interview with the director of the program, whose tack was rumored to be highly confrontational. Gruff and quick, with a needling sense of humor, he was the most searching inquisitor I'd ever come up against. With a gift for the unexpected question, he turned each interview into a high-wire performance. The decisive moment came when he summed up one thread of our exchange with the words "Judge not. . . ." My knowledge of the New Testament was negligible, but without a pause I responded, "that ye be not judged." This was hardly consistent with my reason for being there, for I *was* being judged, but it showed some acquaintance with a gospel different from my own. I suspect it clinched my fellowship, and we became fast friends for years afterward.

This generous program enveloped me like a family. It also became my introduction to a larger America, a Christian, midwestern America, not rural and philistine, not hidebound and conservative, as this provincial New York Jew might have expected, but socially responsible, at times even radical and pacifist—the very marrow of the old Protestant conscience. Just before the academic year began, fellows from all over the nation would assemble on the tranquil shores of Lake Michigan. It was a kind of boot camp of social communion, with evening vespers at the water's edge and speeches by Christian radicals like Mulford Q. Sibley, a seasoned pacifist whose vision combined religion and reform, peaceful protest with courageous militance. This proved to be a humbling lesson in American social history for someone who knew radicals only as urban intellectuals, labor militants, and working-class Jews.

One unexpected dividend of these orientation sessions was getting to know a few veteran Yale graduate students, who took me under their wing. They warned me off teachers whose names I recognized, and sent me to others, invariably younger, whose work was new to me. Cleanth Brooks's book *The Well Wrought Urn* had been one of my bibles as an undergraduate; it taught me to read poems like Keats's "Ode on a Grecian Urn" attentively, looking out for its undercurrents and subtexts, the delicate precision of its imagery and the timbre of its voice. Once an academic outsider as one of the original New Critics, Brooks, a diminutive, genteel, silver-haired southerner, was now at the conservative Anglo-Catholic heart of the department. But like so many scholars, he reserved his best insight for his writing and lent only his presence to his teaching. Now he took a gravely Christian, faith-based view of literature, as he announced mellifluously in an informal public program before my first semester began. He knew many modern writers, he said, but their work gave him, as a Christian, "no reason to doubt," a self-satisfied remark that, unfairly or not, disqualified him in my eyes. Skepticism and doubt, the misgivings of the modern mind, were deep in the grain of my education, hard to set aside or leave behind.

Instead of old-timers like Brooks, whose day was waning, my new Danforth friends urged me to sign up for relative newcomers like Martin Price, a rising star in eighteenth-century literature; Charles Feidelson, whose only book was a difficult but influential work on symbolism and American literature; and R. W. B. Lewis, a genial comparatist, fluent in French and Italian, who was also a pioneer in American Studies. I faithfully followed these insider tips and was rewarded with keener teaching, richer reading, and less superfluous make-work than most of my classmates. I was a budding Romanticist, already besotted by Keats and Wordsworth, but in pursuing a degree I had gaping holes I needed to fill, especially the neoclassical eighteenth century and the basic canon of American literature. With those deficits to be covered by working with Price and Feidelson, I felt free to take Lewis's course in modern European and American fiction for the pure pleasure of it.

Thanks to those advance pointers, I felt less estranged and had a less grueling year than anyone I knew. Their groaning filled our few idle hours. Gracious and polite but harried-looking, already graying in his early forties, Price was a shrewd, understated critic. He moonlighted as an omnibus fiction reviewer for the *Yale Review*, and his eighteenth-century course concluded with five delicious weeks on the poetry of William Blake, whom most scholars annexed to the Romantic era. (My first encounter with Harold Bloom was as a visitor to that class, where he gave an impromptu two-hour lecture, a nervous, virtuoso performance, on one of Blake's most gnomic poems, "The Mental Traveller.")

Charles Feidelson appeared as relaxed as Price was nervous and intense, with a wry, winsome smile that made him seem faintly amused by everything. He spoke with the musical lilt of a highly assimilated southerner, but he was also the first and only Jew awarded tenure in English at Yale, thanks to the unexpected success of his book. (Bloom, already a far more prolific writer, would eventually be the second.) Unlike most of his graduate colleagues, Feidelson was a lecturer who made each class count. His classes were like improvised essays in which he aimed to crack the code, to uncover the key, of each writer's work. After tackling the classics from Poe and Whitman to Henry Adams in the fall, we spent the whole spring term on Henry James's work, which kept me brooding about James for years to come. This would become Feidelson's own undoing. His career took a terrible turn as he struggled for decades, through draft after draft, to complete a book on James that stubbornly refused to come together. Only a small fragment of it was ever published, a talk he gave to Yale alumni on *The Portrait of a Lady*. This was a fate reminiscent of the James stories he asked us to read, such as "The Madonna of the Future," in which an artist never fulfills his grand ambition—to do a contemporary equivalent of one of Raphael's Madonnas. After a lifetime of preparation, he leaves behind only the merest sketch, something he did spontaneously at a moment of crisis, yet it is masterly.

Dick Lewis, only recently arrived at Yale, prematurely but youthfully gray, was something of a European aesthete and a stylish, elegant writer. A man of letters more than an academic, he seemed out of place at Yale, and he would ultimately make his greatest mark as a biographer of Edith Wharton and of the James family, not strictly as a literary scholar. His course on the novel was like a great-books seminar. He came in with little preparation other than three or four lines of typed notes, as if waiting for something intriguing to happen. Once he spoke with envy that many of us would be reading Henry James's seminal tale "The Beast in the Jungle" for the first time, an experience he could never recapture. Lewis's approach was unassuming, conversational, but the knockout syllabus was the selling point. Ranging from Stendhal's seductive *Charterhouse of Parma* to Camus's haunting last work, *The Fall*, it had nothing to do with my Ph.D. requirements in English. Instead it offered a Cook's tour of modern fiction, more in the spirit of my undergraduate courses. Like the class on Dostoevsky with René Wellek that I was auditing in comparative literature, much to the department's disapproval, it was my gift to myself, answering only to qualities banished from graduate study: pleasure, the sense of beauty, and the personal relation of reader to writing.

SCHOOL WORK seemed to take up a hundred percent of my time, yet I somehow found fugitive hours to publish my first articles and, almost simultaneously, to fall in love. Perhaps I was simply at the right age to strike out on my own, but writing and love also went hand in hand. Keen writing could only be founded on love, even baffled love, while strong feelings instinctively reached for electric language to express themselves. My relation to fellow students was based on some kind of love as much as on mutual suffering. This included an attraction to the smartest, least available women I knew at Yale. One of them, a woman with beauty and style beyond her years, soon married one of our more shallow classmates. Later, she went out to teach on the West Coast, and had a child before the marriage broke up. She would eventually become a celebrated biographer. The other was the daughter of a lesser-known abstract painter. She had straight dark hair, chiseled features, and one of the most cutting minds I had yet encountered. I had a sentimental soul, whereas she seemed tart and full of vinegar. This acid manner in a good-looking woman delighted and frightened me, but I guessed that her relationships were mostly with the faculty, not with fellow students.

Neither of these women was Jewish, an insuperable barrier for me at the time, but I also had nowhere near the confidence to approach them romantically, even though my self-assurance as a student spilled over into an arrogance I tried hard to conceal. I peppered them with conversation, an endless flow of chatter about books and ideas. No Don Juan, I had dated only a handful of women in college, always shyly, covering my diffidence with a bright, chirrupy manner. To the question of "What do women want?" I found it hard to imagine myself as an answer. It did not yet dawn on me that the exercise of intellect itself, as a way of being in the world, could be attractive to some women, precisely the women who would most appeal to me.

Few if any of the men in my class matched the self-possession of these smart women. It was hard to recall that women had been admitted to graduate study in English at Yale in significant numbers only a few years earlier, over the determined objections of some of the older faculty, including the world's leading authority on the work of George Eliot. I shudder to think of what life at Yale would have been like without them. Most of the male students I knew were diligence personified, already heading down the straight and narrow path of specialized scholarship. They were very different from the brainy nerds I had fallen in with at Columbia, whose interests were scattered all over the map, but who also moved to the exotic gyrations of whatever was currently happening in culture and politics, no matter what academic paths they had chosen.

The early sixties was not a moment to shut oneself up in a cubbyhole of premature specialization. Politically, the cold war was coming to a head with serial confrontations over U-2 flights over the Soviet Union, proxy warfare in the former Belgian Congo, the abortive Bay of Pigs landing in Cuba, and the Cuban missile crisis, which put us frighteningly on the cusp of nuclear war. But the cold war was also beginning to break up, and the signs of change were everywhere: ban-the-bomb demonstrations like some I had joined at Columbia, where we refused to take cover when the air-raid sirens sounded; worldwide student unrest, from Turkey to Japan; turbulent domestic protests against hearings by the House Un-American Activities Committee, the major relic of McCarthyism. These were well documented in the committee's own propaganda film, *Operation Abolition*, designed to expose and defame opponents of the committee. Instead, showings of the film on college campuses, like one I saw at Columbia, led to further agitation against the committee and the whole blacklist regime. From afar I admired the direct actions of civil rights demonstrators, such as sit-ins at segregated lunch counters and brave integration marches in the South. The cold war had muffled political dissent but now things were opening up, as if echoing the cacophony of radical voices we idolized in the political culture of the thirties.

There were also momentous changes in the arts that kindled and channeled the new rebellious spirit: often scandalous Beat poetry readings before immense audiences like one at Columbia in 1959; the lively bohemian folk music and coffeehouse scene that blossomed in Greenwich Village and in college towns, its roots in the old left-wing protest culture of the 1930s; the mind-bending new wave of foreign and low-budget independent films that challenged the Hollywood system and ushered in an exceptional moment of moviemaking and cinephilia; a vibrant modern jazz scene, linked with both Beat poetry and abstract expressionist art; and a restless, adventurous off-Broadway theater featuring the most innovative modern playwrights like Luigi Pirandello, Samuel Beckett, and Bertolt Brecht alongside provocative young American writers such as Edward Albee and Jack Gelber. Even in New Haven it was hard not to feel the tremors of this shifting landscape; they shook the cultural moorings of the stable world in which I had grown up.

Because few of my fellow students in English seemed moved by these new vibrations, I bonded with a handful of improbable characters in comp lit who were much more tuned to these upheavals. As curious, mercurial intellectuals rather than professionally focused scholars, they dealt with literature in a way that was usually more philosophical, more abstract than mine. Unknowingly, they were the advance guard of the turn toward theory that would take hold by the end of the 1960s, especially a strong revival of Marxism, which would play out in the streets as well as in the classroom. Shortly before arriving in New Haven, I had first heard the name of the Hungarian Marxist critic Georg Lukács from a young historian, Ronald Sanders, whom I had met in August on a fifteen-day sea voyage from Haifa to New York. Though as yet virtually unknown in England and America, Lukács, the major modern theorist of literary realism, was a legendary figure on whom Thomas Mann had modeled the character of Naphta in *The Magic Mountain*. He had twice served as minister of culture in short-lived Hungarian governments, first after a radical uprising soon after the First World War, later in Imre Nagy's reform cabinet in 1956. He was an orthodox Communist, Ron told me, but had been secretly executed, like Nagy, for his role in the 1956 revolution against Soviet domination.

This bit of news turned out to be false, but it triggered my warm friendship with a comp lit student from Brazil, Roberto Schwarz, whose hybrid name reflected his mixed background. He was born to professional Jewish parents in Vienna in 1938, but his family emigrated to São Paulo two years later, after the Anschluss had joined Austria to Nazi Germany. Already a consummate Marxist intellectual yet literary to his fingertips, Roberto was thoroughly ingratiating with men, charming and seductive

with women. His Viennese and Latin roots not only inflected his manners
but made him the most cosmopolitan personality I met at Yale. Despite his
radical politics, which later forced him into years of exile from Brazil, he was
as amused and fascinated by American life as he was engaged by European
ideas, especially the humanistic, Hegelian Marxism of what came to be
called the Frankfurt school. Roberto's thick, dark-rimmed glasses gave him
the look of a bohemian, someone at home in the cafés of the Left Bank,
but he had an infectious chuckle, as if the world's oddities never ceased to
amuse him, and an eccentric way with the English language that was all his
own. Thinking at once in several languages, he called much of the United
States west of the Hudson "the inner of the country."

We first met outside the office of the director of graduate studies in
English, a tough-talking medievalist named E. Talbot Donaldson, where
Roberto sought permission to take the Feidelson course in American literature. Somehow our conversation came around to Lukács, and he was
thunderstruck when I mentioned casually that I'd heard he was dead. (I
was prone to assume a knowing air on subjects I had only just encountered.) Later Roberto would provide not only a reader's guide to Lukács but
an early introduction to the work of Theodor Adorno, Max Horkheimer,
Walter Benjamin, and Ernst Bloch, all cultivated Marxists little resembling the hard-line style of the American Left, so deeply compromised by
Stalinism. Their aphoristic brilliance and theoretical heft swept me up,
in part as a refuge from the unimaginative scholarship that surrounded
me at Yale. They were gifted dialecticians whose work reminded me of
Hegel more than Marx. For years I would read these writers sporadically
in French translations, since little of their best work could be found in
English. But several members of our little circle, all fired up by Roberto,
went to Frankfurt to study directly with Adorno, the most difficult of all
of them, eventually becoming among the chief scholars and translators of
their work.

Unlike most Marxists, Roberto was concerned less with advanced
capitalist societies than with the special problems of underdevelopment,
which he saw crystallized in the fiction of the Brazilian novelist Machado
de Assis. He would work patiently for decades on Machado, and the books
he eventually produced, worthy of Adorno in their conceptual rigor, would

make Roberto one of Brazil's most respected critics. Much as this caught me up, my own bent, even as an apprentice critic, took a different tack. As an undergraduate I had begun reading *Partisan Review* and *Commentary*, the main literary outlets of the New York intellectuals, just at the moment when *Commentary*, under its feisty new editor, Norman Podhoretz, was shifting from liberal anticommunism toward a sixties-style radicalism. At Columbia I had studied with some of their leading contributors—Lionel Trilling, Fred Dupee, Daniel Bell, Steven Marcus. In my New Haven exile these magazines—along with others like the *Evergreen Review*, featuring the Beats, and the *Village Voice*, reporting on the avant-garde—were my lifelines to the New York cultural scene.

I led a Janus-faced life, for these splashy new currents in the arts were as alive to me as any literary scholarship. I saw Trilling when I was in New York and corresponded with Marcus, whose nineteenth-century course had been a highlight of my senior year. My impassioned letters about the chronic pains and occasional pleasures of graduate school must have impressed him, for a few months later he asked me to review a collection of essays by Herbert Gold for *Partisan Review*, beginning a connection that would survive, with many ups and downs, till the magazine folded over forty years later. Another review soon followed, of a similarly named writer, the novelist Ivan Gold. In maintaining the gold standard, I was off and running as a novice critic, writing for the rarefied upper reaches of a general audience, somehow finding the time to write in hours stolen from the punishing demands of my course work.

If Yale, almost against my will, made me something of a scholar, *Partisan Review* helped transform me into a writer. It worked muscles and sinews different from academic writing: more direct argument and the freedom to generalize, more punch and wit and polemical verve. The aim was to hook and even stun readers, not simply to enlighten them. The editors discouraged straight exposition, the academic habit of marshaling tons of illustrative detail, as well as the journalistic compulsion to explain everything, pitched to the least-knowledgeable reader. For me this meant less quotation, less reliance on pedantic step-by-step evidence that can make academic writing seem so . . . academic. Where Yale, one of the outposts of strictly formal criticism, demanded methodical research and close reading, the literary quarterly encouraged aphoristic writing, bold speculation, the flying aperçu. If Brooks, the New Critic, relished paradox, irony, and ambiguity in poetry, the New York critics inflected such destabilizing devices into their critical writing. Academic essays were invariably too long, pedantically repetitious, with far too much spelled out; literary essays were often too condensed, their views validated mainly by the tenor of a persuasive voice. For academic work in those days—how times have changed!—you donned the mask of impersonality; for magazine writing you put on the trappings of personality, the opinionated tone of a living person actually thinking, speaking, braving discriminations. One pretended to objectivity; the other made a show of being frank, even blatant in its partiality. They amounted to two different ways of claiming authority.

Partisan Review in those days was a byword for highbrow writing, a brand well known enough to draw a laugh in sophisticated stand-up comedy. The prospect of contributing to the magazine excited and terrified me, yet I took on the review with foolhardy self-assurance. I have no idea where that confidence came from. Sheer innocence? The habit of tackling school assignments? My first piece was a sweeping putdown of writing since the Second World War, complaining that too many novelists had shifted from concern with the larger society to a narrower preoccupation with the private life. It elicited a warm note from Irving Howe, already a luminary of the New York intellectual scene, inviting me to write for *Dissent.* This was the radical magazine he had founded in 1954 in response to what he called "this age of conformity," a phrase that was an indictment as much of the complacent comfort of his fellow intellectuals as of the whole Eisenhower era. Though most of them had briefly been Communists in the 1930s, then radical Trotskyists, all the New York intellectuals were now fiercely anti-Communist. But Howe and his friends remained socialists and social critics, while others, he felt, had made unholy accommodations to conservative forces that dominated American life since the war. They had largely defaulted on social criticism, turning their backs on the poor and the working class, but had also been weak in defending civil liberties against McCarthyism and witch-hunting.

Even with the 1960s barely under way, I was already on Howe's side of this issue, pining for a revival of the radicalism I dimly associated with the

1930s. But my own way of thinking was more literary than political, and the article on Lukács I proposed to him, after much dithering, duplicated one he already had in hand from Harold Rosenberg, the most brilliant and unpredictable of all these writers. As it turned out, I found no occasion to write for *Dissent* until a special New York issue twenty-five years later, and didn't actually meet Howe until the early 1970s. Yet I felt that his stamp of approval was an initiation into the intellectual scene I had admired from afar. By the time we finally met, the world of the New York intellectuals had fractured irretrievably, torn apart by the tumult of the preceding decade.

IF YALE and *Partisan Review* pulled me in opposite ways toward the world of scholarship, books, and ideas, where I dreamed of finding a place, other loyalties kept me solidly anchored in the Jewish world in which I had grown up. I still kept kosher, more as a familiar—and familial—tradition than as a matter of belief. Any other course was as yet unthinkable, and this kept me socially linked to like-minded Jews. One setting for these encounters was the kosher kitchen at the Young Israel of New Haven, an orthodox synagogue a mile from campus, offering dinner four nights a week for a handful of Yale graduate students. A year or two before I arrived, someone had trained a robust Polish housewife to make traditional Jewish meals, so that we, the fortunate few, might feel as if we had never left home. Yale was not a congenial university for observant Jews, who were very few then. Its atmosphere was strongly Anglo-Christian; it made no provision for Jewish holidays, religious services, or kosher food. Jewish kids fell back instead on the local community for whatever support they needed. My chemist room-mates, Marcel and Eli, introduced me to this kosher eating group and, if I was in town on weekends, to the services at the synagogue. There some families often invited students back to their homes for Sabbath meals. For the most part, town-gown relations in New Haven were either nonexistent or actively hostile, but the congregation's young rabbi, Aaron Gelman, had intellectual ambitions and was eager to reach out to Yale, since it offered so few options for Jewish life to its students. Thanks to the synagogue and the kosher kitchen, I met other equally isolated graduate students and felt much less displaced at Yale than I might have been.

～

JUNE 1962. The school year is over, but one chore still hangs over me, a language exam. I had passed French and German my first day at Yale, the latter with difficulty, despite some help from my rusty Yiddish. The third requirement, Latin, was beyond me, for I'd never studied a word of it. That would be my main challenge in the upcoming summer. Though I signed up for a crash course at the uptown branch of Hunter College, I wasn't exactly looking forward to it. There was something too churchy about the language that had always put me off. My love of the Greek classics had never extended to their Roman conquerors, whose fabled exploits were more martial and technological than cultural. If the Greeks were poets and philosophers, I thought, the Romans were, well, soldiers and engineers. Like the Roman character itself, Latin seemed a cold language, a tool of discipline for Victorian schoolmasters, besides being the lingua franca of the Catholic Church in those days that preceded Vatican II.

But before that Latin course got under way, my roommate Eli, who reminded me of the chunky, big-hearted kids I had grown up with, was set to get married. To my surprise, since we weren't bosom friends, he tapped me to be part of the wedding party; he was not a man to exclude anyone from a happy occasion. He had met his bride a year earlier on a boat trip from lower Manhattan to Bear Mountain, a state park on a breathtaking site forty-five miles up the Hudson River. The annual excursion was sponsored by a Zionist youth group called Mizrachi Hatzair, and Eli, to celebrate his upcoming nuptials, would take us all on the same outing in the hope that we might prove as fortunate in love as he did.

To make sure that happened, he and his intended had arranged for one of her friends to be my "date" for the day, without tipping me off in advance about their plans. Put out by this, I seethed quietly to myself and tried not to be rude to my designated companion, though we had little in common. I was feeling bored as well as annoyed when a striking woman, lean and dark-skinned, with wavy brown hair over a high forehead, came up to say hello; she recognized me from the food line at the seminary, from our days on Morningside Heights. L had finished at Barnard a year earlier, when I had left Columbia. Her Orthodox Jewish upbringing, like mine, was receding into the past but remained a bulky element of both our lives, something so deeply internalized it was hard to set aside. She had grown up in New Haven, and her family, I soon discovered, was busily involved with the same Orthodox synagogue where I had spent many hours the preceding year. She too had no connection to the sponsoring Zionist group and wondered what she was doing on this boat ride to nowhere. A sad-looking older man, perhaps a refugee, had attached himself to her early in the trip, and like me she was trying to get unglued. "I know you," she said to me. "You dated my friend Ina in college." "Who are you?" I piped up, a bit truculently, surprised to be spotted by someone I didn't recognize. After a few such awkward exchanges it came out that we knew many people in common. No shrinking flower, she seemed at once determined and delicate, forceful yet gracefully feminine. Within a few minutes we were exchanging stories and, soon enough, got on swimmingly—quite literally, since a highlight of the trip was an afternoon swim in the pool at Bear Mountain State Park. (She later said we exposed just about everything we had on the day we met.)

By the time the boat headed back down the Hudson, passing the Palisades as dusk settled in, L's middle-aged admirer had finally left us alone, and she firmly refused to give him her phone number. "Do you have any nice friends?" he asked in quiet desperation. As the boat docked at the Battery, we were singing our way through the entire catalog of Rodgers and Hammerstein, with a few other shows like *My Fair Lady* thrown in. Two twenty-two-year-olds wrapped up in each other, we'd grown oblivious to everyone around us. At one point we turned around and the ship seemed completely deserted. Where had everyone gone? L and I raced down to the lower deck, only to see that all the passengers had disembarked; the boat was prepared to sail to where it would dock for the night—in fact had already set off. As it began moving a tiny space opened up between the deck and the dock. "Jump, jump," I shouted, expecting to follow, but she cannily refused to make the first move. I had a vision of us—something out of Mussorgsky's frenzied tone poem—spending the night at Bear Mountain. Instead the boat docked at the weathered Forty-Second Street Circle Line pier, with an amused crew and the two of us as its last remaining passengers, as if the whole voyage had been for our sake alone, as in many ways it was. How strange to think that the course of my life was determined on that day. I can still recall the quiet excitement of our walk along dark, deserted streets from the empty pier and the hours of passionate necking that followed in her tiny flat on West Seventy-Seventh Street, where I felt I had stumbled into the garden of earthly delights. Agitated, impassioned, I'd rarely felt so quickly at ease with anyone I'd just met.

Many such evenings followed all through that summer, usually in mid-week, since I crammed Latin at Hunter's Bronx campus during the day and drove my parents to their country bungalow on the North Shore of Long Island most weekends. One Sunday I invited L to come along for the day, and as she stepped into the car my mother, forthright as ever to her rival, whom she'd never met, said, "I don't approve of single girls having their own apartments." It was a rare but honest display of her sexual imagination. Such an unchaperoned space would lead young women to immorality and young men, her son in particular, to perdition. For her generation, girls went directly from the home of their fathers to the care of their husbands. This was the immutable order of things. It was fine for L to work, that was perfectly normal—unmarried girls from modest families usually did—but living on your own was a waste of money and a source of temptation. L's independence was a moral threat to the son she adored but also an unpleas-ant reminder that he was growing up and moving away just as the world itself was changing.

Oddly, my mother had never spent a week languishing at home since she graduated from Washington Irving High School, just east of Union Square, in 1930. Small, dark-haired, voluble, Anna was the least domes-tic person in her large family. She seemed the most restless of any of my friends' mothers. Housekeeping bored her. She was an uninspired cook with a limited meat-and-potatoes repertoire, all delicious to me since I had grown up on it. She cleaned house haphazardly, only for major holidays. She hadn't seriously thought of going to college—her interests were not at all bookish—but she had a head for business and always loved the social give-and-take of waiting on trade. So she helped out, first in Reitman and Sons, the glass and mirror establishment of her pious, full-bearded father, Morris, after whom I was named, then in the pocket-sized dry goods store of her older sister on Madison Street, on the Lower East Side, and finally working for more than forty years alongside my father in the larger dry goods emporium, quaintly named Anne's Thrift Shop, that they opened in Queens in 1948. For her father and, after he died, for her brothers, she kept the books but also dealt with customers and learned to cut glass, including heavy plate glass, which she would still boast about in old age.

L, alongside her proper German mother, had worked just as hard in her father's delicatessen in Waterbury, Connecticut, and in his catering business. When she wasn't in school, L would lug crates of cabbage, peel bushels of potatoes, wait on tables, and, if the dishwashers didn't show up, she would wash hundreds of dishes. Only going to college, which her parents discouraged—they suggested secretarial school—offered L any real prospect of a middle-class future, of seeking out a profession and working with her mind rather than her hands. She had been a premed in college, but organic chemistry stymied her, and her parents, always tight with money, had categorically refused to pay for medical school. Instead, she remained in science and worked in a lab. When we met she had started a job as a science writer for a high school edition of *Collier's Encyclopedia*, working her way straight through the alphabet.

The summer of 1962, after my first year at Yale, was the first I'd ever spent in the city. My family considered the city no place for children, especially during the years of the polio epidemic. From the year I was born there had been summers of sun and surf in what was then a small working-class town on Long Island's North Shore, Rocky Point, where most of the Reitman clan had built or bought modest frame houses. This tumultuous childhood paradise, in which I was always surrounded by boisterous aunts, uncles, and cousins, was also where some rules were suspended and the strict demands of Orthodox Jewish practice took a summer break. There was no synagogue for miles around, and the beach was essential, even on the Sabbath, so long as we made our way there on foot. These early years were followed by teenage summers when I worked in a Catskills resort, then three years as a waiter and counselor in a summer camp in the Poconos, and finally, after college, an eye-opening summer knocking around Western Europe and Israel with my college friend Sam when we traipsed through half a dozen countries.

By contrast, 1962 was the summer of Latin and the summer of L. By day I struggled with conjugation, declensions, tenses, cases, and a word order unlike that of any language I knew. (It seemed perverse that you could recognize every word yet still not nail down the meaning of the sentence. Those damn endings! It was an "inflected" language, I learned, so that even the dictionary offered only limited help.) On weeknights, when I got together with L, I had glimpses of a different world, free of the awkwardness that had afflicted me with the opposite sex, free (or freer) of the sexual inhibitions in which I had been raised. I had gone to boys-only schools from kindergarten to the end of college. Never much of an athlete, I remained on awkward terms with my own body, though it had never let me down. I had never seen my parents naked and rarely seen them physically affectionate. Though their marriage looked like a happy one, it seemed based less on love than on hard work, child-rearing, and a bottomless faith in family, and only family, as a haven in a heartless world. My father, ever stolid, was given to long, brooding silences, my mother to an animated flow of conversation with anyone and everyone she met.

For months L and I, though powerfully drawn to each other, stopped short of "going all the way." I felt this would somehow ruin what we had, a rapport deeper than anything I had known outside the family. I felt ravenous for sex and love yet held back from pursuing them, caught between raging desire and an inbred constraint. I wanted to be with her but on some idealized plane that was not "merely" physical. My moral qualms served as a mask for insecurity. I worried about disappointing her, and myself. For L the difficulties lay elsewhere. I later learned that she was in the midst of a destructive relationship that unfolded on weekends when I was usually away. This soon came to an end. I simplified her life as she complicated mine.

Both the Latin and the love story came to a head not long after I returned to Yale in the fall. Despite the course I had taken at Hunter, I failed the Latin test again and again. I was sure I was at risk of being thrown out of school. Professor Donaldson himself, a medievalist who had sown his wild oats teaching Latin in prep school, took me personally in hand. My Latin literacy, or lack of it, became his own project. In the next test, my fourth try, I was given a passage of medieval Latin that actually made sense to me, and as he went over the finished result with me I felt a sense of triumph; I had somehow escaped the scaffold without knowing exactly

how I'd managed to do so. There was only one sentence I partly miscon-
strued. After pointing this out to me he said, with surprising cheer, "Well,
you flunked." I sat there gaping at him in disbelief. "But I'll never do better
than that," I said. "That was a fluke, a lot more than I actually know." He
looked at me with a malicious grin: "Well then, I guess you'll never pass."
The balding skin was stretched tightly over his skull like a death's head, a
menacing omen. I went straight from his office to the cathedral-like Yale
gym, stripped naked for a swim, and dived into the pool with no intention
of surfacing again. I liked the idea of leaving the earth as I had come into it.
I wasn't seriously suicidal, merely in abject despair, locked in a conundrum
I could not untangle, unable to imagine a way out. I have little recollection
of what went through my mind in what seemed like an interminable time
at the bottom of the pool, only the memory of rising slowly to the surface,
involuntarily, as if the body itself had taken over, with a terrific buoyancy, a
lightness of being. Some animal instinct lifted me up as if born again; the
creature strangely wanted to live.

As it happened, there *was* a way out. Donaldson ordered me to sus-
pend work for my classes and spend the next ten days focused only on
Latin. Then I would take the exam for the fifth and probably the last time.
The days passed in an impenetrable fog of Latin grammar and Latin sentences. In the past I had performed stupendous feats of cramming; now I
felt unable to assimilate an additional word. Yet when I sat down to take
the exam, I saw in front of me a passage I'd been handed before, the first
time I had failed, and it was familiar enough for me to fumble through. My
cunning torturer must have decided that I had suffered enough, or realized
that I'd learned as much Medieval Latin as I ever would. I could go back at
last to the modern literature I came to study.

WHILE ALL this was happening, L and I fell seriously in love. Her other
relationship had ended, much to her relief, and we were now spending
many weekend days together. A new flatmate, Herb, had replaced the now
happily wedded Eli, and one weekend when he was away I led L into his
room and we made love for the first time. She was in town visiting her
parents, who lived less than half a mile away. After months of anxious hes-

itation, it seemed like the most natural thing in the world. My feeling for L had cracked me open like a nut. After what seemed like a lifetime of gamboling among ideas like my brilliant college friends, I had signed on for an education in the senses, a liberating adventure after so much brooding over Latin and slogging through graduate classes. From the age of thirteen, sex had crept up on me unawares. Many eager, jittery adolescent boys must joke about it, watching their own and each others' bodies for the first signs of puberty. Later they compete with each other in jerking off. Not me. As a yeshiva boy I was something of a monk in training. When I had erections or saw the first tufts of pubic hair, I vaguely assumed they had always been there. The first few times I had a spontaneous ejaculation I had no idea what it was. One of my more devilish classmates, a rabbi's son, who came from a family of eight or ten children, told a fantastic story of what happens on the wedding night, *but only that night*, that enables a couple to conceive children. It was too bizarre for words, and I didn't believe it.

Someone must have told my parents that they had neglected their son's sex education. No hint of the facts of life ever crossed their lips. There weren't many books around the house, but one day I picked up one lying on the coffee table—it was by one Eustace Chesser, M.D., called *Love without Fear*—and the whole story, the machinery of man and woman, love and desire, came pouring out, like fuel on a smoldering flame. For days afterward I felt a heat radiating from my groin, as if I were about to explode. The world as I had known it suddenly looked like a huge lie, a conspiratorial cover-up that finally had been exposed. I took to whacking off like one possessed, under the covers, as if making up not for lost time but for prior ignorance, all that time in the dark. But it remained a separate compartment in my life, still largely a life of the mind, where I knew none of the clumsiness I suffered in sports, the uncertainty I felt about my own body.

When I was growing up, athletes seemed like a breed apart. Between ages nine and seventeen I remained a fanatical baseball fan, following the larger-than-life Yankees and the neighboring Giants—and demonizing the luckless Dodgers—like the devotee of a demanding religion. These were the Yankees' greatest years, with five consecutive World Series titles beginning in 1949, and no one loved a winner more than I did. DiMaggio, Mantle, Berra, Rizzuto, Billy Martin—these players were all legends for me.

But baseball was a spectator sport to me, a form of acute mental activity, a game to be mastered, not played. I became a walking encyclopedia of baseball statistics going back to the beginning of the twentieth century. L, on the other hand, growing up in a verdant corner of New Haven, had actually played baseball and was good at it, a natural athlete, often the only girl on the team, though her mother was aghast at raising a tomboy, a girl who didn't mind skinning her knees and shins.

I was drawn to L partly because she was my opposite in many ways. She stood for a life I secretly envied, a different way of being in the world. She related to her surroundings not simply through her eyes, that most detached of the senses, but through her fingertips. She was a sculptor when we first met, and she taught me to relate to sculpture with my hands, to run my fingers over the shape and texture of it, a form of touching that invariably upset security guards at museums. L also loved food and really took pleasure in it. My mother's cooking rarely extended beyond scrambled eggs, spaghetti with ketchup, and overcooked pot roast and chicken. L's father was a professional chef, and she shared his gustatory appreciation of food. The first meal she cooked for me was a duck à l'orange, something I'd never imagined, let alone tasted. Later she wished that she'd taught *me* to cook instead.

It was all very well to awaken my senses to art and food, but sex belonged to a different order of experience. In my wallet all through my teenage years I carried a tattered love letter, if you could call it that, from my first girlfriend, whom I had met in synagogue when I was about thirteen. Our relationship consisted of long walks and talks during breaks in holiday services, occasional furtive kisses, and at least one party for her school friends at which we all played spin the bottle, yet another kissing game. At such social gatherings I felt as much the misfit as I did at stickball, where old broom handles and mop handles served as the city boy's substitutes for baseball bats. But with L my awkwardness and shyness were miraculously dispelled. We felt right together, made for each other. I cared not a whit that she seemed more experienced than I was—who wouldn't have been?—and I had very little curiosity about what that experience had actually been. Instead I felt loved, wanted, by someone who knew more about life and love, and especially about sex, than I did.

For years and years, along with that love letter, I carried in my wallet something even more indispensable for teenage boys, a condom, for who knew when I would get lucky, and shouldn't a fellow be prepared? I went through an agony of embarrassment when I bought it in a pharmacy, waiting patiently for the place to be deserted, anticipating a leering smirk or a look of incredulity from whoever would sell it to me, if indeed anyone would. I carried it so long it eventually formed a telltale ring on the outer surface of the leather, which came to symbolize the circle into which I longed to be initiated. Such recollections beggar belief yet remain indelible to me today.

My memory of the week after L and I first slept together feels even more vivid as I think back on it. We decided that I would come into the city the following weekend, without telling my parents. I would stay with her since her roommate would be away. This was a dramatic turn, some kind of commitment to each other. We had never spent a whole night together, and I had never misled my parents about where I was. Though I had been away from home so many summers and traveled through Europe for months, I had a new feeling of being off on my own, setting sail in unknown waters. All week the upcoming weekend loomed up for me as an astonishing adventure, a barely imagined moment of fulfillment. L and I had already slept together, but now we would become a true couple, installed in the grown-up world of sexual beings for the first time.

It's no doubt impossible to remain physically aroused for a full week—four hours, we're now told, is enough for a man to declare a state of emergency—but in my memory of that week I'm in a perpetual state of erection, in class, at meals, in the library. At times I imagined everyone was looking at me, as if my feelings were writ large on my face, yet I felt no embarrassment. I could barely focus on anything else, walking around in a private dream in which I felt at once smug, satisfied with my good fortune, and quivering with anticipation. The fresh memory of our time together was heightened by the runaway fantasy of the coming weekend. I had an almost tangible sense that I could reach out at any moment and touch her soft skin and tender flesh. For a dreamy intellectual, this tactile sensation was a novel experience.

The weekend lived up to expectation in every way, as did all the weekends that followed. L and I slipped into one another's lives as if we had always been meant to be together. We seemed never to tire of each other's bodies, nor did we run out of things to talk about or places to go—concerts in which my ears seemed to open up for the first time, art shows where her keen attention gave me lessons in seeing, an aesthetic education. I felt claustrophobic in L's tiny apartment on West Seventy-Seventh Street—she shared a single narrow bedroom with her roommate—and after a few months she moved to a larger place on Riverside Drive and Ninety-Seventh Street. There she had her own room, so at last we could have some privacy. On nights when I rolled out of bed and came home to my parents' cluttered apartment in Queens at 4 a.m., my mother was overwhelmed with anxiety yet said little, out of fear of saying the wrong thing. The following morning, since she couldn't mention sex, she would invariably ask what we were doing at those ungodly hours. "Just talking," I said. Of course she disapproved. "How do you find so much to talk about?" This from a woman who could talk to anyone, in any place, for any length of time—one of the secrets of her success in business.

One night after I had left L's place in the wee hours my mother called her. She was apologetic but she was worried, almost beside herself. She couldn't sleep. L assured her I would soon be home, and she begged L not to tell me she had called. When L did finally tell me, years later, I was surprised, not at my mother's fears—she was fearful of everything—nor at her desire to keep me innocent, keep me close to her, but at the unusual restraint of her not wanting me to know, not wanting me to feel that she was intruding on a part of my life that was just beginning, that would carry me off to another place, the next stage of my life. L too must have been impressed, for she kept it from me for a long time, then made me promise never to say I knew. And I never did.

Two

BEGINNINGS: ROCKY POINT

W HAT WAS THE WORLD I was fitfully leaving behind? It was bound up with a warm, slightly suffocating family life as well as the modest places we called home: the three-room apartment on Henry Street in the Lower East Side where we lived till I was nine; the small, cluttered rental apartment behind the dry goods store in Flushing, Queens, to which we moved in 1949; then, five years later, a larger place across the street, this time above the store, where my parents would remain for the next forty years. But what comes back most forcefully is a handful of rough wooden bungalows in Rocky Point, then a mostly Italian town on the North Shore of Long Island.

There my mother's extended family gathered summer after summer beginning long before I was born. It was here that I and my sister, Doris, spent some of our happiest hours; here I could actually be an ordinary child and a blooming adolescent rather than the closely monitored yeshiva boy who spent all his waking hours in school. Suffolk County, Long Island, in the 1940s and 1950s was never very wild but still genuinely rural and undeveloped, barely electrified, not yet suburban, dotted with potato and duck farms. Its pristine beaches were covered with clam shells, mussels, and the large remains of horseshoe crabs, with their long, swordlike tails. Away from the shore were woods dark and deep enough to frighten an impressionable city child.

Rocky Point today is a typical middle-class town, about sixty-five miles east of New York City, heavily populated with small- to medium-size frame houses. Unlike most of its neighboring towns, it has an unusual history. In the seventeenth century it was a sparsely populated farming community inhabited by a few families, such as the Hallocks, whose name can still be found on village roads and in the local graveyard. Its graceful shoreline was dominated by high dunes, sandy cliffs, and the pebbly beaches that must have given the town its name. The surf of the Long Island Sound was gentle, the water crystalline, except when the whole island was pounded by August and September hurricanes, an annual drama for which we were never fully prepared.

Up through the first half of the twentieth century, the northern part of Rocky Point, bordering the shore, was heavily wooded and unspoiled. To the south lay a vast area of pine barrens which, in the 1920s, attracted the interest of the Radio Corporation of America. It purchased the entire tract. There the company erected huge transmitters that by 1927 had led to the first wireless radio contact with Europe. Another media company was drawn to the woodland north of Route 25A, bordering the shore. The *New York Daily Mirror*, created by Hearst to compete with Colonel McCormick's fabulously successful tabloid, the *Daily News*, bought up a huge parcel of land and subdivided it into building lots, offering them as an incentive to subscribers. They were sold to readers on the installment plan for $89.50 a lot, with $12.50 as a down payment and $3.50 due each month thereafter. In one stroke it brought the lovely beaches of the Sound and the chance to build a second home within reach of New York's working class, especially those living in cramped apartments and small houses in Brooklyn and Queens. The plunge was taken in 1929 by my mother's older brothers, who had arrived in America with their mother only eight years earlier.

Their father, my maternal grandfather, had emigrated from the Polish/Ukrainian shtetl of Lubin (or Labun) in 1913, but before he could raise enough money to bring the family over, the war intervened. He left when my mother was a year old, her younger sister only six weeks old. (They had had eight children, six of whom survived into adulthood. His departure must have been the only form of birth control they knew.) When my mother saw him next, as if for the first time, it was on a New York pier and she was nine or ten, her pitch-black hair in long ringlets. In the Ukraine during the intervening years, through war and civil war, her own pious mother had managed to feed a family of six by keeping a still, not for Jews but for the thirsty peasants of Lubin and the surrounding villages. My mother remembered being hidden under haystacks, somehow avoiding the thrust of bayonets when marauding soldiers—or simply townspeople on a drunken binge—went out looking for Jews. Arriving in New York on the SS *Kroonland* on August 9, 1921, she saw a man with a long beard, who frightened her so much she hid behind her mother's skirts. She later recalled eating a banana for the first time, something she had never seen.

The family's name in America was Reitman, but coming through Ellis Island it was, as I recently discovered, Chajtman, a name unlikely to smooth the path to success in the promised land. Along the way their Yiddish first names were also Anglicized, if only for legal purposes. My grandfather Moische, after whom I would be named, had already become known to the world as Morris; his wife, Dubbe, was soon Dora, which would lead to an explosion of D's among her grandchildren two generations later: Doris, Dianne, Doreen. The oldest son, Zyna ("son" in Yiddish), was renamed Julius, just as Szrul became Sam and Nojach (Noah) soon became Louis, though the family knew them all, and always would, by their familiar Yiddish names.

The brothers were rough-and-ready men, carpenters handy with a hammer and saw, used to physical labor, but it was the three sisters who were to play a larger role in my life. Lily (Leja, or Tuttel), my mother, Anna (Chana), and the baby sister, Fay, or Fanny (Fania, in Russian, Fradl in Yiddish), remained inseparable all their lives, though their personalities were altogether different. Tante Lily, as I always called her, was as obstinate and cantankerous as her older brother, Zyna, and it was no surprise that they never got along. Both of them were barely five feet tall, he a fireplug of a man, with a stentorian voice, all muscle and bluster, she a tough, hard-nosed, gray-haired peasant woman, inured to difficult times, who looked middle-aged even as a girl. Both had a powerful will and an ornery streak of independence, and it was hard to imagine that they had ever been friends. Family legend had it that he could lift a cow back in Europe. We knew he had pierced his eardrums to escape the czar's draconian twenty-five-year draft, which left him hard of hearing and loud of speech all his life, with a foghorn voice that perfectly suited his headstrong temperament. His mother despaired of trying to rein him in, or so I was often told.

Zyna's fiancée, Sarah, traveled with the party that left for America in 1921, and he was said—by the sisters, who were not his greatest fans—to entertain her handsomely at every stop as they made their way from their Ukrainian village to the port of Antwerp, in Belgium, from which they would embark for New York. Meanwhile, as one family legend would have it, his mother was beside herself as the money and food were running out. The same pattern was repeated in America. He took pride in being the head of the family, especially after his father's death in 1936, yet was often at loggerheads with his brothers and sisters, who chafed under his domineering ways. He was active among the landsleit of the Lubiner Society—its main function was to recall old times and to bury its members—and he even organized a Reitman family circle, which lasted only a few years. The Reitmans' peculiar mixture of kinship and conflict, sibling loyalty and rivalry, became even more important after he led the family to Rocky Point, where he and his three sisters, unable either to stay together or remain apart, each built or bought the bungalows that became their summer retreat for the next forty or fifty years.

My grandfather was in glass: plate glass, window glass, mirrors, and frames. "Is your father a glazier?"—that's what another kid might complain to me if I was blocking his way. And I could honestly say yes, for glass was the family trade. From my childhood in the 1940s I can still remember the dim, musty interior of the Reitman and Sons glass emporium on Chatham Square, between the Lower East Side and Chinatown, with plate glass and mirrors propped up along the wall and long, frayed, cloth-covered counters for cutting them to size. Unable to get along with his father and brothers, Julius, prickly and independent, had split for Queens by the late 1920s, opening his own glass business on Roosevelt Avenue, in Jackson Heights. He and Sarah raised their growing family in an apartment above the store, their bedroom only a couple of feet away from the elevated Flushing Line, whose trains roared by their windows every few minutes. (In the country, they said, the silence kept them awake.)

Julius was also a seat-of-the-pants carpenter, fearless, proud of his skill, though rarely very precise in his measurements—nothing he built ever fit exactly. After buying two lots in Rocky Point with his brother Louis's help, he built his own house, starting with a couple of rooms, then repeatedly adding on. It was no architect's dream but simply a warren of connected cubicles, some of them not much larger than the double bed and dresser that filled them up. Since the piece of land was only two lots—forty by a hundred feet—little space was squandered on closets or hallways. The result was a railroad flat in a pastoral setting; one room led into another and, as in many immigrant lodgings, privacy was a thing unknown.

The house sprang up in a remarkably spontaneous way: it just grew. After the first rooms were built, even before its plasterboard walls were in place, family and friends piled in on weekends to dig out a basement, attach additional rooms, build a roof over their heads, construct tiny outbuildings at the corners of the property, and provide a foundation instead of a few cement blocks, adding a basement for storage and tools. A well was dug and the water brought to the surface with a hand pump. The sanitary facilities were first limited to an outhouse in the backyard, something they knew well from the village back home. Yet for newly settled immigrants who lived in crowded city flats it was paradise: stomach-busting meals—still kosher, no doubt—after a day of hard work, a spotless beach a mile away, a nowhere town that felt like the frontier, and some welcome distance from their aging immigrant parents still set in the ways of the Old World, especially the religious ways. Soon Tante Lily and her husband, Dave, built a house just up the road—only two rooms at first—helped along by Julius's carpentry, frequent advice, and generous interference. Thanks to their proximity here on Laurel Road, Julius's four children and Lily's three grew up in each other's hair, sometimes as bosom friends, sometimes as rambunctious rivals, sometimes reproducing the feuds of the previous generation. It was one little family world, an endless uproar of siblings and cousins.

After I was born, in 1940, we often came to stay at one of these two houses, tiny as they were. These were dormitory conditions but I loved being out of the city, walking and playing along old country roads, loved the beach, adored being surrounded by all my older cousins, whose less supervised lives seemed more open to chance and impulse than my own.

I took a thrilled, child's-eye view of them as teenagers; they seemed wild, unmanageable. In the hubbub of being there, surrounded by family, even my parents let their hawklike attention wander, and I felt liberated from the usual adult oversight. Sometimes my folks went back to the city and left me or my sister, four years younger, the apple of my father's eye, to the benign neglect of this extended yet easily distracted family. I was lucky not to be an only child; the full weight of my parents' anxieties would have been difficult to bear. My only recollection of my sister's arrival, on the last day of August 1944, is of being taken soon afterward to a park outside Beth Israel Hospital to wave to my mother, whom I couldn't see, for she was lost in the glare somewhere on a high floor.

In 1948, for the princely sum of fifteen hundred dollars, my parents bought the modest house that lay between the two family cottages in Rocky Point, since their own skills, strictly in retail sales, never extended to construction. Nestled in the corner of a slightly larger piece of land, three lots rather than two (all of sixty by a hundred feet), it belonged to Danny, a local fireman, who must have felt hemmed in by the brood of noisy Reitmans on both sides, virtually the only Jews in this Italian American village. Our newly acquired property became the demilitarized zone between Uncle Zyna's patriarchal authority, which he was never shy to assert, and Tante Lily's stubborn contrarian temper, which made her my favorite of all these relatives.

The house my parents got for their money, little enough even then, was a sturdy wooden structure propped up on cinder blocks, with an outhouse instead of a toilet. The house was divided into four tiny rooms, including an eat-in kitchen that held a sink but no running water, two small bedrooms, and a "living room" that was scarcely used except to pass through to other rooms. Once the center of the house, it had been displaced by another sitting room, a spacious screen porch, cool in the evening, where all the real socializing—the endless talk, the children's games, the men playing cards—took place.

Each room had a dim ceiling light and perhaps one electrical outlet, but also kerosene lamps with glass chimneys for use during the frequent power outages. My bedroom, its original pair of windows now looking out onto the porch, was completely taken up by a high double bed and two ancient dressers, yet it was the only time I had a room I didn't have to share with my parents or my sister. In the corner, standing on its side, was a folding bed, an *aufstellbettl*, to be wheeled out and opened up for company. As part of the deal my room doubled as a guest room, and I gave it up on weekends when my aunt Fay and her husband, Lou, came to stay, before they built their own house just down the road.

This last building project led to one of the worst family quarrels. Fay and Lou hired the irascible Julius as the contractor to put up the framing of the house, though they themselves planned to finish it. But eventually, inevitably, the two men quarreled bitterly over the bill as the family looked on. Lou, young, handsome, a little vain, had had a rough childhood. Abused by his despotic father, he was sent out to factory work at twelve, and this helped mold him into a tough union man and a fervent Communist, touchy, perhaps a little paranoid. With a nasty temper, he could be mean and autocratic, though, like many working-class Communists, he was also a thwarted intellectual, always eager for argument. During the war, he had seen combat on Okinawa and other blood-drenched Pacific islands. The arrangements for building the house had no doubt been loose, probably an oral agreement, and neither man was the sort to give in. Both were proud, self-righteous, easily wounded. The negotiations, the accusations, punctuated by plenty of shouting, took place on neutral ground, the porch of our house. All the others kept their distance, as if the affairs of nations hung in the balance. I don't know how the quarrel was resolved, but there were hard feelings, and the two men did not speak to each other for decades.

Our house was rudimentary, bare of comfort, yet I treasure the memories associated with it. By the time we bought it, Julius and Sarah, always the first with any new convenience, had installed indoor plumbing. But we, like my aunt Lily next door, still depended on outhouses perched on far corners of the lot, actually two on our side; the first one was oversubscribed and now served as a toolshed, since the house had no basement. It's hard to wax nostalgic about an outhouse, a bona fide shithole, but I was a dreamy kid, rarely alone, and it was at least a private space, nothing like a busy army latrine. In my sensory memories I can still recall the pungent odor of lime and other disinfectants that were poured down the hole. It was not the worst way to live: we were in the "country," roughing it, free of labor-saving modern gadgets but free of the hot, crowded city as well. This rude life must have reminded my elders of the shtetl where they had once lived, just as it gave me a distant taste of their bare early lives.

Our water supply came by way of gallon jugs that we filled at the tall iron pump behind Lily's house, probably the most frequent exercise I had as a kid. For a city dweller it was a good sensation to draw cool water from the earth; we felt like children of the soil on a collective farm. Eventually town water reached our road, pipes were laid to our house, and my mother engaged her brother to build a real bathroom, just a square annex attached to the side of the house. (For her it would have seemed a breach to give the job to anyone else—a quarrel would have ensued, ugly recrimination. She also had an immigrant's mistrust of anyone outside the family.) A hot-water heater was soon installed, offering creature comforts beyond the cold out-door showers we took after a day at the beach. Even the screen porch was eventually enclosed by actual windows. The bungalow was turning into a real house but still felt like the rough summer cottage it had always been, a scene for the endlessly unfolding drama of frolicking children and their bickering elders.

I don't know who laid out the busy grid of roads in Rocky Point, per-haps surveyors brought in by the *Daily Mirror.* Most of them were named after plants, sometimes in alphabetical order—Apricot, Aster, Begonia, Canary, Daffodil. We were on Laurel, between Maple and Juniper, a stretch of dirt road that led virtually nowhere. Just beyond Lily's house the road curved up a steep hill surrounded by woods. The hill was a serious chal-lenge to the jalopies of the time, and it was attempted by no more than two or three intrepid drivers a day. Unpaved, it didn't provide much of a playing field for us and the Italian kids across the road, whose devoted immigrant families—two sisters, each with two children—reminded me of our own tight clan. Laurel Road was dusty, twisty, and narrow. Really serious games like punchball and stickball took place at the foot of the hill, on Locust Drive, tarred and flat, where the Dugan's Bakery truck stopped to sell its loaves of white bread and frosted cupcakes, and the Good Humor man tinkled his chimes at twilight, soon after supper, bringing all the kids in the neighborhood running.

For the grown-ups the evening's entertainment was gossiping on the

lawn as the sun went down and the heat of the day subsided. This was the
women's hour: the three sisters chattering rapidly in English and Yiddish,
dishing dirt on everyone they knew, taking stock of the clothes and makeup
that others wore, the food they served and wasted, the money they spent,
the ups and downs of their children. They rehearsed old family slights—
the wedding someone had missed years earlier, the expected *yerusha*, or
inheritance, that had somehow melted away. They spoke of distant cousins
and of landsleit from the old country, who sometimes arrived in Sarah's
house to visit for a week or two, for she craved company and was a formidable cook, happy to entertain. The sisters on the lawn were joined by
Lily's older daughter, Pauline, in residence for the summer with her small
children. Sometimes their sister-in-law Sarah sat down as well, despite the
animus just below the surface; more often she was the subject of their catty
comments, rarely delivered to her face, since she had a sharp tongue. Her
older daughter Millie could be there too, but she was not one to gossip;
amazingly for this family, she tended to see only the best in people, which
made it difficult for her cousins to take her seriously.

The men rarely sat in for these twilight sessions, which were focused
on *weibishe sachen*, women's matters. If they were in residence, it was usually on the weekend, and they could be seen on the porch playing poker or
pinochle for very low stakes. When it had grown too dark to play on the
road, the kids joined the women on the lawn, where they were expected
to sit by quietly: heaven help them if they tried to join the conversation.
Zvayten tug yontif, my mother would say—that is, the redundant second
day of many Jewish holidays—thus putting the pipsqueak in his place, the
wan little voice piping up from the peanut gallery. Whatever the weather,
every few minutes my mother would bark at my sister or me to put on a
sweater—"You'll catch cold, you little bastard!"—and this became a running family joke: Anna says she's cold, so the kids have to put on sweater; a
light breeze could prove fatal, a cold could turn into pneumonia, the world
was full of perils and pitfalls, especially for the young, and their mother
would inevitably be blamed.

This was the comic side of my mother's never-ending anxieties about
her children; we always seemed to her in grave danger. As the next-youngest
child in her family, she had grown up feeling at once protected and vulnera-

ble. Her father had been away in America during her first decade. She must have relied on her older brothers and sister Lily for protection. Somehow this had left her strong-willed yet timorous; her emotions had an operatic cast. Thanks to her fears, which must have seeped into my bones, I didn't learn to ride a bike till I was thirty-five, far away on Cape Cod, well after my own children. These phobic warnings contributed to another running joke. At the Passover seder, when I was asked what I wanted in return for the *afikoman*—the piece of matzo I'd found in the treasure hunt, without which the seder could not proceed—I always said a "two-wheeler," even when I was already a college student. My parents laughingly said yes, but somehow I never got it until, years later, I bought one myself.

Anna's stream of invective was another source of family amusement. Her way of disciplining her children, a very ineffective way, was to hurl a volley of abuse at them, curses no one ever took seriously. "You little bitch! You bastard! You're ruining my life. You're killing me!" They were colorful but never obscene, since she was a deep-dyed puritan. They were the music of hysteria, spontaneously produced and instantly forgotten. Her sister-in-law Sarah, on the other hand, was as earthy as a Russian peasant. She would joke about farting and screwing and belching, all in Yiddish to kids who had no idea what she was saying. She liked twitting their clueless innocence. As a way of saying, "Up yours," she would protrude her thumb between her fingers, perhaps as an insult, or else to make her fist look like squashed genitals—the meaning of this gesture dawned on me only years later. She too was from Lubin, the same town as the Reitmans, but her Rabelaisian spirit was the obverse of their prudery. The three sisters thought her vulgar and unrefined, a good match for their coarse brother Julius, whom they saw as a blowhard and a braggart. Worse still, they said he was more generous to strangers—a real sport, especially with the goyim—than he was to his own family, a cardinal sin.

By putting down roots in this blue-collar Italian town, the family was able to distance itself from its own immigrant roots, especially the religious regimen that still had to be maintained in the city. There were no synagogues to attend, no kosher food except what could be brought out from New York, as it invariably was. To be observant in Rocky Point, as Tante Lily was, as my parents were, meant not using the automobile on the Sabbath, which was easy—only Julius had a car (as well as a pickup truck). Anyway, walking the mile to the beach was more fun than driving, since there were so many different routes, hilly and flat, twisty and straight. Somehow, being Jewish here didn't require staying home to daven, to say Sabbath prayers. All that could be saved for the fall, put on hold, along with my schooling, until September rolled around.

My father didn't own a car until the mid-1950s, learning to drive (badly) when he was almost fifty. By the age of ten I knew Rocky Point inside out, having tramped every conceivable route to the beach or to the Bohack supermarket or the laundromat in the village. My cousins, ten or more years older, all drove, and sometimes they took me with them to the bowling alley or the pizza place in town, or to the movies eight miles away in Port Jefferson, the end point of the railroad line, where third-run Hollywood movies were shown. I loved tagging along, but as a yeshiva boy I wouldn't actually *eat* pizza, merely nibble at the crust, for even the cheese was not considered kosher, let alone the *chazerei* that came along with it. Out of the house my cousins ate what they wanted, as I could not. My unbending restraint, along with my obviously repressed urge to sin, was a source of amusement to them. They must have seen me as the priggish model child they never wanted to be: the star pupil, the compliant son. I in turn wanted nothing more than to be just the opposite: some kind of wild delinquent, fractious athlete, or unrepentant troublemaker. I had a notion that eating forbidden pizza would be a good start, since more serious transgressions were as yet beyond my imagining, yet I got no farther than the tasty crust.

As part of my bright-child impersonation, I sometimes spoke up on subjects I knew nothing about. Once, when the chatter on the lawn turned to the subject of "birth control," whatever that meant, I spoke up proudly, "I don't believe in birth control." I was pleased but puzzled by the gales of laughter that followed. I thought I had scored a hit, said something clever, but what was it? Damned if I knew! I thought birth control meant, well, not having children, but after all, having children was a good thing, wasn't it? There were certainly plenty of kids in the family. Soon this comment became part of the family lore and was often repeated. I couldn't tell whether it made me sound precocious or clueless, probably both. Mostly I sat and listened to the soap-opera turns of minor grudges nursed for thirty years, the unfolding saga of adult life that I only half understood.

Thanks to the family compound in Rocky Point, I grew up amid this gaggle of cousins who were as demonstrative as their feuding parents. Pauline, Lily's older daughter, had married her childhood sweetheart, the lovable Poogie, when he came back from the war, where he had seen the worst of D-day, beaches littered with dead and bleeding bodies. By 1948 she was in residence for the whole summer, raising her first child, Stewie, who repeatedly bit my hand as I walked him up and down the road. He seemed like mischief incarnate. Pauline's brother Bernie was the blond, brainy one, lean and hardened like a marathon runner. He was the favored child of the family; its fortunes rode on his becoming a doctor, so his parents imagined. After a wartime stint as a teenage recruit in the Merchant Marine, he was rejected by every medical school—they still had quotas for Jews—and studied instead in Switzerland, on a near-starvation budget, before being admitted here. He married a woman—Trude, like L the daughter of German Jews—who had gone to Queens College with his tough, forthright younger sister, Barbara, the hell-raiser in the family, the first to go in for psychoanalysis. Trude, genteel and cultivated, always soft-spoken, brought a touch of class but also a touch of snobbery into the family. She and Bernie quickly had a son and then twin girls, who were almost never exposed to the rough rural delights of Rocky Point.

Even before his marriage Bernie was too busy studying to spend much time in the country, but his sisters, Pauline and Barbara, always at each other's throats, supplied some of the drama of my childhood. Their father, Dave, had contracted rheumatic fever when he was young. By the time I knew him he was a gaunt, cadaverous man with a damaged heart, so that he could scarcely work. He and Aunt Lily had fallen out many years earlier and, stubborn as they both were, shared living quarters but no longer spoke. She would prepare his dinner, set it on the table, and leave the room; this went on until he died in his sleep, a man barely over fifty. His two daughters made up for this silence by quarreling incessantly, yet later in life, when their children were grown, they became unexpectedly close. As I watched one of them chase the other with a pair of large dressmaker's scissors, raised aloft like a dagger, I relished the drama, the wild passion, the freedom missing from my own more orderly, uneventful home.

Were the lives of my cousins really as quirky and colorful as I felt they were, or was I simply seeing them through the wide eyes of the child, vicariously enjoying the tempests of their young adult lives? I got to know Julius and Sarah's children less well, but they too seemed larger than life, literally so in the case of their oldest, Irving, who returned from the war and simply grew, perhaps to more than four hundred pounds. He never married—my mother said his problems were "glandular," whatever that meant—and he warded off mockery by becoming the town clown, habitually making fun of himself. He was "Tiny" to his friends, and at the annual Labor Day parade in Rocky Point he swaddled himself in a huge diaper made up from bed sheets. And indeed there was something babyish about him, not only in the layers of fat on his hips, buttocks, tummy, and breasts but in his undeveloped personality, which seemed immature, presexual. Something in his endocrine glands, but also in relations with people, must have taken a wrong turn, from which he never recovered. He liked the company of children, and would offer them rides in the pickup truck, though he had little to say to them. He died in his late fifties, still chauffeuring his elderly parents around, never having managed to carve out an independent life for himself.

The cousin closest to me in age, two years older, was Avrumi, my uncle Louis's son, orphaned as a difficult teenager and raised in Julius and Sarah's freewheeling household. His mother was in her thirties when she died of breast cancer, his father in his forties and newly remarried, with a child on the way, when he died too. I'll never forget my aunt Sarah's keening at his funeral, complaining loudly to the dead man, as his coffin moved down the aisle, that he had left his children parentless, undefended. It must have been the first funeral I was allowed to attend, and one of the most wrenching I would ever see.

Even before his mother and then his father died, Avrumi cast himself as the bad boy, getting kicked out of yeshiva after yeshiva for acting out, talking back, or simply not showing in class for days at a time—his father was always being called in. He lasted about a year and a half in my own school, where I was a well-behaved star and he, deliberately, a dark star, a kid whose rambunctious freedom secretly thrilled me. His freckled, Tom Sawyer face always bore an impish grin. Living with his father on East Houston Street after his mother's death, he subsisted almost entirely on soda, or so the family thought. The apartment, without a woman's touch, seemed the epitome of chaos and squalor, strewn with empty Coke bottles. Years later he suggested, with a trace of resentment, that my mother tried to keep him away from me as a bad influence, which no doubt was true. He was the brother I never had, mischievous, hoarse, mocking, but also a born Mr. Fixit, eventually a college dropout trained, or self-trained, as an engineer, as good with his hands, as expert with machinery as I was inept. As a grown man he had many moneymaking schemes, which grew vague as he would describe them to me, but they always came to naught. Eventually he landed in Southern California, where at last he made a happy marriage. He died young, barely fifty, and only then did I realize how much I missed him.

ALL THE REITMANS had first settled down on the Lower East Side before taking off for the outer boroughs, and it was here that my mother and father met in the late 1930s at a dance sponsored, oddly, by an old-age home. My father was shy, hardworking, and still unmarried in his early thirties. My mother was in her midtwenties, with long curly black hair. Later she loved to reminisce about the offers she had turned down. One of her near suitors, fair-skinned and redheaded, became the father of one of my classmates. He was said to be a good catch, but she wasn't attracted. When her father, always terrified of doctors, died in surgery in 1936, he left a generous dowry of five hundred dollars for each of his younger daughters to make sure they were properly wed, with pomp and ceremony bespeaking their middle-class station in life. Soon afterward Anna's kid sister, Fay, married the handsome but difficult Lou, a working-class man with a chip on his shoulder, harboring that streak of bitterness going back to his childhood.

After a brief courtship my mother and father married too, in 1938, at the Little Hungary, a popular catering hall on East Houston Street that served the Lower East Side Jews for generations. Soon afterward they moved into a three-room apartment in a handsome, fairly new building at 131 Henry

Street, a place passed on to them by her brother Sam, who arranged it with the landlord as he moved out. For all their conflicts, the siblings somehow took care of each other. The Depression was still on. My father had a steady but low-paying job as a shipping clerk. Young families in New York moved constantly, sometimes attracted by months of free rent, but an apartment in hand could not be allowed to go to waste. It would stay in the family, passed on to Aunt Lily after my parents moved to Queens.

Well before my grandmother's death in 1942 the family began to scatter. These children of immigrants were outward bound. Fay and Lou had moved just across the bridge to Williamsburg and my grandmother Dora, now widowed, lived with them in her final years. As she lay dying, the night of the first Passover seder, I stood at the foot of her bed and spoke to her: "Don't die, Baba. Look, I'm wearing my new sailor suit." I was barely over two. Perhaps what I said was prompted by my mother, who may also have kept this memory alive, yet I'm sure it is my earliest, most vivid memory. My mother was inordinately superstitious. Her faith in me, or simply in a child's powers, must have made me feel like God's gift, as if I could ward off death, put everything right, save the world. Despite these awesome powers, my grandmother died the next morning.

On the surface I could not have been a happier child, never praised to my face, for that would have attracted the evil eye, but often singled out. I had the swagger of the precocious kid, always merry and bright, who spoke early and said clever things. Yet I felt somehow on trial, rarely free of my parents' watchful eyes. Our block of Henry Street, between Pike and Rutgers, had an old Catholic church on the corner, Saint Teresa's, and eight or ten *shtieblach*, tiny synagogues, on either side of the street, each with roots in a different Eastern European town. The block was a world unto itself, only a few streets over from the East River, even closer to the Manhattan Bridge, but for a child as vigilantly overseen as I was, these could have been miles away.

Unlike the decaying, overcrowded brownstones that filled the block, which must have been divided into many small flats, 131–33 Henry Street was a relatively modern apartment house, a five-story walk-up with four apartments to each floor, an incinerator chute for garbage, and up-to-date kitchens and bathrooms, small as they were. My parents felt a cut above the working-class Jewish families who filled the building, for we were still observant, which made us feel more genteel. They made few friends there and disapproved that my best friend in the building was Leon, a small, scrappy kid who already had the rough hands of his father, a truck driver. We would huddle in doorways with the girls down the block, who would offer to take down their pants if we took down ours. Riveted but shy, I sometimes refused, at times went along. We burned with curiosity, tempered by embarrassment, about the hidden parts of each other's young bodies.

On the corner opposite the church was a small pharmacy that served as our medical dispensary. Mr. Franklin, the bespectacled pharmacist, was our provider of first aid, as well as an all-purpose authority on minor mishaps. To him we went to remove the cinders that often lodged in our eyes, perhaps from the coal-burning furnaces, or to prescribe cures for cuts, bruises, and ear infections. My most lasting memories of Henry Street in the 1940s were of the block parties that came at the end of the war, when the whole street became a carnival, with food and music as everyone danced to celebrate the servicemen's return.

Two years later, the block was completely blanketed by the great blizzard of '47. Afterward the snow was plowed into a giant fifteen-foot mound near the entrance to our house, and we played on and around it for what seemed like months. Gradually it turned hard and black, as if seamed with veins of coal. Once a year one of the idols of the Lower East Side, the pop-eyed Eddie Cantor, arrived to visit an elderly lady whom he or his wife had known while growing up. The whole block gathered to greet him, delighted that, unlike other celebrities, he never forgot where he came from, his modest beginnings in this Jewish neighborhood.

Only a block away was the school I began to attend in 1945, a yeshiva, the Rabbi Jacob Joseph School, named after a man who had been brought over from Europe in the 1890s to be New York's first and last chief rabbi. Driven to distraction by all the quarreling factions of the Orthodox world, he died unhappy and almost destitute in 1902. The outpouring of grief and guilt among the Jews of the Lower East Side led to a massive funeral procession, the likes of which the city had never seen. On its way it was disrupted by anti-Semitic taunts, by missiles hurled by Irish workmen from the windows of a printing press factory on Grand Street. It proved a bitter moment of truth for New York's immigrant Jews, who fought back and were clubbed by the police. The old ghetto was as much a war zone as a melting pot, with ethnic groups often at each other's throats, the kids worst of all. Such hostilities had died down by the time I arrived, though I recognized them in novels I read from the 1930s.

The yeshiva, founded at the turn of the century, was quickly renamed in honor of the late chief rabbi. Its mission, unlike the small cheders and Talmud Torahs of the neighborhood, was a modern one for its time: to provide a durable secular as well as religious education to young Jews. The secular subjects were much like those in any public school, but on the religious side the emphasis on Talmud, with instruction in Yiddish, was a throwback to the rabbinical academies of Eastern Europe. Since the 1920s, thanks to the burgeoning of Zionism and the Hebrew Enlightenment, there had been a Hebrew track as well, but I was not enrolled in it. The new world of Hebrew as a living language, the vehicle of a revived Hebrew culture, meant little to my parents, for whom Yiddish was still the language of family and tribe.

I would remain at RJJ through the twelfth grade, at first perfectly content, then, as an adolescent, increasingly restive, and finally in continual rebellion. But this belongs to a later phase of the story. I must have been a nerdy kid, perhaps insufferable. My second-grade teacher, the broad-bottomed Miss Heller, marked me down as a chatterbox. On my report cards she repeatedly gave me Ds and Fs for conduct (or "deportment"), much to the fury of my mother, who for years afterward referred to her contemptuously as "Miss Heller, the klutz." But I loved to study, loved showing off what I knew, and certainly basked in the approval of most of my teachers—perhaps also in the envy of other students—long before I began to wonder why I was still there, and what this absorbing parochial education meant to me.

THE GREAT CHANGE in my life came when we decamped from the neighborhood. My uncle Sam moved away before we did, after his life took a rocky turn. His wife, Sylvia, barely in her thirties, died of cancer in 1943, and he moved to Florida with their young daughter to make a fresh start.

There he was married again, to a woman the family (the sisters!) never really came to like, an attitude she resented more and more as she grew older, when she would call my parents to harangue them for not calling her. The sisters rarely accepted their brothers' wives unless they died young, which made them seem angelic, like martyrs, especially in contrast to the grasping second wives, who obviously took advantage of a widowed man's loneliness and helplessness. The sisters' own husbands were accepted only when they joined the family on *its* terms, whole hog, as my father did but Lou, the Communist, emphatically did not. For this he was often cast as one of the villains of the family saga, especially since he could be cruel and demanding in the way he treated my aunt Fay, the most shy and vulnerable of the three sisters.

My parents stayed on the Lower East Side till 1949, when the wholesale clothing firm where my father worked went out of business, and he opened his own dry goods store in Flushing. Turning thirty-five in 1940, newly a father, he was slightly too old to serve in the armed forces. Instead, he earned a modest income all through the war, always imagining that businessmen were making their fortune. He was not one to change jobs—or change anything—too easily. For twenty-five years he had worked at S. Blechman and Sons at 555 Broadway, a "jobber" in the clothing industry, the middle-man between manufacturers and retailers. This market disappeared after the war. Large department stores began buying directly from manufactur-ers, and when the company went under my father was determined to launch his own business. The kind of small, independent store he envied, though it freed him from being a wage slave, was not exactly the wave of the future. With my mother's full-time help it did well enough at the beginning, yet the long hours six days a week would eventually consume their lives, *become* their lives. It was a more viable business than the tiny grocery that Bernard Malamud described in *The Assistant*, but its demands—long hours on your feet, small profit with each transaction—were much the same. I read that painful novel in the late 1950s with a chilling sense of recognition.

Moving from the old Jewish neighborhood to distant Queens, where there were few Jews, was a dramatic turn in my childhood. But I never fully left the Lower East Side, since I continued in school at the yeshiva, just a block down from our old tenement building on Henry Street. The long trip from Queens was extraordinary for a nine-year-old kid in the fifth grade: a bus ride to Main Street, Flushing, then two or three different subway lines to East Broadway, where I would exit near the old Garden Cafeteria and the *Forward* building, both hangouts for the Yiddish literati. In the crowded subway car at rush hour I found I could read almost anything standing up, a book in one hand, hanging on with the other. A few times, in the crush, I was disgusted to feel a disembodied hand along my midsection, inching toward my genitals. What was *that* all about?

Since school itself lasted from nine to six, this saddled me with a twelve-hour day. Despite handball games at lunch hour and a laughably inadequate gym, there was little time for recreation. I began going to lunch at the home of our former neighbors Esther and Jack, who lived across the hall from our old apartment. They had moved in as newlyweds a month after I was born, the very day of my *pidyan ha'ben*, the ceremony of redemption of the firstborn male. Jack was never well. His lungs were in dreadful condition, though we never knew exactly why. He wheezed at the slightest exertion and often paused to catch his breath while walking on the street or climbing the flight of stairs to his first-floor apartment. He was said to have asthma, or a punctured lung, but his profession was even more risky than his health. Though Jack was legally on the books of his brothers' clothing business, he was actually a bookie, or perhaps a numbers runner, and occasionally his disappointed clients got rough and beat him up.

In some ways Esther was as vulnerable as he was. Nearly all her family had perished in Poland during the war, except for two brothers who landed in London, whom she never saw—Europe was far away then. She was a petite woman, less than five feet tall, quite pretty, even a little vain with pitch-black hair that was always perfectly groomed. She wore lipstick and powder and visited the beauty parlor every week, something that my mother, who cared little about her appearance, never did, even when she had a wedding to attend. Esther never learned to read or write English, and her fluty, high-pitched voice and broken English, dotted with Yiddish, was never less than colorful. "Ersgusting," she said about anything that offended her. Nearby Clinton Street was always "Clincoln Stritt." She got all her news from the Yiddish papers, though the news scarcely interested her. She loved the group activities at the Educational Alliance on East

Broadway, an institution founded by uptown Jews to bring culture to the immigrant hordes, but she must have skipped the English classes or done badly in them, for they never took.

Jack doted on her, helpless and childlike as she often seemed, and he served as her link to the practical world. He was a Damon Runyon character who called women "tomatehs," lived a shadowy life, and endlessly shuffled small pieces of paper covered with numbers. Her sphere was the home, where she cooked, expertly, the Eastern European Jewish dishes my mother never dreamed of making: borscht (beet soup), *schav* (sorrel soup), pirogen, blintzes, and kreplach (all forms of dumplings), holishkes (stuffed cabbage), tzimmes (carrot stew), and kugel (potato or noodle pudding). All I knew about Jewish cooking came through Esther. My mother, having next to no interest in homemaking, confined herself to chicken (usually boiled) and pot roast (cooked over onions), with boiled carrots, canned peas, and boiled potatoes on the side, all seasoned only with salt. For a Jewish family this was simple maintenance, but it was the homely fare I grew up on, and mostly loved. About food, certainly, I had a lot to learn.

Esther and Jack were childless, perhaps because his health was so precarious and she was so high-strung—her tremulous fears made my mother, with all her anxieties, seem rock-solid. Gradually Esther and Jack adopted us, my whole family but especially my sister and me, so that when we moved to Flushing it seemed inevitable for me to eat at their home, even sleep over occasionally if the weather was really bad. For all this they would never accept a farthing of payment, only the modest gifts—some aprons, for example—that my mother would bring from the store whenever she visited. My mother, who thrived in the give-and-take of a retail business, the constant whirl of people and talk, was glad to off-load some of her parental responsibilities, which Esther and Jack were only too glad to assume. Every summer, though she disliked the beach and couldn't swim, Esther would spend a week or two in Rocky Point, to make sure the kids could remain in the country while my mother went back to work in the store. I was always "Maishele" to her, the son she never had. Thus I grew up with not one but two Jewish mothers, both worrying about me enough that I should never have had to worry about myself, though I did.

One benefit of having such surrogate parents, as my mother and father saw it, was that I could continue at school on the Lower East Side; to them this was the only authentically Jewish place in America. I had to carry on there to keep from going astray, but also to make up for their own departure, however arduous my daily trek might be. Though our corner of Flushing had a small conservative synagogue, to them the area was a *goyishe* wasteland, not really a place to raise Jewish children. It was an Irish and Italian working-class neighborhood—they had first heard about it from one of their Italian neighbors in Rocky Point—but so it had to be: this was my parents' trade, their *parnasseh*, or livelihood. But placing their son and heir in the local public school would have been a step too far. I had to be that much more Jewish to make up for their transgressions, which were built into living there. After a few weeks' trial they found it impossible to keep the store shut on the Sabbath. They had tried, and I can imagine how much anguished discussion went into this big step. Otherwise they felt they couldn't survive.

My duty was to carry the Jewish life they had so compromised into the next generation. The Lower East Side, the yeshiva, were links to their youth, ways of keeping faith with their Eastern European roots. On Sundays, when the store was closed, they traveled back to the old neighborhood, with its kosher delicatessens and dairy restaurants, to buy real pickles at Guss, genuine rye bread and marble chiffon cake at Gertel's, and ready-to-wear items at cost on Orchard Street, both for themselves and for their customers. This was where much of their families still lived. Though many immigrant Jews and their prospering children had fled—the ghetto meant poverty to them, poverty and Old World ways—for my parents the neighborhood where they had been raised could never really be replaced.

I'VE WRITTEN about my mother and her clan, the extended family in which I grew up, but where was my father in all this? She had the more stormy personality, her pure soprano voice radiating waves of emotion. Abe was diffident and soft-spoken. Physically compact, wiry and muscular, with tortoise-shell glasses and a receding hairline, he seemed to embody a quiet authority rarely exercised. His mood was usually stoical—you could hear it in his slow, heavy, deliberate tread on a stairway—but he turned angry on some occasions, almost giddy with laughter and high spirits on others. When he blew up in momentary anger or exasperation, my mother instantly shrank back. His spasms of fury passed quickly but they terrified me as well. Two or three times he whacked me for grave offenses I can no longer recall, but this kind of discipline was as unusual as it was unforgettable.

Abe was a self-educated man; he came here at seventeen in 1922 with little schooling and only a few words of English. He learned English in night school, in the jobs he held, and by reading newspapers. I don't remember seeing the *New York Times* as a child, only the working-class favorite, the *Daily News*, and Dorothy Schiff's liberal *New York Post*, but by the late 1940s he read the *Times* every day, partly as relief from the daily grind of his business. For the next four and a half decades it would be his university, his graduate education. Since he kept his views to himself, you might not have guessed how intelligent he was. He followed the stock market's ups and downs closely, day after day, though he told me he'd last invested in it (in a small way) in 1928, until things began to look shaky to him. From then on it became his cherished spectator sport, the dramatic scene of his fantasy life, filled with unexpected turns of fate and fortune. If he saw me as a vehicle for his thwarted ambitions, he doted fondly on my sister, found it hard to deny her anything—ice skates, roller skates, a bicycle, fashionable clothing that he could usually pick up wholesale. His daily conversation was about the store, which he came to detest; about the synagogue, where he became the gabbai, or sexton, who distributes the honors that were sprinkled through the service; and about the family, a never-ending saga. But he also followed politics intently, almost religiously, like the stock market. Growing up poor had made him a lifelong liberal; feeling powerless, he kept a watchful eye on those who were in charge, as if his own fate hung in the balance.

Not long ago I dug out an old audio cassette made by Jeremy, my son, in 1982 and listened to it on a Sony Walkman I had not used in years. Miraculously, the tape and even the old batteries in the Walkman were in perfect condition. Then just fifteen but sounding even younger, Jeremy was interviewing his seventy-seven-year-old grandfather for a high school history class. Much of it was about the American history of the previous six decades, from Warren G. Harding to Ronald Reagan. The questions touched on the stock market crash, the Great Depression, the war, Truman,

McCarthy, Vietnam. My father, like most Jews of his generation, was an unshakable Democrat, a devoted union man who had actively maintained his membership, partly for the benefits, even after he went into business on his own. About history and politics he proved surprisingly knowledgeable and spoke with conviction. He could recall the presidential election of 1924, when he had just arrived in America. No, he said firmly, Harding was not reelected before Calvin Coolidge succeeded him. Installed by a clique of corrupt advisers, he died in office. Then Coolidge defeated a forgotten conservative Democrat named John W. Davis. Such distant recollections of forgotten candidates were scarcely on anyone else's lips.

I wished there had been more personal questions, for I wanted to hear much about his life that I had never bothered to ask. On the tape he became unusually animated as he talked about his fears during the Depression. "I was worried day and night," he said. Each worker had a punch card, and by Friday, which was payday, he said, "we were shivery, scared," that the card would be missing, an indication they were laid off. "We were constantly in a jittery state of mind." Another moment of truth comes at the end of the interview, just when I'd given up learning more about his personal history. Jeremy asks him if there's anything he'd like to add, any story he wants to tell. He had always acted as though nothing could be less interesting to him, or to any of us, than his early life, though I'd heard a few bits about how they had been displaced from Dembitz (Debica), their Galician town in southern Poland, during the First World War, and spent part of the war in a refugee camp in what later became Czechoslovakia. Now, suddenly, the tape became a message in a bottle, an unexpected legacy, and I heard the whole story for the first time.

His father, Shabse, like my mother's father, had left for America before the war to earn enough to bring the family over, but within a year the war broke out. Not long afterward, when my father was nine or ten, they were warned that the Russians were coming and would soon overrun their corner of Poland, then still part of the Austrian Empire. With his mother, who had a heart condition, his grandmother, and his baby brother, Nachum, they were evacuated by the Austrians in cattle cars, first to Vienna, where they were turned away—the place was already swamped with refugees—and then to the Czech city of Brno (or Brin, as he called it). My father described this journey in terms eerily reminiscent of accounts of the Holocaust, with "hundreds of people in each car, no place to urinate or leave your waste." (He was not usually given to talk about bodily functions.) But at Brno, in a makeshift refugee camp, they were cared for by the local population for more than a year before being told it was safe to return home; the Russians had retreated. Transported back, the family found that "the town was burnt to the ground. There wasn't a single house standing." For the next several years they shared crude barracks with several other families, sleeping on the floor, until they were able to join my grandfather and two older sons in the United States. The tape is silent about *that* journey, but the seven-year ordeal from 1915 to 1922 explained a great deal about my father's anxieties during the Depression, as well as the caution, the stoical determination, with which he lived his life over the next half century. As he saw it, all people lived their lives on thin ice; their world could give way at any moment.

MY MOTHER'S FAMILY, as I've said, was a tight matriarchy. The men who married into it were expected to fit in, as my father seemed glad to do. He remained remotely loyal to his own family but their dour temper, which my mother quietly mocked as typically *Galizianer* (Galician) gloom, and their stern, forbidding religious outlook made them seem so different from her boisterous Russian clan. (For those times such a match was considered intermarriage.) I scarcely knew my father's parents, since his mother was already dead when I was born and his father, with his gray rabbinical beard, whom I dimly recall, died when I was four. My one possession of his, which I value, is an inexpensive set of the Five Books of Moses, surrounded by Rashi and other medieval commentaries, but its pages are as friable as old newsprint, as ephemeral as the past itself. I well remember my father's three brothers: Szrul (Israel), the patriarch, peremptory and domineering, like my mother's eldest brother; Charlie, who married a girl from the southern Jewish merchant class and moved to Savannah, freeing himself from his big brother's authority; and Nachum, the baby brother, not entirely right in the head, with a marked facial twitch, who peddled merchandise on the streets near Union Square, lived in a furnished room, and never married.

When I was a child we sometimes visited Szrul, his wife, Hinda, and their four children on Columbia Street, near Delancey, where my father had lived before he was married. Their flat always seemed sepulchral and dark, perhaps because we were invariably there on *Shabbes*, when it *was* dark, since few lights were left burning. With a bathtub in the middle of the kitchen and an elevated toilet tank with a pull chain, it belonged to an older, poorer section of the Lower East Side, all eventually torn down to make way for public housing. By that time Szrul and his family had moved to Crown Heights, an attractive Orthodox neighborhood in Brooklyn, and over the years we saw them mainly at the weddings of their numerous grandchildren, more than twenty of them, as they married into large, even more observant Chasidic families.

I sensed that my father feared his elder brother's judgment of him, and gradually came to prefer my mother's family for its more tolerant, easygoing ways. Szrul certainly knew that my father kept his business open on the Sabbath but, in an unwonted act of self-restraint, had made up his mind never to mention it. He was less restrained one of the last times I saw him, at the cemetery, when his wife of more than fifty years was buried. I had grown a beard just as the sixties ended. He eyed me suspiciously, tugged at my facial hair, and said, "You can't fool *me*. That's the wrong *kind* of beard." Did this reflect his sense of humor, or mine? If my beard was evidence of conversion, it was in the wrong direction. My apostasy to the yeshiva world, perhaps my father's defection as well, was written satirically on my face.

Long before, even as I had begun to rebel, our congregation in Flushing still thought of me as the great white hope of Judaism. As the neighborhood's only yeshiva boy, I was expected to become a rabbi—something I never considered, though my busy synagogue life might have suggested otherwise. Since I loved to sing, on Friday nights I led the junior congregation. For guidance, the cantor had cut a ten-inch LP recording of the entire service for me, and I imitated his pure melodic flow with teenage zest, even showmanship. I had a good voice and I was shamelessly vain; I longed for applause, for appreciation, and I got it. Yet something deeper must have been at work. To this day that service—beginning with five or six ravishing Psalms, followed by *lecha dodi*, the most beautiful prayer in the liturgy, welcoming the Sabbath as a winsome bride—resonates for me like an island of tranquillity in a sea of troubles.

A more demanding synagogue responsibility came soon afterward. I had learned to read the Torah for my own bar mitzvah service; two years later, at the age of fifteen, I became the regular Torah reader, the *lehner*, for the whole congregation. The task demanded serious hours of weekly preparation, since the Torah scrolls lack vowel signs and musical markings—they had to be memorized. On a few occasions I even gave a substitute sermon, as if I were the young rabbi-in-waiting. I worked hard at it, making sure that everyone was blown away. What I got in return, besides the pleasure of mastering difficult things, was a radiant glow of attention, the warm element in which I surely basked. But the words and music of the service and the chanting of the weekly readings sank into the subsoil of my emotions at an impressionable age, never to be rooted out.

At eleven I eagerly joined the local Boy Scout troop, and though I did my share of hiking, camping, dodgeball, and rope tricks with ingenious knots, essentially I became the troop's orator, making speeches at semiformal occasions when parents and friends were invited, especially the annual celebration of the founding of the scouting movement. If there could be such a thing as a Boy Scout intellectual, that was me, facile and silver-tongued, ever ready to sing out the ideals of the movement and comb through its history. In all this I somehow missed living a boy's life. My friendships with other boys were starved, shallow; I was overflowing with energy but my animal spirits were impoverished. Long days at school (including Sundays), duties at the synagogue, piano lessons on Friday afternoons, and enforced idleness on the Sabbath, when I would ransack the local public library, left little time for physical activity, though time enough for extended bouts of reading. I had a terrible hunger for knowledge yet found myself pulled in too many directions, though I didn't understand this until years later. Only the carefree summers in Rocky Point relieved the inexorable pressure to ingest the world, to read everything and know everything, to excel and to impress.

If I was overextended, one small traumatic moment should have put me on guard, though it did no such thing. Szrul's three sons, all older than me, studied at an even more traditional yeshiva than I did, on East Broadway, just around the corner from where we lived before moving to Flushing. It was headed by Rav Moshe Feinstein, a shy, self-effacing man but also the most revered authority on halacha, Jewish law, in America. Like a judge in a rabbinical court, he issued innumerable rulings that applied Talmudic teachings to the innovations of modern life, especially scientific advances. Perhaps out of deference to him, or to Szrul and his family, along with others who still lived on the Lower East Side, including Tante Lily and Esther and Jack, it was decided that my bar mitzvah would take place at that yeshiva, which I'd never attended. A bar mitzvah then was not such a big affair as it later became among middle-class suburban Jews, but it was a serious milestone. I was told that it was the moment you became responsible for your own sins; until then they were logged on your father's spiritual account.

I duly prepared, tutored by my old first-grade teacher, Rabbi Lazar, and after six months of practice, rehearsing again and again, I read the long maftir (the concluding Torah portion) and the haftorah (the week's selection from the prophets) with aplomb. (I had a decent musical ear and still remember them more or less by heart.) But during the kiddush, the reception that followed, I looked around at a sea of venerable but unfamiliar sages, grew confused, and began reciting the wrong blessing over the wine. I was quickly corrected by the murmuring beards and I carried on, but the feeling of shame seemed to reach into the core of my being and I flushed to the very fingertips. For years afterward, whenever I thought back to that moment, I could feel my face redden, my breathing quicken, as if it were some kind of disgrace I would never live down—the humiliation of seeming unprepared, of making such an obvious mistake. I felt exposed before the elders, who expected more of me, but the real problem was what I demanded unforgivingly of myself.

A comical version of this public embarrassment came two years later when I landed my first summer job. I had outgrown Rocky Point and somehow found a job in a very religious Catskills hotel. There were more elderly rabbis there than in the yeshiva, and the hotel was so strictly observant that it had no pool, though swimming was the only thing that might have saved the summer. Too young to be a waiter or busboy, I was hired to work in the tearoom (where guests could snack on cake and cookies between ample meals) but also to chant the Torah on Sabbath mornings. This part of the job led to my downfall, but also to my unexpected liberation.

A pair of Torah portions, including some quite long ones, are sometimes joined together for the weekly reading (except during leap years, which add a month to the lunar calendar). My luck: just such a marathon affair was on tap for my very first week at the hotel. Taking a first look through the seemingly endless reading, I quickly realized that as a novice there was no way I could learn it all. One of the two portions would simply have to do on its own, or so I imagined. And why not, since it was more than long enough? I was only fifteen, with minimal experience: what more could they expect? I rehearsed for several days and when the time came I simply began to read, not letting anyone in on my sensible plan. By the first break everyone realized what I had in mind. A buzz of horror, no, of scandal, swept through the room as if I were trampling on the sacred writ, editing it for my own convenience. I finished my reading and someone else, no doubt a veteran relief pitcher, picked up where I left off, but I was duly disgraced.

Instead of feeling shamed I was amused and outraged. The punctilio of ritual, the unbending Orthodox need to dot every *i*, suddenly struck me as ludicrous. The next day my father came up from the city to see how I was doing, and I begged him to rescue me, to get me out of there. He called a friend who was part owner of a hotel not far away in Ferndale, and he agreed to take me on. My duties were the same—I led Sabbath services and worked the tearoom—but the atmosphere there was lax and permissive. I could do exactly what I wanted, which was whatever the big boys did. Tagging along with the college kids, the waiters and busboys who had the real jobs in the hotel, I became their watchful disciple. The yeshiva boy had stumbled into new freedom. With no one to answer to, free of the pressures of family, the expectations of teachers, I felt as though my separate life had finally begun. I would stay for three summers, all through my high school years, earning only meager tips and, after the first year, a minimal salary of ten dollars a week, but enjoying every moment of my freedom, as if I'd finally taken one of the larky turns I envied in my cousins' more adventurous lives.

This liberation could not last. Returning to school that September in 1955, I felt that a weight had settled on my shoulders. I loved my English and history classes—the teaching was good, even challenging—and I had fun with French and math, though my teachers were eccentric misfits who had somehow landed in this yeshiva backwater. Science, as always, was a black hole that I could safely ignore, then simply cram for the state Regents exam at the end of the year. But the religious subjects that occupied me six days a week from nine to one, limited to advanced study of the Talmud, had gone completely dead for me.

I had already spent the preceding year in incipient rebellion, refusing to learn as much as an additional page; the Talmud had grown tasteless to me, completely irrelevant to my life. My teacher that year, as I later realized, must have been a hapless Holocaust survivor, a refugee who knew scarcely a word of English. No doubt he barely escaped the carnage in Europe with his life, a fate that personally touched no one in my family, who all arrived here by the early 1920s. With the special cruelty of the young, I sometimes taunted the man to his face. Or else I concealed other books under the oversized tractates of the Talmud. When he asked me (in Yiddish) why I wasn't paying attention, I said, "Because it's spring, tra-la, and the birds are singing." The class was in an uproar, laughing aloud, and he looked stricken and befuddled. This impudent retort became a school legend. Of course there were no birds in sight; under the weight of age-old texts we were all pale prisoners, condemned to an indoor life in a dingy setting, the building's shabby synagogue, since they were short of classrooms. Even as logic or dialectic, this enforced study of ancient legal debates had ceased to interest me.

Ten years later, when I had my first college teaching job, a friend (Herb Leibowitz) and I would regale the other assistant professors with routines from the Talmud, drawn-out, legalistic exchanges utterly remote from the life we lived. We had started, as all eight- and nine-year-olds are started, with simple laws of tort: what can be done when an ox gores a neighbor's cow, or when an ox gores for the fourth of fifth time. But even before we reached puberty we were dealing with the laws of marriage and divorce (divorce first!), long, difficult tractates that required more knowledge of anatomy and human behavior than we actually possessed.

One memorable period was spent entirely on the rules pertaining to "unnatural intercourse." A mischievous student raised his hand with a question, in Yiddish of course: "Rebbe, can you tell me what is unnatural intercourse?" No fool, the rabbi shot back, "First you tell me about natural intercourse, and then I'll explain unnatural intercourse." End of discussion. We were meant to explore the intricate rules and arguments without fully grasping what they were about, just as we'd been taught to recite our prayers in singsong Hebrew without understanding what they meant. I grew fiercely alienated from such a sterile formalism unconnected to actual experience. This was less the fault of the Talmud than of how we were being taught. We were directed solely to the halacha, the legal side of the Talmud, while ignoring the aggadah, the tales, legends, and reports of everyday life that might have engaged us more, besides giving us some sense of the actual world, the lives of Jews in their Babylonian exile, where these arguments unfolded.

A peculiar standoff developed between me and my Hebrew teachers. I adamantly refused to study any more Talmud, but still was passed along from grade to grade, making each teacher miserable in turn. One of them, having spied me reading something behind my Talmud volume, swooped down on me and seized not a comic book, as he expected, but a slim volume of the Yale Shakespeare—appropriately, *As You Like It*, a play about leaving the city and the court behind, to find passion and regeneration in more natural surroundings, just what was missing on the Lower East Side. Instead of tearing the book up in front of the class, as he would have done with a comic book, he stared at it blankly, as at a foreign body that had insinuated itself into Jewish life.

I was arrogant, unapologetic, stubbornly holding my breath through two more years, making a beeline for college while trying to break free of a way of life that had shaped me. Meanwhile, on the secular side, I shifted from adolescent reading, much of it about sports, to "serious" novels. In the public library opposite the railroad station I stumbled on Somerset Maugham's egregious abridgments of ten great novels, including *Wuthering Heights* and *Old Man Goriot*, which were catnip to a reader as slow and pedantic as I was. But I was also taken with books like *Marjorie Morningstar* that surprised me by making literature out of the Jewish world I knew.

On many Wednesday afternoons I would cut classes with a friend, Willy Kantrowitz, to take in a Broadway matinee. In this way I saw half the popular plays and musicals of the decade, from *South Pacific* and *The Caine Mutiny Court-Martial* to *The Teahouse of the August Moon* and *Inherit the*

Wind. Had I been more hip I might have discovered the jazz scene, but that was as remote as a distant planet. Instead, I joined the Literary Guild and, worse still, the Reader's Digest Condensed Book Club, so that I could keep up with the latest bestsellers. I loved the feeling of being in the know, up on what everyone else was talking about. In short I had the makings of a perfect fifties middlebrow, taking baby steps toward serious culture without really knowing how demanding it could be or what it had to offer.

Since I could scarcely imagine going away to college—how would my parents afford it?—I set my sights on Columbia, to which I could commute from home. I knew next to nothing about it other than its reputation as the best university in the city. A couple of the waiters I knew in the Catskills were Columbia students. One of my English teachers also did some teaching there, and the school principal, Mr. Winter, was a proud graduate. I had some gift for writing, which seemed to come easily to me: little hand-written essays for my courses, articles and editorials as editor of the school newspaper, the *RJJ Journal*, and polemical speeches for the debating team, which competed energetically in the yeshiva debating league. (I recall Alan Dershowitz, who was a year ahead of me at a school in Brooklyn, as one sharp-tongued opponent.)

I enjoyed the research for these debates, though the topics, pure off-shoots of 1950s politics, were less than inspiring. Should Red China be admitted to the UN? (Yes, it was always called "Red China.") Should wiretapping be legalized? (Justice Holmes, I discovered, called it "a dirty business.") Should we build the St. Lawrence Seaway? (Hard to recall why *that* was controversial.) This helped me understand that there *were* issues: there was more than one side to every question; writing and speaking were acts of persuasion that demanded coherent arguments and an instinctive, tactical feeling for one's audience.

All this busywork must have helped me get into Columbia, and so did my helter-skelter reading, which ranged from Herman Wouk to Kafka. On my application I mentioned Winston Churchill's recent *History of the English-Speaking Peoples* among my favorite reading, though I'd read only the lavishly illustrated four-part abridgment in *Life* magazine. (Churchill cheated too; he didn't really write most of it, but added only the incomparable Churchillian patina.) My interviewer, a young professor of international relations, Kenneth Waltz, fastened on this choice. "So you like reading Churchill," he said. "Oh, yes," I piped up, and I did. I was a sucker for grand style. Whether he was impressed or amused I could not tell. Years later it dawned on me that the grandiloquent Churchill was not exactly the hot ticket among academics as a writer or historian.

My trajectory toward Morningside Heights was nearly derailed several times, not least when I took the wrong train to the interview and landed in the middle of Harlem. From where I exited the subway I could just make out the colossus shimmering on the hill above me like Kafka's unapproachable Castle. The trek I made along West 116 Street and through Morningside Park, later a battleground between the community and the university, seemed to represent the social distance I was traveling from Henry Street and the Lower East Side.

I was a little frightened, somewhat awed by the path I was taking. Friends from the preceding class had entered Columbia and instilled terror into us when they returned to RJJ for a visit. One of them, Alan Feld, who later became a law professor, was carrying a copy of the unpronounceable *Oresteia* of Aeschylus, which looked absurdly difficult—far beyond what I was then reading. He displayed it like a badge, a sign that he was now playing in the big leagues. I wondered: would I measure up? I took the test for a National Merit Scholarship but didn't qualify, and the assistant principal, Mr. Sternfield, couldn't resist telling me how much hope they had invested in me and how I had disappointed everyone.

Shamefaced, I redoubled my efforts to prepare for the College Boards, drilling myself in math problems and methodically memorizing forty new vocabulary words every night. I hadn't realized I possessed such discipline. In the early spring, while waiting to hear from colleges, I went through a sudden religious revival; my adolescent fervor, welling up out of nowhere, surprised everyone around me. Turning away from my Columbia plans, I put in a late application to Yeshiva University, which would have been a safe way to keep to the path I'd followed since the first grade. With unexpected passion, I slipped into a paroxysm of faith and prayer, donning my tefillin each morning as I'd long since given up doing. The bubble burst an hour or two before the first Passover seder in April when a telegram arrived offering me a General Motors Scholarship, which would cover not only tuition at

Columbia but the cost of living there. Telegrams were a rarity in our home; everyone was dumbfounded. In the light of this offer, my weeks of focusing on Yeshiva evaporated like a morning fog, along with my newfound religious zeal.

I had always assumed I would commute to college, never dreamed I might move out, but my uncle Lou, the Communist, always the family troublemaker, who had himself been deprived of an education, pointed out the practical benefits. "They're willing to pay for you," he said. "You'd get so much less if you were just living at home." This was impossible to pass up. Even my parents could not resist the financial logic, though they must have been miserable at the thought of my leaving.

I went to see an assistant dean at Columbia, Henry Coleman, who picked up the phone and arranged for a dorm room, though space was at a premium and, as he had first told me, freshmen from New York City were not being offered housing on campus. This would be a tremendous break from the sheltered yeshiva life and home life I had led, even more than the summer jobs that offered brief, exhilarating periods of independence. It was a thrilling though scary prospect, for I could hardly guess at what I might do with the freer yet more uncertain life that lay before me in the great world.

Three

MORNINGSIDE HEIGHTS

S KIP LIGHTLY to a bright sunny day in June 1958. My freshman year in Columbia College had come to a hectic close with a battery of exams and papers but I had somehow gotten through it. At home in Queens I'd slept off the exhaustion of the exam period, surprised that such bone-weariness and sleep deprivation could be shed so lightly. Now I was back on campus to return a book to the library, strolling along College Walk in a languorous mood. The strain of a difficult year was a distant memory. It was well past commencement, the tents and folding chairs had been carted off, and the Morningside campus, usually buzzing with students and faculty, seemed completely deserted.

Free of the stream of humanity that usually flowed through and around them, the grand classical buildings looked like well-preserved remnants of antiquity shimmering in the light of early summer. The campus was eerily quiet and peaceful. To my left I could see the statue of Alma Mater, seated with her arms outstretched, symbolizing the university as a seat of learning that nurtured young minds. Behind it, atop a long sweep of stairs, were the imposing marble columns and vast circular dome of Low Library, once an actual library, now the university's administrative center. The architecture, so different from the Gothic imitations of other Ivy League campuses, spoke silently not of ecclesiastical beginnings but of classical and secular culture.

On my right I could see the flat façade and decorative colonnade of Butler

Library, shielding the multistory windows of the main reading room. Just below the building's roof, chiseled in stone, I noticed, as if for the first time, the names of writers I had been reading in the college's Humanities course, those venerable landmarks of the Western tradition: Homer, Herodotus, Plato, Sophocles, Aristotle. Without warning, I found myself in a blissful frame of mind, tranquil and contented. Between the sunny warmth of the day, the unruffled peace of the elegant campus, and the stately procession of the writers' names, I felt curiously happy. It struck me all at once: here was what I had been looking for all my life, a home away from home where I could settle in, at least for the time being, which at eighteen seemed like forever. Without realizing I was going anywhere, I had nonetheless arrived; a glimpse of my future opened up before me.

Part of this serenity was a feeling of relief that I had come through, since that first year of college had been anything but trouble-free. The names on the library, like the book in my hand, told one story, a tale of discovery that matched the sunny June day itself. The book I was returning was a little volume of lectures, *Don Quixote's Profession*, written by a teacher of mine, Mark Van Doren. I had just taken his course "The Narrative Art," which included a slow journey through Cervantes's novel as well as Homer's *Odyssey*, some tales from the Hebrew Bible and the Apocrypha, and, as if from another universe entirely, Kafka's unfinished novel *The Castle*.

Much as I admired the soft-spoken, silver-haired Van Doren, he was not exactly a role model for a Jewish kid from Queens and the Lower East Side. He had been a fixture on the college faculty since 1920. With his midwestern reserve and air of timeless wisdom, he seemed quintessentially rural and American, a more academic version of his friend Robert Frost. As a poet, critic, and teacher he trod softly, holding himself in abeyance. I found it difficult to remember anything specific he put out in his lectures, but the books he spoke about seemed to glow more brightly, to glisten under his warm inspection. He retrieved tiny details, a terse biblical phrase, some striking lines of dialogue, a curious wrinkle of character, and made you pleased to notice them. As a reader and critic he disappeared into the object of his attention. These stories, the way they were told, the people in them, the role of the gods in their all-too-human lives, were an endless source of wonder to him. Reading his book was my way of extending his course, for I had enjoyed it with a surprising passion, moved by its spirit of sharp-eyed appreciation. It was not officially open to freshman but I'd talked my way into it, since students loved it and I learned he would soon be retiring.

It was a somewhat distracted young man who sat in his class twice a week and wrote brief papers on which Van Doren bestowed a few gracious words of approval. Though it seemed to go smoothly at first, college life had not been an easy transition for me. The initial challenge, after twelve years as a yeshiva student, always under the vigilant eye of parents and teachers, was how much of my deeply ingrained religious practice I could (or wanted to) keep up. During freshman orientation week we had all worn silly blue Columbia beanies, the mark of the unfledged newcomer. Would I now uncover my head? The Israeli fashion for small knitted yarmulkas had not yet come in; I had lived my street life under a series of Yankee baseball caps. Although we were not close friends, three or four of us from our yeshiva had stuck together through freshman week, foraging for dinner at nearby kosher delicatessens. What then? One solution was the dining hall of nearby Jewish Theological Seminary, where I began to take classes three days a week on top of my Columbia courses. Some of my father's very observant family were indignant to learn that I studied in this citadel of Conservative Judaism. "I'd sooner send my children to church than to a place like that," one of his nephews told him. My father, a mild-mannered but sensitive man, was amused by this but may also have felt pangs of remorse at being so cavalierly judged for letting me go my own way.

At the seminary I could treat myself to very basic kosher meals a few times a week and find solidarity with other Jews from Barnard and Columbia. But what I most appreciated was the tolerant environment. In the yeshiva world I felt—and was—under constant surveillance. One of my teachers roamed the streets near school in off-hours, pouncing on students who had removed their caps, browbeating them with finger-wagging warnings. At the seminary, though the religious services, even the core values, were quite traditional and reassuringly familiar to me, no one ever preached to me, scolded me for doing something wrong, violating some commandment, shaming my family and my fellow students. I could do just as I wished—once I knew what I wanted to do! That was the crux of the problem, for I hardly knew.

The seminary gave me an education in Hebrew language and culture that had been omitted in the yeshiva, with its Old World curriculum focused on legal rabbinic debate. This in turn eased my transition to a secular university. But every Friday afternoon I would head back to all my duties and routines in Flushing, continuing with the piano lessons I'd started two years earlier, leading the Junior Congregation in the synagogue that evening, then chanting the long Torah portion the next morning and a briefer one later that afternoon, as I had been doing since I was fifteen. It was as if I had never left. On Sunday morning I would return to Morningside Heights, take seminary classes all afternoon, and then try to finish the next big work of literature and philosophy for the Humanities class, alongside the briefer, knottier texts in European history and social thought assigned for Contemporary Civilization. Meeting four days a week, these courses offered a total immersion in the Western tradition—at times superficially, or haphazardly, but with serious impact on our young, unformed minds.

With dizzying momentum, I seemed to be taking a crash course in everything worth knowing. In a few short months I went from being a slow, deliberate reader, savoring each phrase, each sentence, to something of a speed reader; still I had trouble getting through these hefty assignments. I was leading two lives and thought I could do it all: Morningside Heights and Flushing, Columbia and the seminary, piano lessons and *Spectator*, the student newspaper on which I spent at least an afternoon a week as a cub reporter. After all, I had always juggled the complicated demands I made on myself, and no one had ever suggested I couldn't.

For freshman English I had a young but fearsome teacher, Jim Zito—bad luck, I was told, because he was rumored to be the toughest grader in the college. Though still an instructor with a Ph.D. to finish (along with a massive aversion to writing that kept him from finishing it), he was already a legend for his offhand brilliance, someone said to be impossible to please. An explosively compact man with thinning hair, large frame glasses, and a sharp, needling voice, he reminded me of an owl-eyed character actor and radio personality named Arnold Stang, who made a specialty of annoying people. His whiplike manner in class—he seemed almost to spit out his words—was translated into unsparing comments on our papers—and unsparing grades. (Mine started with a C plus.) After four years as a high school journalist, the overly confident editor of the school paper, someone used to valentines from his English teachers, I wasn't prepared for how he took apart my syntax, nailed clichés, crossed out slack or vague words, and rejiggered my sentence rhythms. Mr. Zito did not believe in coddling students or worried overmuch about their feelings. He was partisan to the cold bath approach to education, a firm believer in shock therapy. As a writer I was humbled, abashed, tossed into purgatory. In his distant and seemingly heartless way he became my first college mentor, a model of relentless, cruel intelligence.

His own mentor was the equally demanding Shakespearean Andrew Chiappe—my faculty adviser, as it happened—who had taken over the department's Shakespeare course from Mark Van Doren more than a decade earlier. Portly, walleyed, thickly bespectacled, he spoke with a cultivated accent that was impossible to place; precise and refined, it seemed vaguely British yet continental. He was the epitome of the bachelor Oxbridge don, a closeted type I had not yet encountered in the flesh, but he recited Shakespeare with a mellifluous voice that brought to mind John Gielgud. (Gielgud's peerless anthology of Shakespeare readings, *The Ages of Man*, was one of the first recordings I ever bought.) Chiappe's genius, like Zito's, was oral; he was completely blocked as a writer and, as I heard, had not written anything since his unpublished Cambridge University thesis in the 1930s. Yet in a volume he passed around in class I came across his handwritten translations of five Shakespeare sonnets into French, something he must have dashed off as an exercise. Though Van Doren published a great deal while Chiappe and Zito published nothing, between them I got an inkling of the literary life as an almost religious devotion to great writing, as attentive to language as to character and experience.

I was close to drowning in the great books yet under pressure to be more rigorous, more finely focused in how I dealt with them. There would be no more vague, passionate arias of appreciation. My teachers didn't care that I loved a book; they wanted to know why. My education was plunging forward at a swift clip even as I was caught up in contradictions that were making my life hard to manage. I had been lucky to have good English teachers in high school, but the books they assigned were few, and we read them so sluggishly they didn't hang together. Taking the core courses at

Columbia was like stepping from a puddle into the roiling sea. At the same time my seminary classes in the Bible, the Hebrew language, Jewish history, and Jewish philosophy, all conducted in conversational Hebrew, had little connection to the work I had done (or not done) at the yeshiva, in Yiddish, focused almost solely on the Talmud. Now I was working my way through Homer's *Iliad* and Sophocles's Oedipus trilogy by day and grappling with the conjugation of Hebrew verbs in the evening.

Whatever the toll this disparate work was taking, the late 1950s was a fortunate time to pursue a general education. Freshly minted translations by Richmond Lattimore and other classicists had made ancient Greek literature more accessible yet more fascinatingly strange. Where earlier translators like Alexander Pope had turned the classics into their own polished idiom, the loose hexameters of Lattimore's *Iliad* suggested the textures of the original verse in ways the Augustans and Victorians had shunned. The paperback revolution had just taken off, making classic works cheaply available; series like the Penguin Classics offered fluent, uncommonly readable translations of prose works ranging from Herodotus and Thucydides to Rabelais and Cervantes. We were exposed to the texts of the Western tradition in contemporary ways, not as scholars but as untutored readers, no doubt missing or misconstruing a good deal of what we read.

As innocents wandering among masterpieces, we were short-circuiting the specializations and transgressing the national boundaries that had balkanized literary study. This had elicited furious controversy between the two world wars when the courses were first introduced. Departments of literature, history, and philosophy had walled off their turf; scholars had defended their critical specialties, their methods of research. General education seemed to them irresponsibly superficial, especially as taught by nonspecialists. We could not know that part of the original goal of these courses was to civilize the unwashed, to acculturate the large numbers of children of immigrants, at that time mainly Jewish, who had been making their way into the university. In other ways this acculturation was the goal of the seminary too, for its curriculum, a product of the Haskalah, or Hebrew Enlightenment, was partly a reaction against the scholastic learning and pious homiletics of Talmudical academies like Rabbi Jacob Joseph. Each in its own way, Columbia and the seminary were joining forces to pull me out of the ghetto and set me down on the secular soil of the modern world.

Though I was awed and attracted by these new horizons, I resisted giving up the world I came from, partly out of inertia, partly from fear of the unknown, of losing my moorings and drifting off. But the strain between my overcrowded days on Morningside Heights and the busy weekends in Queens eventually extended me to the breaking point. Two of my freshman roommates were deracinated Jews, remote from any religious tradition, but the third, Mike Gidos, was a fervent Catholic from Buffalo, and we shared a study in the sitting room of our suite in Hartley Hall. As he sat working under the large crucifix over his desk, I would don a yarmulka to prepare the next week's Torah reading, humming to myself in a low drone. We understood each other very well while our suitemates, though Jewish by birth, hardly understood us at all.

But something in me was beginning to crack, something that would leave me emotionally stricken, barely able to go on. It began in midyear, in my parents' synagogue, where I had always felt so much at home, so welcome. Ordinarily I loved reading the Torah aloud, loved how the melodic flow accented each syllable, the very cadence of this unbroken tradition. I also liked making a show of it, drawing out the notes and getting the music just right. The congregation seemed to relish every trill, or so I was often told, and I basked in the glow of warm approval. But now, week after week, within moments after I began chanting, I was set upon by a bad case of stage fright. I'd soon grow breathless; my heart would begin pounding, and I felt as though I would explode, pass out, or suffer a heart attack. Then the feeling would slowly pass and I would carry on. But each succeeding week I was dogged by the fear that it would happen again, and this metastatic fear of fear ensured that it soon did.

One Friday early in April, soon after I boarded the subway heading out to Queens, I was beset by the same symptoms, the shortness of breath, the wildly beating heart, the overwhelming sense of panic: I began to feel I would never get off the train alive. At Main Street in Flushing I stumbled up the flights of stairs and onto a waiting city bus. Once home I went to the family doctor, who was only a block away, and he injected me with a sedative and ordered me to bed. Dr. Israel was no shrink—his main form of treatment was a shot of penicillin—but he turned psychologist that day as he realized how much I had on my plate. "Give your son a break," he told my father. "He's under stress, doing all these jobs, coming home every weekend." No one was more of an oracle to my parents than any doctor. They hung on every word. I got a great deal of sleep that weekend, and after I returned to school I didn't get home again for another seven weeks, not until the semester ended. The two-dollar piano lessons with the virginal Miss Olt proved dispensable. The affable Rabbi Zwillenberg himself took over the Torah reading. The umbilical cord that still linked me to home and synagogue, to my old way of life, was stretched if not wholly severed. At last I was flying solo, as I should have been when the school year began, if only I could have made a cleaner break.

I too had immense respect for doctors, perhaps too much, as time would show. "Take it easy" became my mantra for the rest of the year. "Let yourself go!" For the first time in my life I felt licensed to do . . . absolutely nothing. For the next seven weeks it felt as if I never cracked a book, though I must have kept up with my course work in some fashion. I savored the novelty of weekends in school, including late Sunday breakfasts at Prexy's, the slightly pretentious diner on the far side of Broadway. As if I were a tourist from the boondocks, the city itself became my oyster: movies, music, an off-Broadway play, an opera at the old Met on Broadway and Fortieth Street, where I first discovered the emotional power of opera, seeing *Carmen* from the family circle seats for $1.65. I began reading serious books for pleasure, not for classes. In league with a friend in the dorm I discovered Conrad and Joyce, and we exchanged notes on each book and story. I had never read prose as lush as Conrad's sea stories or as spare and suggestive as Joyce's *Dubliners* and *Portrait of the Artist as a Young Man*, exactly the right work for someone wrestling with religion, tradition, and the taste of freedom.

Conrad's *Heart of Darkness* exposed me to the existential mysteries of the modern mind; its grim view of human nature seemed not so far from the fateful outlook of some Greek tragedies I had been reading—or from *King Lear*, which plunged me into the depths of another kind of nihilism, its own heart of darkness. I grew incensed, almost protective when I stumbled on F. R. Leavis's takedown of Conrad's Congo journey in *The Great Tradition*—

he found it hollow, rhetorical. For me it became a touchstone of serious literature, a glimpse into an abyss of moral horror.

LATE IN THE SPRING of my freshman year, Esther's husband, Jack, died suddenly of a respiratory infection. He was not a surrogate parent as much as she had been—his poor health and quiet, uncertain manner made that impossible—but he had always been open and generous with me and, with no children of his own, he was especially fond of my kid sister. I knew his hoarse, breathless voice and halting step as well as I knew my own. Upset by his death, I grieved that I had not gotten to the hospital to see him in his last few days. I was enjoying my new, independent life at school. My parents assured me he would be fine, and I was all too ready to be reassured, since it lifted a burden from me. But when he died it left a weight of guilt that would not lift, a consciousness of death I had not known till then. It left Esther all too vulnerable—bereaved and inconsolable, as she would remain for many years to come. Always girlish and emotional, painfully dependent on a husband who had long shielded her, she had few skills for navigating life on her own. I wondered how anyone could ease the pain and sense of grievous loss that struck another human being.

I was well on my way to becoming a teenage existentialist, appalled by the absurdity of life as a moral vacuum that led inexorably toward extinction. Without religion, without a trusting faith, life seemed to lose all meaning. But the spring readings of the Humanities course, which took us from Augustine's *Confessions* to Dostoevsky's *Crime and Punishment*—the twentieth century was left to fend for itself—made it impossible to settle into any single outlook. Earlier we had gone in quick succession from being Platonists to becoming Aristotelians and then Lucretian materialists. The course moved quickly past the Hebrew Bible—its role in shaping the Western mind was virtually ignored. But the Book of Job, by challenging God's justice, seemed to offer us a darker view of life, in which good fortune and terrible suffering were dealt out arbitrarily, as if by some capricious power. It was novel to read a biblical work infused with a wrenching skepticism rather than unquestioning faith.

As the new semester took hold, we moved along swiftly from Augustine's religious conversion to Montaigne's resolutely secular introspection, from Rabelais's ribald satire to Swift's precise misanthropy, from Cervantes's vast human comedy to Dostoevsky's psychological maelstrom. Reading Conrad on my own, I found the modern mind full of dark places—the "horror" of Mr. Kurtz was the emblem—but this older literature offered an almost limitless range of human possibilities, especially to a young man whose own experience was confined and confused. I barely began to make sense of these books—not until I taught the course myself almost a decade later, when I felt as though I were reading them for the first time—but they seemed to open up a new world to me, a vista of historical time and imaginative space, a bottomless well of the inner life. This was one source of the deep satisfaction I felt walking across the campus that day in June, despite the emotional upheaval I had gone through. A different reality had beckoned to me, both in the books I was reading and in the secular life I was now living, and it helped produce that strange sense of taking possession, of being home at last.

In time this led me to think about what I might actually want to do with my life. The endless conversation about ideas was mesmerizing, but ideas and conversation were not a profession. The notion of the intellectual had not yet crossed my mind, but I could see my friendships shifting from those who came as I did from a world of yeshivas and synagogues to those who came from demanding public high schools, where they had been exposed to more rigorous teaching and college-level work. By the middle of my sophomore year I had fallen in with a troop of kids from the Bronx High School of Science, one of New York's elite public schools, admission by exam only. Despite its name it spawned a legion of would-be intellectuals, not science nerds but readers without borders, boys who read widely, haphazardly, as if on some devotional quest for meaning. They spoke with fear and reverence about one of their English teachers, who had inspired them, chastised them, and fired their ambitions.

Somehow they had learned to think and write. Separately and together they had discovered books, plays, theories of every kind. They tended to get heady with talk, slightly drunk with big ideas—life and death, faith and reason, love and aggression, history and imagination. Within this group, which gradually adopted me as an honorary graduate, I was perhaps the most anchored in the workaday world. I actually had friends who were fraternity boys. I went along merrily on panty raids on the Barnard dorms, with sex-starved boys demonstrating in the courtyard and girls shouting abuse or encouragement to them from the windows. Week after week I covered ordinary campus news for the *Daily Spectator*. Most of the Bronx Science kids were Jews but their ties were cultural, not religious. They had grown up in bagels-and-lox Jewish families, not homes dominated by Orthodox rules and rituals. Their lives were not conditioned by immigrant fears or by customs brought over from Europe that went back many centuries.

A few quick portraits of my colorful new friends: Sam, a man of remarkably few words, was so gaunt, so ascetic-looking that his appearance stood out when we took our College Board exams together as high school seniors. The room was filled with at least mildly observant Jews, since it was a special Sunday session for those who were excused from taking tests on the Sabbath. Sam looked exotic, vaguely foreign, not at all like anyone else I knew. I later discovered that his background was part Russian, part French. He had the precise mind of a trained philosopher but a dour demeanor, as if in permanent contemplation of human folly. This may have been rooted in his family's history. His father had escaped from the Soviet Union and taken refuge first in Istanbul, where Trotsky briefly became his neighbor, and then in France, where Sam was born in 1940 as the family fled westward from the Nazi conquest. Sam had grown up in Washington Heights in a cosmopolitan environment in which his parents spoke French and his grandmother spoke Russian, which helped make him trilingual, though he was not especially keen with languages. His family still had French roots, since his father served as the New York representative of one of the most venerable Jewish institutions in France, the Alliance Israélite Universelle, a notable human rights and welfare organization.

Through Sam I met Marshall, who didn't live on campus but commuted to Columbia, as I had always expected to do. With his wavy brown hair and ruddy face, he was as rotund and rubicund as Sam was lean and pallid. A superb student and a gifted though sometimes blocked writer, he majored in history, not literature, but seemed to take the whole field of knowledge as his terrain. He gave the impression that his parents had been thirties bohemians who took special pleasure in the urban carnival of New York life. But his father died suddenly when Marshall was almost fifteen and his sister much younger, and in some ways he was still in shock when we met three years later. As the only male in an extended family of women, he remained as emotionally dependent on them as they were on him. Yet he also had a girlfriend, unusual in this circle, the darkly voluptuous but emotionally unstable Rita, an exotic but deeply troubled young woman.

Another new recruit, not a Bronx Science graduate, was Bob, a physics major but also a wide reader, witty talker, and wildly funny storyteller. There was a touch of the Borscht Belt tummler about him. "If we had meat," he would say, "we would have meat and potatoes, if we had potatoes," a line Kafka would have understood. Though he felt outclassed by some of the geniuses drawn to physics, he was a born teacher, for there was nothing in science he could not break down and explain, often amusingly, in ordinary language. As a Red diaper baby he had grown up surrounded by politics; it was the air he breathed. His father was a Communist, a true believer, yet also a small industrialist who drove around in a Cadillac, that convenient symbol of the exploiting class. When I visited their home in the private community of Sea Gate, off Coney Island, I could never avoid arguing with him about the Soviet Union, which as he saw it could do no wrong. These arguments reached a peak when I mischievously brought up the growing Sino–Soviet split; he dismissed it as "theoretically impossible," a fabrication of the capitalist press, as if theory trumped reality hands down. In college Bob was emancipating himself from Stalinism in exactly the same way I was breaking free of Orthodox Judaism. In this way our paths converged, and we eventually became roommates.

I spent as much time blowing smoke with these guys as I did on my course work; it was part of my education, a way of chewing everything to pieces, taking the world apart to find out exactly what held it together. This was naive, of course, but it suggested a way of life I wanted somehow to chase down. This was a pivotal moment to be taking baby steps into the life of the mind, for the cautious, conservative culture of the postwar years was beginning to break up. For the newcomer, just learning to think, to read, there was a whirl of inviting old texts to be freshly read, a rush of poems, plays, novels, and movies, old or new, an exhilarating first taste of edgy critical debates in intellectual journals. Now, as the fifties ended, the political scene was shifting as well. Even a callow undergraduate could sense that the frozen political climate of the early cold war years had begun to thaw, especially since the end of the Korean War. My antennae were tuned in to politics, perhaps because my mild-mannered father followed it so closely, almost as a blood sport.

At ten I drew a large map of the Korean Peninsula on which I penciled the shifting battle lines from week to week. I followed the long ordeal of the Rosenbergs from their arrest in 1950 to their execution in 1953, perhaps because they were so markedly Jewish. Their fate, the faces of their orphaned children, became a source of anguish for me, as it did for many Jews who knew nothing about their guilt or innocence. Some felt that a pogrom was in the offing, thanks to the way McCarthyism and the blacklist had targeted the old Jewish Left. I didn't know any Communists except my uncle Lou, but the demise of Stalin in 1953 left me in shock for weeks afterward, as if one of the pillars of the stable world—the only one I knew—had suddenly buckled and collapsed. I took it personally, like the Rosenberg case, and was stunned at how easily our lives could be turned upside down.

Change was in the offing, yet no one knew what form it would take. The cold war had seemed immutable, almost a fact of life. But it was clear that Stalin's death, on the cusp of bloody new purges, and the subsequent summit meetings between President Eisenhower and the new Soviet leaders created options unseen since the war. The world was awakening as if from a long paralytic trance, and I began to feel that a new generation was finding its own way. Not long afterward, in 1960, the Kennedy campaign brought this feeling home. Though he ran for president on warnings of a nonexistent missile gap, his youth and energy galvanized us with hopes for political renewal. He spoke famously for the next generation, "born in this century," as he would put it in his inaugural address. It felt like a quiet revolution, a leap into the unknown.

In the cultural world, the in-your-face iconoclasm of the Beats had the same effect, though they were at first mocked yet brazenly publicized as apolitical dropouts. They renewed the oral power and public reach of poetry, long muffled by the difficulty of so much modern writing. My friends and I grew nostalgic for the political activism of the 1930s, though we knew nothing of the dire conditions that had brought it about or the sectarian conflicts that hobbled its influence. I was instinctively drawn to what Lionel Trilling called "the bloody crossroads" where art and politics meet. In 1959 I picked up my first copy of *Partisan Review*, still the great forum for the modernism and anti-Stalinism of the older generation, but also began sampling the countercultural *Evergreen Review*. Its rambunctious publisher, Grove Press, trumpeted the wares of every radical new writer— and some old ones as well, as it brought out the banned books of a previous era beginning with D. H. Lawrence and Henry Miller.

At home and school I'd been raised with stern standards of morality, an ascetic sense of self-denial, yet my adolescent self, hooked into the Dionysian side of modern culture, yearned to break free. *Partisan Review* was perched on both sides of this divide, weaned on modernism, saturated with Freud, ambivalent toward the Left, obtuse about the Beats. But its fierce attacks on Allen Ginsberg and Jack Kerouac were also signs that they were taking them seriously, unlike most other literary journals that simply ignored them. The crosscurrents of American and European writing—of intellectual debate in general—seemed to be running through the magazine, from Robert Lowell, who was turning to confessional poetry, to Boris Pasternak, whose work reached back to pre-Soviet literary traditions; from the Yiddish-inflected stories of Bernard Malamud, which read like modern folktales, to the philosophy-tinged fables of Iris Murdoch. The first issues of *PR* I bought included Trilling's controversial birthday tribute to Robert Frost and Diana Trilling's involuntary tribute to the Beats, James Baldwin writing from the South and Alfred Kazin musing about psychoanalysis, Gore Vidal on the theater and Harold Rosenberg reviewing a one-of-a-kind novel by Paul Goodman, *The Empire City*, which proved more enticing to read about than to read. Much of this was well beyond me yet it staked out a territory where I thought I might belong, a tradition of the new, as Harold Rosenberg called it, a feeling for the avant-garde, for bold experiment and risky innovation, that had weakened after the war and now was breaking out.

I took an instant dislike to some of what I read in the magazine. One early copy I bought of *PR* featured a polemic against mass culture by Dwight Macdonald, a name that meant nothing to me. It was clear that he was the wit and gadfly, the great contrarian, among these tricky critics.

The piece proved to be a wonderfully lively satirical assault but also, I felt, a bald piece of cultural snobbery. The target of his entertaining scorn was not popular culture—beneath discussion except as a symptom—but middle-brow versions of high culture, such as Thornton Wilder's down-home play *Our Town*, Stephen Vincent Benét's book-length poem *John Brown's Body*, and Archibald MacLeish's verse play based on the Book of Job, *J. B.*, which had just enjoyed a great success on Broadway. As a teenage culture maven I had gobbled down these works and resented being told what bad taste I had. Like many earlier satirists, Macdonald took his stand on traditions for their own sake, whether or not they maintained their original vitality. The *Evergreen Review* writers, on the other hand, looked ready to try anything novel, incendiary, provocative, whether it worked or not. Some of it seemed merely sophomoric, even to a sophomore, no more than a garrulous sprawl, awash in self-expression.

Part of me would dance to the tune of the new avant-garde, but for now I was also busy picking up the beat of the older culture. The names engraved high up on the Columbia library were still the peaks I most wanted to climb. Yet the Beats too had left their mark on Columbia, where Ginsberg, Kerouac, William Burroughs, and their friends had first hooked up in the early 1940s. The night they returned for a famous reading in 1959 I went instead to a Shakespeare performance across town at the Heckscher Theatre, the winter home of Joe Papp's fledgling New York Shakespeare Festival. But a few days later my physicist friend Bob, who worked at WKCR, the campus radio station, brought me to the studio to hear a tape of the reading. Ginsberg's passion and unexpected humor took my breath away. I had missed the moment but somehow the moment caught up with me, and soon afterward I made my way down to the Lower East Side to hear Ginsberg read from an unfinished poem called *Kaddish*, a liturgical lament for his mad Communist mother, Naomi, that also demonstrated how Jewish he himself had remained.

I was hooked on Ginsberg and soon on his friends Gregory Corso and Lawrence Ferlinghetti, though I did not read Kerouac's *On the Road* until years later, deterred by a fierce putdown by Norman Podhoretz in *Partisan Review*. But when the magazine published Diana Trilling's evocative account of the Columbia reading I had missed, I found myself irritated by her condescending tone, though it was leavened with a streak of maternal affection. The wife of Ginsberg's teacher and Columbia's leading literary critic, a tough-minded observer in her own right, she was at least willing to give these bad boys a hearing, but little more. When she got home she found her husband meeting with W. H. Auden and Jacques Barzun—together the three served as gatekeepers of a highbrow book club. Mischievously, she reports that Auden, the mandarin poet, voiced his disapproval, as if she had gone soft, taken in by childish shenanigans.

It was in the pages of *PR* and *Commentary* that I learned that Columbia's faculty led a busy and contentious life outside the classroom. No one as yet labeled their contributors the New York intellectuals, but the *PR* crowd had strong links to the university, where some of them taught and many others had studied. Several others, like Irving Howe, the often embattled editor of *Dissent*, had gone to City College, majoring in political disputation, or, like William Phillips and Delmore Schwartz, had worked at New York University with the hard-nosed philosopher Sidney Hook, once a Communist, now the most polemical of the cold war anti-Communists. Already I recoiled from everything about the cold war. I felt that it had suffocated American politics and undermined civil liberties, yet I strongly identified with this older generation, as if I had lived through all their family quarrels.

In his anti-Communist zeal Hook was matched by Elliot Cohen, who founded *Commentary* in 1945, but I began subscribing only when Podhoretz became editor at the beginning of 1960. I was taken with his exceptionally well-argued essays in *PR*, especially one on Norman Mailer's first three novels. In a sign of the times he moved *Commentary* to the left and, in his first three issues, serialized Paul Goodman's *Growing Up Absurd*, a highly unconventional piece of social criticism. Goodman was an anarchist, bisexual, a Gestalt psychologist, educational theorist, and utopian city planner, as well as a haphazard poet and fiction writer. He had been publishing in little magazines at least since 1940, to no public attention whatever. Now the spotlight was on him, as it would remain all through the 1960s. When *Growing Up Absurd* came out I read it as social poetry, a call to community as well as a troubling vision of the world in which the young had no causes, few genuine satisfactions, little to grow up to. The Beats, he said, and the young juvenile delinquents who were much in the news, the cause of a great deal of editorial hand-wringing, were two sides of the same coin, the products of a society that offered them neither fulfilling work nor admirable role models. Between Ginsberg and Goodman a new day was dawning, the cultural equivalent of the election of Kennedy. They became the most charismatic pied pipers of the new decade.

I scarcely knew where I could fit into this emerging culture. I had arrived in college with vague thoughts of becoming a lawyer or journalist. By the time of my sophomore year I was looking for something I myself would find more fulfilling. In high school, reading innumerable popular novels, enjoying big-budget Hollywood movies like *The Bridge on the River Kwai* and *Stalag 17*, I had feasted on sheer storytelling. I had even tried to versify in the Victorian manner of Palgrave's *Golden Treasury*, putting adolescent feelings into singsong rhyme and meter. A cruel but accurate English teacher had stomped on my attempts at verse. Now I'd stepped into a turbulent world of ideas, felt the thrill of discovering genuine literature, the passion of ideological debate.

I glimpsed these new horizons through my teachers, in the books I was reading, in late-night gab sessions in the dorm, in magazines that featured cuttingly intelligent and abrasive writers. I took pleasure in new poetry like Robert Lowell's directly autobiographical *Life Studies*, which includes a sharply etched prose memoir; in the provocative stories and essays in Norman Mailer's *Advertisements for Myself*, as fresh in their style as in their challenge to live dangerously; in the apocalyptic Freudianism of Norman O. Brown's *Life against Death*, with its muddy but (to me) exhilarating appeal for a "resurrection of the body." All three of these books were published in 1959, almost a prologue to a new decade, and their impact built steadily.

The political world was churning as well, with civil rights protests attacking racial discrimination and ban-the-bomb peace rallies directed against the atrophied stand-off of the cold war. The ground was shifting beneath our feet and we felt its vibrations in our very bones. The 1950s had taught me and my friends to cherish cultural traditions going back to Athens and Jerusalem, London and Paris, Weimar and Petersburg. But the culture had also hardened into an ice age of small, pinched poems and novels, prudish sexual morality, and circumscribed political debate. We may not have heard of the New Criticism, but our teachers were shaped by its often blinkered yet also enlightening methods of close reading, so well suited to the classroom. The narrow limits of debate and dissent were enforced by blacklists, congressional witch-hunts, perjury and espionage trials, loyalty oaths, and an intimidating atmosphere of character assassination and guilt by association. This had come down especially hard on the old Jewish Left, with its roots in the pervasive working-class socialism of the ghetto and in the vigorous political ferment of the 1930s.

It was not clear why all these issues mattered to me except that they did. I was no Red diaper baby, raised by Communists like my friend Bob, but my father was a typical Jewish liberal, a longtime member of a CIO union. Without being especially political, I seemed to have politics in my veins, or at least a worrying concern about the future of a society that seemed prosperous and free yet felt somehow stifling. The hard-won anti-Stalinism of the New York intellectuals, forged in the ferocious political debates of the 1930s, had been overtaken by the crude, repressive anticommunism of the 1950s, tarring every expression of political dissent. That enforced conformity was now beginning to come apart. My own way into the new culture would be mostly literary, not political. I had tried my hand at poetry and fiction but the gift escaped me. My verses were earnest, jingly, and flat; my stories remained unfinished. Where would I go?

I always left myself some specially promising books to read when the semester ended. A year earlier Mark Van Doren had been my idol as a critic—I imagined dedicating my first book to him—but that seemed like a century ago. I saw him as a *goyishe* Sholem Aleichem, wryly amused at human foibles, timelessly wise. But that midwestern voice, so homey and receptive, would surely falsify me if I tried to emulate it. Two books that now piqued my interest were Jacques Barzun's *Teacher in America* and Lionel Trilling's collection of essays *The Liberal Imagination*, handsome and handy in their compact Anchor editions. The first, by Columbia's provost and longtime history professor, told me something I hadn't realized, that it was possible that someone would be willing to pay me to go on doing what I was doing—to read books, talk about them, and write about them—a happy discovery. Having learned that, I never needed to look at Barzun's book again.

But the second book, by Barzun's close friend and teaching partner, was even more telling, for it gave me an inkling of how that work might be done. It offered a model for criticism in a subtle, personal voice that was neither ponderous nor academic but was itself a form of literature. Trilling's seductive conversational style gave me the impression—or was it a carefully crafted illusion?—of a mind in motion, a man actually thinking things through as he weighed the alternatives and probed the issues before him. It was not the irreverent voice of the coming era but the ambivalent, ruminative voice of the more reflective decade that had just passed, a genuinely engaging voice. Despite its Anglo manner, polite and reserved, it was also a Jewish voice, rarely assertive, honeycombed with ambivalence. It conveyed a sense of the tragic; it spoke not of revolutionary change but of "moral realism." And Trilling was a professor at my own university, in my own department, a leading contributor to the magazines I had just begun reading. He had been Allen Ginsberg's teacher, Podhoretz's role model, and the difficult mentor to a dozen other writers and critics who rarely managed to gain his full approval—and were sometimes driven wild by his hesitation in bestowing it.

One essay of Trilling's that caught my eye was on the 1948 Kinsey report, a landmark of enlightened but narrowly quantitative research into the sexual behavior of the human male. As a sexually deprived nineteen-year-old virgin, someone who was forward, even aggressive in class but painfully shy with women, I had very little experience to fall back on. I was taken with Trilling's argument that Kinsey's approach was mechanical, not psychological, that any conclusions drawn about sex would be lame without considerations of feeling, concerns about love. I wanted badly to test this hypothesis for myself. Trilling was a Freudian. His preferred arena for exploring love was fiction, with its dense underbrush of motives, desires, and relationships, not social science.

As an avid novel reader this was meat and drink to me. But when the new cultural radicalism came roaring in, it was the widening campaign against sexual repression, even Kinsey's, that I cheered most: the frank portrayal of a woman's orgasm in *Lady Chatterley's Lover*, which told me some things I never knew; the ribald, predatory, guilt-free sex in Henry Miller's newly published *Tropic* novels; the vision of "polymorphously perverse" eroticism

evoked in Norman O. Brown's book, whatever that might mean; the even
more murky quest for "an orgasm more apocalyptic than the one which preceded it" in Norman Mailer's overheated manifesto "The White Negro";
the Wilhelm Reich–influenced view of sexual release in Paul Goodman's
work; and the surreal and violent erotic visions chanted with half-demented
passion in Ginsberg's *Howl*. I felt that my own devoutly anticipated sexual
breakthrough, though likely to be more tame than any of these, would be
swept along by some larger cultural breakthrough, a loosening of cultural
mores, a mighty blow against repression. The scent of emancipation was in
the air, and I wanted like hell to be part of it.

Still, for all these charged-up fantasies, I admired Trilling for his
skepticism, his nay-saying, his air of introspection and Hamlet-like temperament. He seemed to be of two minds about everything, a tendency I
shared, but his inner demons actually spoke to each other. They made civilized conversation, and his essays enabled us to tune in to that dialogue.
Perhaps these were partly Jewish qualities, combining diffidence with dialectic, though I would scarcely have understood that at the time. Much as
I had recoiled from the interminable, legalistic debates of the Talmud, my
austere religious training still had a strong hold on me, especially the inner
voice of parental morality. For someone growing up in an Eastern European Jewish family, desire and guilt were parts of the same heady brew, as
Philip Roth's work was just then beginning to show.

Trilling agreed with Kinsey that the level of sexual information in the
country was scandalously low. He hoped the report's findings would land a
blow against ignorance and contribute to more-enlightened sexual attitudes
and greater personal happiness. But he also felt that sexual conduct could
not be understood from a behaviorist angle or made more healthy by the
hygienic liberal attitudes his whole book set out to question. The wildly
permissive sixties would put this to the test, and I would find my loyalties in
both camps, my sympathies torn between the sexual ideologues who imagined an abolition of repression and the moralists who warned against chaos,
cruelty, and selfish abandonment. I was raised on a litany of "Thou shalt
not." Moral restraint was in my DNA, along with respect for the thinking
mind, but this made the vision of an ecstatic breakthrough at once fearsome
and enticing. I was drawn by the apocalyptic element in modernism, its

ambivalent appeal to the chthonic and the irrational, from Nietzsche and Dostoevsky to Freud and D. H. Lawrence. Most of all I wanted to be part of the cultural conversation about the changes in modern life and to see how they would play out in my own thirst for experience. With such issues at stake, the calling of the critic, the teacher, the inquiring intellectual was an alluring course to pursue, for me almost inescapable. I longed to be at the center of the action, to plumb the meaning of it. Not yet twenty, I was already aglow, puffed up with a sense of mission, eager to see where it might carry me.

Four

SUMMER WORLDS

M Y PARENTS never went to "the Mountains," as the Catskills were called by the generations of Jews who spent boisterous weeks there. My father had gone up occasionally with his bachelor friends. But once they were married in 1938, my folks preferred Rocky Point, where my mother's extended family had built their ramshackle bungalows. For the first ten years my parents had come as frequent guests, then bought the modest house, free of every modern convenience, where my sister and I could escape the summer heat. Ordinarily, I loved school, a place where I sopped up learning and managed to shine, but I also loved breaking loose from school into a summer world where my skin turned red from the first sunburn and then gradually dark from long days at the beach. There I spent the best part of my first fourteen summers, caught up in that raucous extended family of aunts, uncles, cousins, and visiting landsleit they knew from the old country. But by that last year I grew so restless I painted the house, fending off my mother's nervous sisters who kept trying to get me down from the roof. I wasn't a kid anymore; though the gleaming house, looking like new, gave me quiet satisfaction, I was bored. For the following summer I'd have to look for something else.

In the spring of 1955, having just turned fifteen, I sprang into action. I had no work experience: no paper route, no lawn mowing or leaf raking, none of the jobs that suburban kids pick up to earn pocket change. Staying in the city was unthinkable. Didn't everyone agree that the city in summer was stifling, unhealthy? It had to be a job somewhere out in the country, but where? I went down with my oldest friend to Brooklyn's Boro Park, to be interviewed as a counselor-in-training at a camp so Orthodox it would have made my old summer haunts seem like a Roman carnival. Whether I turned the camp down or it rejected me I can't recall; no doubt we both knew it couldn't possibly work. I'd been raised in a flexible religious household, where the rules about drinking milk after meat or observing the Sabbath grew more elastic when summer rolled around, nothing like the strict regimen observed in this camp. Instead I ended up with an unbearable job as a "tea boy" and Torah reader at the Lake House in Woodridge, a place where every letter of the law was rigidly enforced.

A few days after my disastrous debut at chanting the Torah portion, when I was surrounded by disapproving rabbis, my father arrived to see how I was doing. I asked him plaintively to get me out of there. The atmosphere was dense with Old World piety, and I could scarcely breathe. The room I shared with three other boys, one of them the owner's son, was tiny, and there was virtually no space between the beds. I felt hemmed in by strangers, embarrassed even to undress in front of them; I had never lived with anyone outside of the family in such close quarters. My dad was not well connected, and always quite shy, but he got in touch with a distant friend, a partner in another hotel, who told him to bring me over: perhaps they could find something for me to do. They couldn't pay, but I'd be fed and housed and maybe pick up some tips. I didn't know it yet, but here was the freedom I'd been seeking all along.

The Kanco Hotel in Ferndale, New York, not far from the large town of Liberty, was kosher, of course, though most of the guests were no more than bagels-and-lox Jews. Well, bagels and lox, and kishka, and tzimmes, and pot roast—it was a never-ending feast. But my dad's old friend Al Kanter, part owner of the hotel, wanted to make sure there were religious services on the Sabbath, though few people attended. I took over the same jobs I'd had at the Lake House, with none of the pressure to satisfy a roomful of bearded sages. This was almost a lark to me, something I knew very well how to do, yet it also kept me within the fold, still the yeshiva boy. But in the small room off the lobby that served as a makeshift synagogue, I could handle it my own way and do as I pleased on my own time.

At the Kanco, religion was little more than a formality. I would preside over the tearoom, fill in during mealtimes as a pantry boy, and, relying on years of religious training, keep the services humming for a handful of elderly men. All this was hastily arranged soon after I arrived. A few minutes after my father struck this deal, someone offered him a ride back to New York and he was out the door. I can still see myself standing behind the wooden screen door of the tearoom, watching him scamper away, and feeling bereft and abandoned for the first time in my life. I had been excited about leaving home but suddenly home was leaving me to fend for myself, as if I'd been dropped off in an orphanage, wondering whether anyone would adopt me.

If I felt lost and alone in that moment, I never looked back. I was so happy there I stayed on for three summers, free of stifling rules, with no one looking over my shoulder, though my benefactor, Mr. Kanter, had promised to keep an eye on me since I was underage. I was good at dealing with old people, who thought me clever and adorable, and in the tearoom each morning and afternoon I supplied them with gallons of hot tea (in a glass, Russian style, with slices of lemon, never milk), or prune juice as a morning purge, or hot water and lemon to clean out the pipes. During meals I would work in the pantry, putting together salads, side dishes, and desserts—a guest could request virtually anything. After lunch I was free to swim, play Ping-Pong, or, if I liked, join the outdoor dance lessons. There the youthful staff was encouraged to mingle with the guests, a few of them young and attractive, though many more were aging badly, with leathery brown skin from long winters in Florida. The need for males of any age was desperate, so, like a gigolo, I served as an occasional dance partner to elderly widows and matrons, some barely five feet tall. Ballroom dancing had not been part of my education, so here I was initiated into the fox-trot, the cha-cha, the merengue, the mambo, and even the tango, with its sweep and thrust, the boldest sexual moves of the current Latin dance craze, which I wisely kept in reserve for partners my own age. At just that moment in the mid-1950s, other kids were beginning to dance to different tunes—rock was on the horizon—but for all I knew that might have been unfolding on the dark side of the moon.

I liked the old folks, who were lonesome and kind and grateful for attention, but time with them was almost part of the job. Most of my free hours were spent with the waiters and busboys and day-camp counselors who were years older than me, who adopted me as something between a juvenile tagalong, wet behind the ears, and a voluble mascot they could bring along on their exploits off the grounds. One of my roommates, Roger, a busboy, dark-skinned and thick-browed, amazed me with his down-and-dirty language, using all-purpose inflections of "fuck" at least three times in each sentence: it modified every verb, every noun, and described every person he met or knew. It was the lingo of the locker room or the army barracks, an argot I had never heard. I felt like a country parson's son who had landed in boot camp and gone though basic training in a state of culture shock.

Roger not only talked the talk, he walked the walk. Our bunk was a small wooden cabin with three or four beds, Roger's being roomier than the others. One evening I came back early and, as I tugged at the light chain, heard some rustling in the dark. When the bare overhead bulb came on I saw Mimi, a day-camp counselor, under the covers with Roger, coyly pulling the blanket up to her chin. Cool as ever, he motioned to me to turn off the light as his lady friend giggled with mild embarrassment. I had seen her romping with her young charges, but here was a turn of events I hadn't expected. I look back on this as the moment sex actually entered my life, if only vicariously: My God, they were not just thinking about it but blatantly *doing* it. I was thrilled and jealous as I headed back to the lobby. With a confidential air, I joked with one of the waiters about the scene I had just stumbled into, pretending to be amused, not shocked or surprised. I was a green kid playing a man of the world, making a show of taking it all in stride.

Ballroom dancing and furtive sex were not the only amusements at this Catskills Babylon, with its steamy servants' quarters. Every decent-sized hotel had a casino, not for gambling but as summer stock for Yiddish American music and comedy. The modest Kanco could never attract the popular stars like Jerry Lewis who performed for big bucks at Grossinger's, the Concord, or Brown's. Instead it counted on aging vaudeville comics or the superannuated divas and leading men of Yiddish radio and theater. I remember seeing Seymour Rexite (né Rechtzeit), the Jewish answer to Bing Crosby, and his wife, Miriam Kressyn, who translated popular American standards, even advertising jingles, into Yiddish. The fuel of life in the Catskills was not only the quantity of food but the high-octane nostalgia for an immigrant culture that looked ever rosier as it faded into history. A hush of expectation greeted a legendary grande dame, Jennie Goldstein, who was still in her fifties but had been on stage for half a century. I was too young to have witnessed the show-biz hubbub of Second Avenue, the Yiddish Broadway, but I caught its dying echoes in rural Sullivan County.

At one of these shows I met a girl I'll call Elaine, who was a camp counselor a mile down the road toward Swan Lake. She was at least two years older than me, not really pretty but mature and confident, with clipped brown hair, perfect for summer, and thick, tortoise-frame glasses that gave her the classic wallflower look. By and large, the girls I met those summers did not take me seriously. Why would they? I was too young for a serious job and looked even younger; I had no legitimate working papers and was told to make myself scarce when the state labor inspector came by. Tall but thin as a beanpole, weighing in at 120 pounds, I must have seemed immature; indeed I *was* immature.

I had always gone to an all-male school, and women seemed like complex, enigmatic creatures who would never take an interest in a *pisher* like me. I was often shy with them, fearful of rejection, but with Elaine I struck up an easy conversation that went on for hours: in the last row of seats in the casino, sometimes down near the pool, along the hilly grounds, or on the dark road that led back to her camp. It continued on other evenings when she found excuses to come to the hotel, and I felt myself irresistibly drawn to her, less because of who she was—we scarcely got to know each other—than for the amazing sexual opportunity she might represent.

Though inexperienced, I sensed that Elaine radiated signals of availability, perhaps even desperation, very different from the so-called good Jewish girls I knew, who were impregnably well defended, letting a callow, awkward boy go only so far. I had had a crush on one of them back home in Flushing since I was thirteen, and I had carried around one of her letters, tucked into my wallet, until it fell apart. But somehow the atmosphere of the Mountains made everything feel different; there was a sense of liberation in the air, a radiant summer sensuality that let my fantasies run wild. In dreams I saw myself as the foul-mouthed Roger, the confident seducer ready for a quick roll in the hay.

This was not to be, at least not in the way I had imagined. One night Elaine and I turned off the empty road between Ferndale and Swan Lake and lay down in a bare clearing, under a romantic canopy of trees and stars. Talk soon turned to kissing and kissing to grappling as our arms got tangled in each other's clothes. Somehow I loosened Elaine's bra and intrepidly began fondling her breasts. The touch of her body made me wildly excited; I was astonished that she let me do this. The idea that women might be eager for sex, might even enjoy it, had never crossed my mind. With luck, I thought, they yielded stoically to male desperation. But Elaine, armored behind a tight corset, resisted my wandering hands whenever they ventured below the waist. Was she saving herself for her wedding night or holding out for a more aggressive or more practiced lover? Whispering sweet nothings in my ear, she firmly brought me back to her comfort zone, and it seemed that this sweaty wrestling could go on all night. But when I brought her willing hand between my legs, I soon felt a warm explosion and it was all over.

A few moments later we struggled to our feet and went our separate ways, and for days afterward I felt exhilarated yet mortified. I had never touched a woman's body so intimately—yet also so clumsily, or so I imagined. In the locker-room chatter of the time, I had gotten to first base, perhaps even rounded second, but then had childishly lost control. I wondered what would happen the next time. Would any woman ever have me? The summer was nearly over, and I promised to call Elaine in the city but somehow never did. The high school world of my teachers, my studies, my parents closed in around me. I felt that I had nearly lost my cherry that fateful night but, if the truth were told, I never even came close. Still, that summer in the Mountains, with sex constantly on my mind, had done wonders for my education. This had always been the place where hardworking Jews had relaxed their inhibitions. It gave me an unexpected taste of freedom, an intimation of manhood, and a tantalizing glimpse of some complications of life that lay ahead.

As a high school student I spent three summers at the Kanco, but my life there was more banal and uneventful than this encounter would suggest. No one else working there was my age, and I seemed always too young for whatever was happening. I looked up to the waiters and busboys as college students, working their way through school, especially to one or two who were going to Columbia, but I had no idea what they thought of me. They took me along to late-night movies in Liberty, where I sometimes fell asleep from sheer exhaustion after rising so early. I got no pay that first summer, only some minuscule tips that I recorded on the rough wood of the wall of my bunk. When guests left they tipped their waiter, their busboy, their chambermaid; the tea boy was a rare afterthought. All told I took in not much more than a hundred dollars but I was there for the experience, not the money. Those summers socialized me in ways that my closely watched life at home, in school, or my duties in the synagogue did not. Al Kanter, who had hired me, was an affable man, easy to like, easy to please. Through the rest of the year he was a traveling salesman in the *shmatta* trade, which was how he knew my father. With his permanent tan, balding head, and brushlike mustache, he had a salesman's ingratiating personality. Taking it easy after a mild heart attack, he was the front man, greeting every guest like an old friend, not the real boss who kept the hotel going.

Authority rested with his partners and in-laws, Sam and Becky Cohen, along with their burly son Donny. The Cohens ruled the nerve center of the hotel, the kitchen, with an anxious determination. For Jews of that generation, a hotel like the Kanco was essentially a food business, a vulnerable one in which the merchandise was perishable. It lived or died by the quality (and quantity) of what it put on the tables. Many of the guests had grown up poor and hungry; now they expected, demanded, God's plenty, or more. Sam and Becky planned menus, negotiated with the temperamental chef, who sometimes wielded a meat clever menacingly or, when enraged, threw things across the kitchen. They carefully ordered the food and supplies, making sure nothing, but nothing, ever went to waste. Ripe fruit was recycled into fruit salad, tuna fish was fortified with cheaper no-name fish that came in large wholesale cans, and yesterday's leftovers were fed to the always famished staff. Unsmiling Sam and beady-eyed Becky had a perpetually worried look, as if their fate hung perilously on every meal, yet I had never eaten so well. Working in the pantry, flitting in and out of the walk-in refrigerator, whipping up whatever cold dishes the pampered guests might order, I could feel Becky's eyes on me to make sure I didn't throw anything out—or snack on the side, as I inevitably did. It was a seasonal business and the margin of profit must have been slim, for all I knew or cared, but the food flowed like a perpetual banquet.

I took enormous pleasure in small things, such as getting on the public address system to greet the guests and announce, in the silken tones of a radio broadcaster, that "the main dining room is now open for dinner." Whose voice was that, low and manly, that resonated through the lobby and across the grounds? Was this me, Abie and Anna's eager boy, perhaps too smart (or smart-ass) for his own good? I had even taken on a new name to grasp at a new identity. To my parents, whose formative culture was Yiddish, I had always been Moi-shee, like my late grandfather. (For Esther, whose language really *was* Yiddish, this became—and remained—the fond diminutive Maishele.) But all this sounded too ethnic, too Old World for the beach in Rocky Point, where we were surrounded by goyim and eager to sound less ethnic, less Old World. My aunts and older cousins decreed that I would henceforth be called Dickie, a name that would have made me the butt of a thousand smutty jokes in the Mountains. So I now renamed myself Marty, and soon actually felt like Marty, one of the boys, Jewish enough but not *very* Jewish. For Elaine, who never quite figured out what I actually did at the hotel, I was Marty the maintenance man, a working-class personality that suited me fine. That name survived into my first year or two of college and, with a twinge of nostalgia, I still hear it occasionally at class reunions, reminding me of who I once was.

Though I was by far the youngest person working at the hotel, I saw the job as a step into maturity. I was earning money, pittance though it was, and working hard for it. I was more or less on my own, disposing of my time as I saw fit, mimicking the swagger of the waiters and busboys who treated me as their younger brother, a kid who needed to be wised up. They worked much harder than I did, careening through the swinging doors that led to the kitchen with heavy trays piled high with heaping food or soiled dishes. When there was a collision and one of these trays went flying, the Cohens glowered but kept tight-lipped. It was a matter of good form not to recriminate, for this was the cost of doing business—something I hadn't learned from my frugal parents, who treated every material loss as a tragic waste.

The physical demands of the job were vital for me since my long days in school were so sedentary. I had always been a reader, never an athlete, and apart from basketball, the favorite sport of urban Jewish kids, my high school had virtually no athletic program. Summer had always been my escape from the life of the mind, the relentless pressure to perform and achieve. My confidence in my body was hardly great but the water was my best friend, ever since my cousins taught me to swim in Rocky Point. At the hotel I haunted the roadside pool whenever the guests stayed away—especially after lunch, when they were digesting or sleeping off their heavy meals.

Sometimes I shared the pool with teenage kids my own age, who had come with their parents or grandparents and were thoroughly bored, since the place offered little for them to do. Once each summer my father, who otherwise took no vacation, would come for a week, sometimes with my sister, while my mother held down the store. He came simply because I was there, and we played endless games of Ping-Pong, where I would sometimes let him win. Wildly competitive myself, I enjoyed watching the glee of this normally quiet, uncompetitive man, for whom the American obsession with sports was an alien experience. I caught glimpses of what he must have been like—a much freer spirit—before marriage and fatherhood weighed him down with a heavy load of responsibility.

By the second and third year at the hotel I had proved myself and was paid the same low wage as the waiters and busboys, ten dollars a week, though their tips were far greater. Now over sixteen, I took out legal working papers and no longer had to hide when the state labor inspector showed up. My duties in the tearoom, the pantry, and at the Sabbath services remained the same, but now I could spin them off with ease. The weekly Torah reading had become routine and I needed only to refresh my memory from year to year. Had I returned for a fourth year I would have turned eighteen and perhaps become a busboy myself. I could have used the money to help with college, though my college expenses would be mostly covered by my corporate sugar daddy, General Motors, which generously bestowed on me a four-year scholarship. Or I might have taken over the larger tearoom where the guests and staff caroused from after ten to midnight or later, a more lucrative after-hours job from which I'd been barred by my tender age.

But I sensed that the Catskills had given me all the place had to offer: some halting steps toward independence and self-reliance; a taste of maturity, including sexual maturity, or perhaps just the knowledge that sex was not such a distant and unapproachable land; and, not least of all, a glimpse of the final years of the Catskills resorts to which immigrants and their children had flocked because they were not welcome anywhere else. It offered them a respite from hard work among their own kind, listening to music they knew, laughing at jokes that were old before they were born. It catered to an unappeasable hunger they knew from a deprived childhood; it provided a relief from the suffocating heat of the crowded city in surroundings so beautiful that the poets of England's Lake District, like Wordsworth and Coleridge, might have appreciated them. Earlier I had witnessed the last act of the rich drama of Jewish life on the Lower East Side; now I had sampled its rural counterpart, enjoyed it, and found it good. I managed to miss the really garish side of Catskills culture played out at the large hotels, with their ostentatious Miami Beach lobbies and Broadway-style stage shows, but also the impoverished side, the working-class *kochaleins* and small bungalow colonies that have long since gone under or become ultra-Orthodox havens. With religion on hold, the Catskills had put my hyperactive mind to sleep—there was no way to read a book while working in these surroundings—but opened my eyes and my senses.

SUMMER CAMPS were another Jewish institution I had skipped during my years in Rocky Point, but in my freshman year of college I discovered a camp quite unlike the others, though I can't recall how I first heard about it. Many camps were either charitable operations that lifted poor kids out of the sweltering ghetto or lavish sports complexes that reflected the growing wealth and wider horizons of the Jewish middle class. Tennis and camping in the woods became one of their children's tickets to America. Other camps were routine facilities gussied up with faux-Indian tribal motifs. Camp Massad was different. It consisted of a pair of camps in the Poconos, near the Delaware Water Gap, founded in 1941 by a Zionist family, the

Shulsingers, who were mainly in the Jewish publishing business: prayer books, Passover haggadahs, gift books for Chanukah, Hebrew-English dictionaries. The camps' religious orientation was gently Orthodox but their real mission was to instill Zionism into American youth by immersing them in a wholly (not holy) Hebrew atmosphere. This was exactly what had been missing in my old-style yeshiva, where the primary language, as in Eastern Europe, was Yiddish and the study of Talmud crowded out the rest of the Jewish curriculum. A middle-aged Israeli, Shlomo Shulsinger, abetted by his perky wife, Rivka, ran the camp with a stern voice and an iron hand. Stocky and short, with wavy, iron-gray hair, Shlomo dispensed homilies about the Land—*Ha-aretz*, the Holy Land—and reprimanded anyone caught speaking even a few words of English. His wife, looking equally strict and fit—I rarely saw her without a soccer ball in her hand—ran the sports programs for the girls' camp. They became my image of the new Jew, the Israeli chalutzim, pioneers who had returned to the soil, embraced manual labor, and were making the proverbial desert bloom—except, of course, that he and she were living in the United States, hands-on emissaries for the Zionist cause.

I arrived at Massad the same year, 1958, that Leon Uris's *Exodus* dominated the bestseller list, soon to be followed by an even more popular film version starring Paul Newman as the Sabra hero. They enshrined a tale that left American Jews bursting with unearned pride, easing the pain and unspoken guilt over what had befallen the Jews in Europe. It told how the Zionists had wrested a homeland from the ashes of the Holocaust and how a new kind of Jew, bold, strong, determined, had sprung forth to supplant the persecuted Jew of the Diaspora—the meek, unworldly Talmud scholar, the exploited worker, the small urban storekeeper like my father. This might explain why Zionism had scarcely impinged on my Orthodox Jewish childhood. I had carried around the blue-and-white collection box of the Jewish National Fund, raising money to plant trees in Israel, green forests in an arid land. But many religious Jews, though excited by the David-and-Goliath story of the birth of the Jewish state, saw Israel as a dubious experiment at odds with the fundamentals of the faith. The epitome of Zionism was the kibbutz, which meant tractors, socialism, and free love, with children separated from their parents and brought up in common as sun-baked young pagans. There were religious Zionists too, pioneers in khaki shorts with tiny knitted skullcaps, but Zionism scorned what it saw as the passivity and otherworldliness of ghetto Judaism, as it also spurned the assimilation and material values of America's Jews. For many kibbutzniks the Soviet Union was the preferred model; for others it was European social democracy. Giving up the dogmas of religion, they grew fanatically devoted to political disputation and ideological commitment, a fractured legacy of the European Left.

In my interview with Shlomo Shulsinger he quickly realized that my spoken Hebrew was rudimentary, despite the courses I'd taken at the seminary, which had been my first real encounter with the living language. "There's only one place at Camp Massad for someone who doesn't speak Hebrew," he said. "You could be a waiter this year and, if you learn enough Hebrew, become a counselor next summer." Thus I signed on to wait on tables with the camp's renegades, an unruly crew of young waiters who prided themselves on behaving like a band of outsiders, the camp's recalcitrant counterculture.

The waiters lived in unsupervised chaos in a large bunk at the foot of a hill in the far corner of the camp, near the recreational pull of the ball fields, the basketball court, and the wide lake. In this bunk English reigned supreme, in a spirit of rebellion against Shlomo's severe discipline. But even as the camp's happy outcasts, we were part of an educational experiment that would loom large in my life. My "Marty" identity quickly gave way to Moshe, accent on the second syllable, and it was not long before I actually *became* Moshe, as my homey Yiddish and prayer-book Hebrew gradually receded. Slowly I learned the Sephardic pronunciation of the spoken language, with its hard consonants and trilled *r*'s, so different from the Ashkenazic Hebrew that was second nature to me. Its very intonations seemed to reflect the Sabra myth and the recoil from every model of the European Jew—the pious Polish Chasid, the cultivated Judeo-German, the wry or demonstrative shtetl Russian. Israel was now a decade old; its Hebraic revival was echoed here, altering the established American Jewish culture.

With its daylong schedule of sports, its end-of-summer color war competition between bunks, Massad was in many ways a typical summer camp. Though sports had never been my chosen pastime, during free hours I would swim in the icy lake or shoot baskets for hours on an empty court, trying to improve my game without undergoing the embarrassment of team competition. I quickly bonded with a few other camp intellectuals, some of them future judges, college professors, and rabbis. In the Mountains I had met girls but made no real friends since everyone working there was so much older than me. The good Jewish girls on the far side of the camp seemed remote and out of reach, but I struck up warm male friendships. My two closest chums were both named Shlomo, though they were opposites in other ways. Shlomo B., lean and wiry, was a serious young man and quite a good athlete; with the patience and determination that would later make him a searching literary scholar, he could practice shooting baskets or playing handball even longer than I could. Shlomo R., on the other hand, was already softly rabbinical, with dark curly hair and an ingratiating manner that would later win him a wide following. He had grown up, as I did, in Flushing, Queens, but in a family not at all observant. Now, after a kind of conversion, he was studying at Yeshiva University, catching up with the Talmud classes I had left behind but also embarking on a serious major in classics, pursuing a dual assault on Rome and Jerusalem. Both Shlomos would eventually give up flourishing careers in the United States to emigrate to Israel, one to a professorship at the Hebrew University, the other to found and lead a moderate religious settlement in the West Bank, not far from Jerusalem itself. Camp Massad undoubtedly helped shape their future.

I did not always take easily to becoming a waiter, which stirred up dim anxieties I didn't know I had. The conflicts and insecurities of my first college year came back in a new guise. I developed a low-grade ache near my groin and imagined that I had ruptured something while carrying heavy trays. This kind of intestinal hernia had been a common ailment among workhorse Jewish males on the Lower East Side, the occasion for many jokes, folk wisdom, and finally, for some, a dose of corrective surgery. A medical quack, advertising his surgical skills, had supposedly posted a sign in Yiddish—*Dein killa is mein gedilla*—which translates very loosely as "Your rupture is my rapture." My uncle Julius, after a life of hard labor, was more herniated than most. His bulging abdomen was a ropy terrain of bumps and lumps, like a relief map, but he had the family terror of any kind of surgical procedure and postponed operating on it for decades.

When it came to physical ailments I too had a vivid imagination; the most innocuous symptom, any unfamiliar discomfort, could suggest to me some menacing condition. Having observed my uncle's various belts and corsets, I wrote home to my parents to send me some jockstraps. They must have been surprised I was suddenly taken with sports. At the Kanco I had prided myself in stacking seven cups of hot coffee up the crook of my arm. Now I began using a serving cart rather than shouldering trays. As usual, with each new turn in my life, some resistance was holding me back, a voice saying I was overextended, skating on thin ice. Another voice demurred, and I carried on without too much difficulty, but the cart and the jockstraps served as a crutch, a reassuring placebo. At least this time I was lucky that the ache of fear, lodged in a corner of my mind, did not get the best of me.

As a waiter, living in a rat's nest of young hooligans, I learned only a smidgen of conversational Hebrew, but the atmosphere of the camp had its effect. I stumbled through another interview with Shlomo the following year and was anointed a counselor, a *madrikh*. This brought its own problems. The boys' greatest respect, a mixture of fear and hero worship, was accorded to counselors who were superb athletes, not to dreamy college students in love with world literature. This was less of an issue in the first year, when my charges were five ten-year-olds, nowhere near puberty—one of them still occasionally wet his bed. By the second year I had a larger group of rambunctious eleven- and twelve-year-olds, some of them big and strong enough to knock me down if they had a mind to do so. I was surprised at the personality that emerged in me, warm and big-brotherly when the situation allowed but at times almost military in enforcing discipline. On rare occasions this had to be backed up with strategic blows, a dose of corporal punishment to keep the troops in line. The kids' safety, their well-being, was in my hands, and it tasted more like premature parenthood than army discipline. But it was strangely gratifying to win my bunk's grudging affection for being tough but fair, as if I had conjured up a stern doppelgänger with a keen sense of adult responsibility. As with my drift into Zionism, I was trying on new identities I didn't know I had.

The pervasive Zionist atmosphere in Camp Massad embraced more than the spoken language. Each bunk was named after a town or kibbutz in Israel, usually a place we knew nothing about apart from its exotic name. My first bunk was called Beit Alfa, but this meant little to me. When I visited it a few years later, I saw the most exciting archaeological site in Israel. Its masterpiece was the tiled floor, with strange biblical and zodiac design, of a synagogue some fifteen centuries old. While evenings in the Catskills had been filled with the fading remnants of vaudeville comedy and Yiddish theater, Massad evenings revolved around Israeli dances and songs, such as the lilting tune about a lass called Simona from Dimona. *Hey Simona, mi'Dimo-ona, hey Simona-mona, mi'Dimona*. One counselor joked that, hey, Dimona was no more than a gas station in the Negev; that was good for a laugh. Who could imagine that it was the future site of Israel's nuclear program, and later a magnet for Russian immigration? Even then we didn't quite grasp that this was a song about a Sephardi girl—a *shkhora*, or dark-skinned girl—at a time when these so-called oriental Jews were still an exotic but growing underclass in Israel.

We also sang popular American songs with lyrics transposed into Hebrew, some of them the work of Zvi, the plump and jolly head counselor himself. I can't forget the Hebrew version of "When the Saints Come Marching In" (*Ha'tzadikim, haim nikhnassim . . .*) and the Hebrew lyrics lamenting the end of the summer, set to the main themes of Brahms's resounding Academic Festival Overture (*Ha'kaitz chalaf kvar, he'nay hegiyah ha-sof*). But mainly we sang Israeli folk songs about pioneers working the soil or sitting around the crackling campfire watching the coffee pot, *Ha-finjan*, or about centuries of dreamers on Mount Scopus looking down with longing on the stone buildings of Jerusalem, a city then still in Jordanian hands, off-limits to Jews. We were all young Americans, but we were meant to feel that our exile was ending, that Israel was our once and future home.

The larger buildings at the camp were named not after towns but after Zionist heroes and heroines, though not for living political figures. The main auditorium, where most indoor activities took place, was called Ulam Szold, after Henrietta Szold, who had founded Hadassah in 1912 and later emigrated to Palestine. The visionary Theodor Herzl, the lexicographer Eliezer Ben-Yehuda, the national poet H. N. Bialik, the pioneering essayist Ahad Ha'am, the dying Joseph Trumpeldor, killed in 1920 defending his farming village, the young wartime martyr Hannah Senesh, parachuted into occupied Europe, even the controversial revisionist Ze'ev Jabotinsky, whose enemies labeled him a fascist, were names we heard every day. They were the glowing stars in the Zionist firmament. Alongside such heroic models and the revival of the Hebrew language, the ultimate ideal of Camp Massad was *Aliyah*, emigration, the lodestar of all Zionist indoctrination. The words of Herzl, *Im tirtzu, ein zo aggada* ("If you really will it, it's no legend"), were inscribed on the walls and were ever on Shlomo Shulsinger's lips. To me this was a warm, distant, and unreal notion.

After a two-thousand-year hiatus, Israel seemed an astonishing political creation, an almost miraculous fulfillment of a millennial dream. I don't recall that the Arabs of Palestine were ever mentioned, though the enmity of the surrounding Arab states was a constant theme, an echo of the vulnerability Jews had felt through centuries of pogroms. As I read Moshe Dayan's vivid diary of the 1956 Sinai campaign, I felt at once proud of Israel and anxious about its fate. But in my real life it remained a remote fantasy, though the dances, the songs, the tales of the kibbutz, and the strange yet familiar names of the towns seemed magically appealing; they projected their own vigorous reality. The Zionist project, *Ahavat Tzion* (the love of Zion), the attachment to the biblical land, was reshaping us into different kinds of Jews, and my best camp friends would eventually emigrate, something I was never tempted to do, though I wondered at moments what such a life might be like for me. Zionism made us imaginary inhabitants of a place most of us had never seen.

Meanwhile, to relieve the hothouse quality of camp life, we were emigrating internally; each week on days off we set out for different corners of Pennsylvania, not exactly a stand-in for the promised land. One day a rowdy crew of six waiters piled into an old car and drove to the top of a nearby mountain. On the way back down the brakes failed, or so the driver said. At first this seemed like a joke, but as I looked toward the dashboard from the middle of the backseat I could see the pedal pushed down to the floor, with no braking effect whatever. I heard the driver shouting and watched the speedometer push past 100, taking aim at 120 on the steeply descending road. As we whizzed around slower cars, poky farm vehicles, and knots of surprised people and animals moving along the side of the road, I could only think of the next day's newspaper headlines, the shock waves at the camp, and my parents' bottomless grief. It seemed like the silliest way to die, in some tabloid tale of wild and crazy teenage kids, killed while joyriding. Gradually the road flattened out, the car slowed and came to a halt. I had never till then understood what relief meant. The driver had done well by steering around every possible obstacle, never losing control, but had done rather badly in the first place by flooring the brake and burning it out. Still, we would live to make new mistakes another day.

Once I became a counselor I was taking my days off with the two Shlomos, though none of us drove a car or had one at our disposal. We were city boys exploring the country by hitchhiking, though today it's hard to imagine who would have picked up three nineteen-year-old guys. Either it was a more trusting time, when hitchhiking was routine and few bothered to lock the doors of their homes, or else we looked laughably unthreatening. We took trips to see the natural wonders of the green and lush Poconos, to Scranton, an already dying coal town, where many downtown businesses stood deserted, and even to faraway Philadelphia to see the Liberty Bell, with its famous crack, and other early American sites. Somehow we came and went in one piece, chattering on, exploring a corner of rural America while embarked on our summerlong seminar on what it meant to be a Jew.

This was 1959 and 1960, just before the Eichmann trial, when the Holocaust was still a buried subject. It had yet to impinge deeply on the American consciousness, since both the survivors and other Americans, including Jews, were determined to put it behind them. In the upbeat climate of the 1950s, only the most hopeful and muffled versions of the Jewish catastrophe could be assimilated. I had been deeply moved by *The Diary of Anne Frank* in one of my Broadway excursions, without thinking how this story of an ardent teenager coming of age, experiencing her first love, affirming her unshaken faith in humanity, stopped well short of her camp experience and death.

At Massad, a very different kind of camp, we were sequestered in a self-contained world, keeping the larger world at bay. At home I was a news junkie, engrossed in politics, driven by the curiosity of a budding journalist. But there was no television in the camp, and I scarcely saw a newspaper. Years later I realized that the carnage in the former Belgian

Congo and other crises in the summer of 1960 remained little more than blanks on my mental map, remote rumors I barely assimilated at the time. Even my fanatical love of the Yankees had begun to wane. Nor could I do much reading, since I was on duty or with my campers almost twenty-four hours a day. Summer was my retreat from my own world as a student and would-be intellectual. One summer I did manage to read *The Brothers Karamazov*, about ten pages a night, after lights out, with the help of a tiny flashlight, as if pushing back grimly against the sunny kibbutz-like life I was now leading.

Instead of news and books we were enveloped in Zionist ideals joined with Orthodox Jewish routines. Religious practice was hardly the main focus of camp life. But in all my years in synagogues and at the yeshiva, I had never found myself in a more congenial religious environment, enthusiastic, spontaneous, and brightened by our rural surroundings. At the camp's Friday night prayers, always my favorite service, we welcomed the Sabbath Bride outdoors in white shirts and khaki shorts, singing psalms that should have been enough to convert the heathen and soften the hard heart of the anti-Semite. Back home the restrictions of the Sabbath, which I had once taken for granted, had come to vex and annoy me. The day seemed full of Thou Shalt Nots, in thrall to the letter of the law rather than the spirit behind it. For some Jews these restrictions, like the blessings intoned before even the most trivial act, were full of meaning, a hallowing of everyday life. For many others they were simply habitual—brief pit stops in an unthinking routine. Too often obedience to the rules was all that mattered.

But synagogue music, especially this Sabbath service, so familiar to me, was enough to melt my now unbelieving heart. It gave me an indescribable feeling of peace and joy. At Camp Massad, a hive of activity all week long, the Sabbath offered not only rest and renewal but a numinous sense of being in touch with something Beyond. The isolation of the camp, the unspoiled youth of the campers, the beauty of the setting, the rare sense of communal purpose, all brought such feelings home. At these moments I could feel what Wordsworth called "the sentiment of being" flowing through me and connecting me to the world.

Camp life also did wonders for my knowledge of the Hebrew Bible, which had remained rudimentary at the yeshiva, where it was ignored and taken for granted. My growing comfort with the language had made the easier books, especially the storytelling works, more accessible; the poetry of the prophetic books was more difficult, though I was studying them at the seminary. I now understood much more of the Sabbath prayers I had learned by rote, taught to pronounce without really comprehending them, like the ritual repetition of the Latin Mass. It was as if a veil had been lifted as I grasped the meaning of biblical passages I had sonorously chanted aloud and prayers I knew by heart.

Each year in Israel there was an elaborate *Chidon Ha-Tanakh*, a kind of World Cup of Bible competition. Camp Massad had its local version, and I decided to bone up for it, poring over texts of prophetic books, poetic works, and history chronicles I barely knew existed. With illicit aid from English translations, I plowed through the prophets, major and minor, reread tales from Abraham and Sarah to Ruth and Jonah, and memorized the knotty sequence of the kings of Israel and Judah. I walked away with a small prize, a blue, metal-bound copy of the Book itself, published in Israel, in which I took inordinate pleasure. The competition was more like a spelling bee than real scholarship, yet I learned more about the Bible's astounding range of works and styles—and the history recorded in them— than I had ever known. As with my seminary classes, I was making up for the lapses in my early education, but also for the gaping holes in Columbia's core curriculum, which gave short shrift to the Hebrew sources of the Western tradition.

But the real miracle, for me at least, was becoming comfortable with the Hebrew language, which I spoke haltingly, then more fluently. I had a decent ear and a gift for mimicry, so that even the Sephardic pronunciation, at first so alien, began to come easily. Without noticing it, I passed through the border between translating mentally and actually thinking in a language, the way a musician no longer thinks of the notes he wants to play but lets his fingers do the thinking for him. Despite the Orthodox observance of the camp and the traditional atmosphere at the seminary, I was moving imperceptibly from a religious way of life, marked by punctilious daily practice, to a feeling for the cultural links that bound me to the community, beginning with the newly revived language.

Five

FINDING MY WAY

I T WAS STARTLING, even disorienting, to return to Columbia from my summer as a camp counselor in 1959. I had lived all summer not only in a different language but in an alternate reality. In the Hebrew environment of the camp I felt I'd been light years away. Now I reentered a world at once familiar and hard to recognize. My first two years in college had been taken up with required courses, especially the literary terrain covered by the first year of Humanities and the social and intellectual history packed into Contemporary Civilization. There were also follow-up courses introducing neophytes to music, the visual arts, and, most intensely, the key social issues of the modern world. This last course, embracing major theorists from Marx, Weber, and Durkheim to Friederick Hayek and Hannah Arendt, had always faced stubborn resistance from specialists in the social science departments. It was dropped as a requirement soon after I graduated, yet it furnished a terrific background for every kind of liberal arts major.

As a sweeping introduction to modern social thought, it lent encouragement to generalists, not specialists, motivating students to overstep arbitrary academic borders and delve into relations between one field and another. By focusing on ideas—Durkheim on suicide and anomie, Engels on historical materialism, Arendt on totalitarianism and terror—it resisted the tide of narrow empirical work that dominated the social sciences, just the kind of work that one maverick faculty member, C. Wright Mills, attacked that year in his book *The Sociological Imagination*, inspired in part by Trilling's *Liberal Imagination*. Showing how institutions condition individual lives, Mills argued for a more humanistic, less quantitative form of social observation, something closer to literature than to empirical science. This was the spirit in which Trilling had taken apart the Kinsey report, though Mills and Trilling were far apart politically.

I was never going to be a social scientist but I returned to school with a new job that pretty much demanded that I become a generalist. I'd grown more involved in writing for *Spectator*, mostly as a straight news journalist, occasionally as a reviewer of books and plays. However, the preceding spring the incoming editor in chief, Bill Bishin, had had a vision. Though he himself was a prelaw student, he thought the state of reviewing in America was appalling—middlebrow, complacent, and superficial—especially at its most influential, in the *New York Times Book Review*. He was sure that even an undergraduate newspaper could do better, and he called in me and my pal Sam, also a *Spec* writer, to figure out how it might be done. (We must have been seen as the paper's resident literary intellectuals.) In our no-holds-barred conversations we hatched a high-minded plan for what was essentially the *New York Review of Books*, a full four years before that paper appeared in 1963 in the midst of a New York City newspaper strike.

Our more modest version would be published periodically as a supplement to the newspaper, but we also planned to distribute it separately to college campuses around the city. It would be made up of extended review essays written to severe standards. We would search out contributions not solely from undergraduates but from anyone we admired—faculty members, graduate students, cultural figures. It was set to begin publication in the fall, edited by Sam and me, and its title, *The Supplement*, would be as austere and unflashy as our conception. For me the project would pay back some of the debt I owed for the intellectual awakening of the last two years. It would keep me in touch with new books, plays, music, and art at just the moment they were exploding on the New York scene—in chic and shabby art cinemas, unconventional performance spaces, grungy off-Broadway theaters, and out-of-the-way galleries.

It was a minor miracle that our venture took off at all since college papers didn't usually publish extensive literary supplements. But it also unfolded at the cusp between two decades, a moment when the whole direction of American culture was in play and the staid official culture of the 1950s was loosening up, freeing itself especially from the heavy hand of the cold war. Now the stultifying consensus was coming apart and New York was where much of it was happening. We had ringside seats though without knowing it we were also among the contenders, eagerly looking for new openings.

With his precise mind and exacting sense of language, Sam proved to be a rigorous editor of other people's prose. I loved fingering review copies, spinning off ideas for essays, cajoling reviewers, assigning and editing their articles. It was as if all of twentieth-century culture had become our own playground. We found recent graduates to write pieces on the new paintings of Willem de Kooning; on the films of Eisenstein, including the brilliant second part of *Ivan the Terrible*, which had been shelved while Stalin was alive; on the latest Faulkner novels, *The Town* and *The Mansion*. I myself chose, not so unpredictably, to review a book called *The Cruel God*, a study of the Book of Job by a Christian scholar. Working through my own problems of faith and doubt, I read that peculiarly modern biblical work as an existentialist text about an absurd universe, a challenge to the orthodoxy represented by Job's false comforters, who insist that if Job suffers he must have sinned since God is neither cruel, capricious, nor unjust. This was no news to biblical scholars but momentous for me, a literary as well as a theological adventure. I was taken with the sheer sublimity of God's answer through the Voice from the Whirlwind, God's willingness to engage with his human challenger, coming to meet him, awing him into submission without responding directly to the difficult questions Job had raised.

Most of the subjects covered in *The Supplement* were more contemporary. One of Sam's teachers, a densely brilliant critic, Quentin Anderson, reviewed Leslie Fiedler's sexually charged magnum opus, *Love and Death in the American Novel*, under the provocative title of "All Discontents and No Civilization." Fiedler was very much in the sexual vanguard of the moment, arraigning American writers for their discretions and suppressions, and Anderson respectfully dissented. A recent graduate, Morton Halperin, who had moved on to Harvard—he would later become one of

Henry Kissinger's best and brightest—reviewed work on game theory and nuclear war. We set up a debate between an old-style cold war liberal, James Wechsler, who in the thirties had been a crusading editor of *Spectator*, and Jeffrey Hart, a teacher of mine and a young Burkean conservative—he would later become a fixture at William Buckley's *National Review*. To this I added a commentary that said, in effect, a plague on both your houses. It was a heady time, and we felt that we had the wind at our backs.

Since I was not actually majoring in *Spectator*, at least a fraction of my time had to be spent on my courses. I was now at liberty to take a number of electives. The jewel in the crown would be my faculty adviser Andrew Chiappe's Shakespeare class, which, in the course of a year, promised to take us through nearly all thirty-seven plays. (One exception was that travesty of Falstaff, supposedly written for the pleasure of the queen herself, *The Merry Wives of Windsor*.) Despite his remote, seigneurial manner, the rotund Chiappe was the most mellifluous of lecturers. He was superb at reading aloud, especially with characters like the self-pitying, self-dramatizing Richard II. Yet Chiappe was no preening performer but an analytic reader adept at finding the key to what held each play together—the bold, intuitive patterns of imagery, the layered psyche of the characters, the coursing variety of the language, the themes so arresting they seemed like today's coinage. It was as if he had the playwright in his blood, so deeply had he penetrated Shakespeare's mind and universe.

Chiappe's performance had a sequel, for he went on leave at midyear and my old mentor and tormentor, Jim Zito, took over the class. From the outset, in a rare moment of humility, he prepared us for the cacophonous notes we might be hearing from him. His opening words, delivered as a warning and an advance apology, came from *Love's Labour's Lost*: "The words of Mercury are harsh after the songs of Apollo." Yet as Zito tracked a path through the problem plays and the great tragedies, Shakespeare himself grew more dissonant. As the universe of his plays darkened, the very music of *Measure for Measure*, *King Lear*, and *Othello* turned increasingly harsh. Between Chiappe's fluent insight and Zito's acrid brilliance, I sensed we were taking in more than the genius of Shakespeare or the wild reach of poetic speech. As they plumbed his characters, his language, the remarkable coherence of his metaphors and allusions, we were gaining a better understanding of how any literary works were put together, how to live inside them as intimate human experiences that nevertheless resisted yielding up their meaning.

No one else taught quite the same way, from inside the belly of the whale, yet there were so many subjects I was hot to explore that I often split the difference, signing up for the first half of Fritz Stern's course in modern European history, then the second half of Trilling's course on modern writers. In those days Europe, with its checkered history, salad of languages, and flourishing arts, was all that really mattered to us. It was the great mountain we were trying to climb. Though I kept up with contemporary American writing as it came out, it never crossed my mind to try a course in American literature; we patronized it as a provincial offshoot of great European traditions, something you could pick up on your own if you really cared to. The feeling for Melville and Emerson, Fitzgerald and Faulkner, Cather and Wharton, did not take me by the throat until years later. Some of this was sheer intellectual snobbery, an unthinking contempt for the local and familiar. We prided ourselves on being cosmopolitan, shunning any hint of cultural boosterism. The American writers I had been force-fed in high school, from Longfellow to Carl Sandburg and Stephen Vincent Benét, seemed banal compared with more demanding modern writers like Eliot. But it's also possible that the Christian coloring of early American literature put me off despite the Hebraic roots of Puritan culture, about which I knew next to nothing.

In Stern's course I did my term paper on the notorious Kishinev pogrom in Russia in 1903, a massacre that had drawn worldwide condemnation. Reading up on it, I learned more about Russian history and the besieged, often endangered lives of Russian Jews than I'd ever known, though I was only a generation away from that world. It brought to mind stories of harassment and persecution I'd heard from my mother, distant memories of her childhood in the Ukraine. Slow, patient research, the nitty-gritty of historical documentation, usually bored me, but here was a subject that kept me riveted. I cited everyone from Tolstoy to the Hebrew national poet Bialik on this notorious atrocity. It was a small-scale rehearsal for the Holocaust, about which I knew even less. Soon afterward, taking Trilling's course, I was especially drawn to Dostoevsky, Freud, and Kafka, perhaps the most

"Jewish" of the modern writers, despite Dostoevsky's fierce Christian anti-Semitism, so evident in his voluminous *Diary of a Writer*.

No teacher could have been more unlike Chiappe and Zito than Trilling. He was not at his best in a large lecture class, since his whole approach was musing—conversational rather than analytic. His was the sidelong glance, not the frontal attack. Where Chiappe hovered slightly above his auditors, surveying the landscape of a lush kingdom called Shakespeare, and Zito lobbed brilliant insights, like heavy-duty ordnance, at his amazed student audience, Trilling, seemingly casual, even unprepared, appeared to be mulling it over as if for the first time—the author, the work, its place in the culture—awaiting some shaft of inspiration. Often it never arrived, and only the quest itself, the alert, patient waiting, left an impression. When it did arrive it could be worth the effort. One day he opened a class devoted to Kafka's *Trial* with the lament that he had nothing to say, nothing that stood up to the extremity of the subject. This is a book in which a kind of Everyman is arrested, grilled, charged, and finally executed for a free-floating offense never specified—he is merely "accused of guilt," as if accused of being accused. Trilling described going to each of his colleagues in Hamilton Hall, asking them in turn if they had anything he could say. Each one proved more voluble than the last—this was a faculty of world-class talkers, bursting with clever ideas—but somehow it was not exactly what *he* wanted to say, at least not on that day. Before we knew it the class was over. Without quite realizing what had happened, we'd heard an impromptu lecture on how difficult it was to talk about Kafka's work—indeed, how difficult it was for any reader, especially the boldly interpretive reader, with his will to knowledge, to measure up to the exigent demands of modern literature.

This proved to be the major theme of his seminal essay on modern writing that came out in *Partisan Review* about six months later. But where in class he had mildly satirized his loquacious colleagues, here he turned his artillery on his complacent students, the ones in the very course I had just taken. He—no, the writers themselves—had asked them to gaze into the abyss, and they had politely, affably complied; the abyss had gazed back into them, as Nietzsche had anticipated—and found them hollow. Instead of rising to the challenge, we had greeted the extreme visions of the modern writers with an amiable tolerance, a vast complacency—at least that was how he saw it for the purposes of this essay. Much as we looked up to him as a critic, we were taken aback by the caricature, which also seemed a wild distortion of what had happened in class. To me the modernists of the 1920s—Joyce, Kafka, Proust, Eliot, Yeats, and Mann—were as unsettling as they had been to his generation almost forty years earlier. Far from asking us to gaze into the abyss, he made it clear from the beginning that he was tired of student writing, bored above all by student *seriousness*, and he considered assigning papers confined to straightforward factual accounts of the writers' lives. He didn't follow through on this demeaning threat but the impulse, layered with his customary irony, made his point: he wanted us really to respond to this work—and, to my mind, we did, at least as far as young people could. Our pride was wounded, we felt used, insulted, but there was something admirable about Trilling's crankiness, his restive refusal to settle or be pleased.

Columbia College in those days was full of great teachers, but Trilling, an uneven one, taught in this existential way, as if lying in wait for a genuine encounter. Often the encounter remained tantalizingly out of reach, so that we learned more from reading him than from hearing him in the flesh, especially since he held himself apart, genially inaccessible. Blinding flashes of illumination were much more common in the classroom of Jacob Taubes, an unsung, almost unpublished professor of religion whom my friends had begun following years earlier. Religion was his formal department but the knotty history of modern intellectual life was his actual subject. Lacking any gift for doing philosophy, I had shied away from him despite the incandescent reports. But from the middle of my junior year I began auditing his classes, with mounting excitement. He was the son of the chief rabbi of Zürich, and by the age of twenty-four he had written and published an immensely ambitious thesis on Western eschatology, in German. His publications since then had been tantalizingly few, though we managed to dig them up. He was certainly no scribbler; this added to his mystique. Still, his improvised lectures were so precise they could have been published verbatim. His ever-shifting courses were rich with subjects otherwise left out of the curriculum: metaphysics and existentialism (shunned by the positivists in the philosophy department), psychoanalysis (despised by the behaviorists in the psychology department), and Marxism (completely out of favor in the economics and politics departments). All these were in vogue in Europe, where he must have taken his cues; he was our living conduit to the preoccupations of the modern European mind, especially the line that stretched from Hegel to existentialism.

Above all there was something seductive about him. Radiating charm, intelligence, and mystery, Taubes drew men and women irresistibly into his orbit. Yet from our lowly viewpoint he also seemed to have the perfect family, a beautiful and brilliant wife, the dark-haired Susan, and two attractive children. On the day of a nuclear air-raid drill, when all of us were supposed to take cover, I saw the four of them standing in mute protest on the steps of Low Library, as if on a windswept English heath. This momentary view became an indelible image of a destiny I naively imagined for myself, the youthful fantasy of a life that fused intellect, personal courage, social witness, and family feeling. In my mind's eye I could see myself as part of such a family, striking a solitary pose of courageous dissent.

It was through Jacob that we encountered Susan Sontag, an instructor in sociology who doubled as his teaching assistant. She must have fallen under his spell when he taught at Harvard, where she had done graduate work. We assumed they'd had an affair, though she was also very close to the other Susan, his wife. All of us were madly in love with the mysterious and articulate Sontag. She exuded the combination of beauty and intellectual cachet we also projected on Jacob and his family. Fifteen years later I shared a cab with her as we were returning from a midtown conference. By then she was a star and I had been reading her for years, first in Morningside Heights publications, including *The Supplement*, then in *Partisan Review* and the *New York Review of Books*. A wave of nostalgia welled up, and I began reminiscing about those days when she assisted with Jacob's classes and graded his term papers. She blew up at me, not for the last time. "I was never anyone's assistant," she shouted angrily. "I never graded anyone's papers." I was feeling mellow, aglow with idealized recollections, but she seemed horrified to be reminded of the days when she was not yet famous, not yet somebody. I was shocked yet amused by this absurd fit of pique but even more stunned to hear personal history revised in the presence of a living witness. She had somehow fashioned a myth of her own origins.

Taubes's courses were existential in their own way, for whatever their initial plan they seemed to drift spontaneously. One course was set to open with lectures on Hegel's *Phenomenology of the Spirit*, to be followed by readings in major nineteenth-century thinkers who rebelled against his influence but could not escape it, including Kierkegaard, Nietzsche, and the so-called Young Hegelians, such as Ludwig Feuerbach. Hegel's bravura account of human consciousness, with its dialectical exposition of the relation between master and servant, proved to be one of the most difficult books ever written, yet I found I could follow it under Jacob's tutelage. I was primed to read the whole sequence of thinkers he had influenced, but no sooner had we finished grappling with Hegel than a new star arose on the horizon. Jean Genet's play *The Balcony*, set in a brothel at a moment of revolution, had just opened off-Broadway, and Taubes decided that its action was the perfect working out of Hegel's dialectic. Reading Hegel had long been a hot ticket in Paris but this was an unexpected turn. So the second half of the semester was spent entirely on Genet, France's once-imprisoned, gay, outlaw writer, whose work was then new to New York. More than a decade later the French founder of deconstruction, Jacques Derrida, published his most recondite book, *Glas*, with double columns composed of facing commentaries on, guess what, Hegel and Genet. I couldn't believe that he had not somehow gotten word about Taubes's idiosyncratic course, which turned into a surprising intellectual adventure. It left me with a fascination with Hegel, especially his way of mapping history and consciousness, something I would pursue ham-handedly for years to come.

It's strange that I should be writing about my undergraduate courses and teachers more than half a century later. But the best of these were not simply courses but life-altering experiences. Teachers like Chiappe, Zito, and Taubes not only opened me up to new subjects but left me rapt with excitement, whether or not they could serve as models for what I myself might do. I had just begun to think of teaching as a vocation, thanks to Trilling and Barzun; in my own teachers I could see what made it attractive. They were careful scholars but also freewheeling minds, seemingly interested in everything, following questions wherever they led. It became clear that teaching literature would require a knowledge of different cultural traditions, an understanding of technique in the arts, an ideal openness to new work, a Hegelian feeling for the zeitgeist of an era, a full sense of the larger world in which art and culture were embedded. This was a daunting prospect, though I would never have thought of it in such exalted terms.

It worked to my benefit as a college student that I was still not a particularly fast reader, especially for an English major. I had to resist the temptation to load up with heavy reading courses; this would have left me always behind, playing catch-up. As a perverse way of lightening my load, I signed up for a new language, German, though it met first thing in the morning five days a week. Steering away from excess reading, I signed up for Otto Luening's offbeat survey of the history of opera and Howard Davis's popular course in Northern Renaissance art. I felt a need to educate my senses; my mostly literary mind was too much given to processing everything verbally, abstractly. Words, words, words were my default medium. Instead, I was also learning to hear, to see. Luening was a well-known composer and pioneer of electronic music. Always playful, slightly stooped, speaking gently as he illustrated his points at the piano, he passed quickly over the chestnuts of the nineteenth-century repertory to focus on earlier and later work, on Monteverdi, who helped create opera in the first place, on Mozart and Gluck, on the late Verdi of *Otello* and *Falstaff,* on Debussy's only opera, *Pelléas and Mélisande,* on Alban Berg's *Wozzeck,* above all on opera as drama—the drama in the music, not simply in the story. He skipped Puccini's more famous operas to expose us to his final work, the unfinished *Turandot,* and reminisced about studying with his mentor Ferruccio Busoni, who had died in 1924 with his own opera, *Doktor Faust,* also incomplete. It took years for what Luening called the "schlockmeisters" of the Met to catch up with his taste and broaden its repertory to include more challenging, less crowd-pleasing works.

In the same venturesome way, Howard Davis lured students into his course with the sure-fire promise of the delights of Rembrandt and Rubens, then spent the whole semester on meticulous studies of the delicate craft of earlier painters like the Flemish Jan van Eyck, Hans Memling, and Rogier van der Weyden, whose portraits, religious subjects, and altarpieces were executed with astonishing precision and psychological insight. I loved their minute visual detail, their sense of individual character in relation to social position. They brought religious imagery into the real world yet painted secular subjects with the same exquisite refinement. Having prepared the way, Davis had no doubt we could go on to appreciate the more accessible Rembrandt and Rubens on our own. Both courses bestowed lessons that stay with me even today in the opera house or the museum, gifts that keep on giving.

AMID THESE PLEASURES disguised as course work, the demands of putting out a daily newspaper accelerated. In late March 1960 the departing editors of *Spectator*, soon to graduate, would choose its managing board for the following year. I found myself on the short list to become the next editor. As an English major and perhaps a future academic, not bound for a career in journalism or law like most of my colleagues, I was hardly a perfect fit. The other main contender, Marty Margulies, was cut from a different cloth. He was a prelaw student who readily fit the mold of a hard-boiled reporter, though he would later become a law professor. He smoked too much and burned the candle at both ends. Lean and intense, Marty reminded me of the cynical, tough-talking Chicago newspapermen in the Hecht-MacArthur play *The Front Page*, though his manner with me was always considerate and soft-spoken.

He had earned his spurs as an investigative reporter with a multipart series on the Morningside neighborhood, fluently written in an unvarnished, hard-hitting style. I understood him better when I met his stern, slightly intimidating father, whom he treated with marked deference. Like many kids who grew up under a strict regime, he seized upon the freedom of college life as his chance to break out. Marty belonged to one of the Jewish fraternities, Sigma Alpha Mu, where, it soon became clear, a good number of my classmates were actually having sex, at least at the parties on Saturday nights when girls from Barnard and other schools drifted in. I was envious but hardly a candidate for such casual sex, except in my fantasy life. Fraternities were off the map and women were a breed apart, hard to approach. Though it was situated just across Broadway, Barnard seemed a hundred miles away, and there were barriers that kept its students out of Columbia classes. My social life had dwindled since my freshman year,

when I worked overtime to meet girls. Lacking innate confidence, anticipating rejection, I didn't manage to get very far with those good Jewish
girls across the street. After many frustratingly chaste dates, which invariably ended with a kiss at the door, I'd given up and thrown my social energies into merry but monkish intellectual friendships. There, at least, my
confidence brimmed over.

I was nothing if not competitive, so when Marty was tapped to become
editor—and I became the editorials editor—I was initially crestfallen at
being passed over. I hated to come in second, even for a job for which I
wasn't well suited. Soon enough, though, I felt a wave of relief. From the
frantic lives of previous editors I knew the job was all-consuming. It would
have taken over my life. This indeed happened to Marty, who perpetually
put off work on his senior thesis, so that he was forced to lurk furtively
around campus for fear of bumping into Peter Gay, his adviser. Instead of
running the paper I was happy to focus on writing. The editors met every
Sunday night to thrash out the issues of the moment; Marty and I would
propose topics for that week's editorials. As the days unfolded, he and I
would write them all, usually two a day, a relentless routine I can barely
imagine today. Meanwhile, I kept my hand in at *The Supplement*, which my
friend Sam was now editing brilliantly on his own. It made all the difference that Marty and I got on unexpectedly well. Though he played Humphrey Bogart to my Thornton Wilder, or Ben Hecht to my Billy Wilder, we
never had a moment's quarrel.

Editorial writing presented a special challenge. It was keyed to the
week's news but had to be sensitive to the underlying issues that mattered
to the university: how it was governed (not very well), how it treated students (high-handedly, we thought), and how it related to the surrounding
community (full of poor people it was trying to push out). This kind of
writing ruled out the personal idiosyncrasy that added spice to genuine
literature, but I came to enjoy the anonymity. It served as a corrective to
my usual writerly ego. Speaking for the newspaper as an institution, we
imagined ourselves as the voice of the college and, yes, the moral arbiter
of the university. This pulpit gave us a heady but illusory sense of power,
especially when we skewered the central administration for its sins, such
as its callous real estate dealings as the major landlord in the mixed neigh-

borhood of Morningside Heights. We made lots of noise but I can't say we were taken seriously. In the hierarchical climate of the late 1950s, imbued with respect for authority, the dissonant student voice was easy to ignore; complaint could always be written off as naive adolescent idealism. This would change dramatically in the following decade, when the nation went through a crisis of authority and students found their voice.

Spectator editors, going back to Jimmy Wechsler and Reed Harris in the 1930s, had often been a fiery lot, especially in the tense political atmosphere of the Depression. Under the autocratic regime of President Nicholas Murray Butler, who single-handedly dominated the university in the first half of the century, crusading editors were occasionally expelled as troublemakers, sometimes for offenses no worse than attacking the football program. (Butler had once, scandalously, cashiered recalcitrant faculty members for opposing America's entry in the First World War.) Things had calmed down in the torpor of the postwar years. Butler's long reign had ended and the university was decentralized, but those earlier editors, perpetually embattled, were our heroes and role models.

Whereas Butler was willful and domineering, brooking no resistance, his successors, Dwight Eisenhower and Grayson Kirk, were remote, almost invisible, leaving the real governing authority in the hands of individual schools, which operated as independent fiefdoms. Ike was there only two years before being tapped as commander of NATO, then running for president in 1952. It's not clear whether he ever understood the dynamics of the university. He once was said to have addressed the faculty as "you employees of Columbia University," only to be told, in no uncertain terms, "Mr. President, we *are* Columbia University." Few undergraduates ever encountered these grandees except in an annual tradition preceding Christmas, when they came to one of the dormitories to light the ceremonial Yule Log, a practice unknown on the Lower East Side. For students and faculty alike, Low Library was like Kafka's fabled Castle, distant, indifferent, and inscrutable, just the way the university itself had appeared to me when I approached it as a high school senior.

As *Spec* editors we had a privileged view, for we were granted regular interviews with the college dean (John Palfrey), the provost (Jacques Barzun), and the president himself (Kirk). Palfrey, the epitome of a straight arrow, was frank and trustworthy. He answered every question as directly and knowledgeably as he could. The silver-haired, silver-tongued Barzun, perfectly mannered, a model of personal elegance, was one of the most slippery characters I'd ever met. The smoothest of politicians, he managed never to say *anything.* The pink-faced Kirk was in a class by himself, a figure of waxlike immobility, immured behind the desk in his cavernous office in Low Library. He had a bad stammer, which he concealed behind a pipe, and each of our questions was followed by a long hesitation or a series of stuttering syllables. His public relations man, who sat in the far corner of the room through every conference, would then speak up with the official story: "What Dr. Kirk means to say . . . ." Over many months we came to the reluctant conclusion that Kirk was actually a manikin wheeled out for these occasions, strategically positioned behind the barrier of his oversize desk. But at one of our last meetings, as Marty took out a cigarette and reached into his pocket searching for matches, Kirk leaped up, grabbed an ornate silver lighter from his desk, and raced nimbly across the room to give him a light. We were floored to see this Mme Tussaud figure spring to life. Unfortunately he would prove less dextrous in responding to the student uprising and faculty discontent later in the decade, which would terminate his career. It was something for which few university administrators would be equipped. He had stayed on past his time.

Long before that sixties turmoil erupted, we editors saw ourselves as gadflies, keepers of the social conscience, at just the moment John F. Kennedy was rousing the young to an idealism that lay dormant through the cold war years. Though I had loved the literate speeches and witty, civilized manner of Adlai Stevenson, Kennedy was a much more adept politician. I was thrilled when Marty knocked out our long front-page editorial supporting his candidacy for president. His campaign and his eloquent inaugural address, as well as his call to service in new institutions like the Peace Corps, set a tone for the generational rebellions of the new decade. His demeanor, ironic wit, and energy made us feel he was one of us, despite his privileged upbringing. The snide, shifty, self-pitying Nixon, who had used contemptible McCarthyite tactics to win previous elections, was a specimen of everything we hated in American public life in the 1950s: the burial of real social issues, the obsession with the enemy within, the jingoistic, sometimes paranoid rhetoric of the cold war. Kennedy, on the other hand, seemed to combine activism and intellect, culture and sly humor, class and style. It was no wonder that writers like Norman Mailer, who were searching for a clean break with the past, came unduly to idolize him.

With the publication of his outrageous collection *Advertisements for Myself* in 1959, Mailer himself became a key figure of rebellion for my generation, or at least for me as a would-be radical. Another was Norman O. Brown, the author of *Life against Death*, who caused a local sensation when he delivered the Phi Beta Kappa address at Columbia in the spring of 1960. I had no business being there, I was not part of the graduating class, but when I heard that Brown was speaking and Robert Lowell would read a new poem for the occasion, I found my way in. I was mesmerized by the urgent, immediate attack of Lowell's poetry, with its musing confessional tone and arresting images. He helped retire the gnomic, allusive manner and craftsmanlike ironies of too many postwar poems, including the densely charged work that had made him famous.

I was even more enraptured by the prophetic prose-poetry of Brown's passionate address, a revealing signpost in the turn toward the 1960s. Under the title of "Apocalypse: The Place of Mystery in the Life of the Mind," he cited Blake, Nietzsche, and Emerson's own Phi Beta Kappa address, "The American Scholar," to conjure up the dark, chthonic forces at the root of intelligence and education itself. Like his great predecessor E. R. Dodds, the author of *The Greeks and the Irrational*, like Nietzsche before him, this wayward classicist located a divine madness, with its spiritual (and sexual) abandon, at the heart of culture. (Diana Trilling later complained that the presence of Lowell, with his history of mental breakdowns, should have reminded him of the steep price of the mundane horrors of madness, but Brown had no knowledge of Lowell's troubles.) Whereas Kennedy and Camelot were Apollonian, issuing a call to the best and brightest to take up the torch for the next decade, Mailer and Brown, like Allen Ginsberg, were flagrantly Dionysian, promoting a dizzying descent into the unconscious, the unknown, even the unknowable. They looked to the dark gods for renewal, the shadowy recesses of our nature. With no sense of inconsistency or confusion, I imagined we could set off in both directions at once. I longed to put my straitened youth behind me, along with the deadly mediocrity of the postwar world.

It was the good fortune of my in-between generation to come of age on the cusp of a new era. The 1950s, hemmed in by conformity, fear, and intimidation, bedeviled by anxieties arising from the cold war, had fitted us for a political straitjacket yet spawned a powerful literature, including memorable novels by blacks and Jews like Ralph Ellison and James Baldwin, Saul Bellow and Bernard Malamud. Now, like a return of the repressed, those constraints were stimulating a vigorous counterculture. The cultural ferment of the late 1950s, from folk and rock music to stand-up comedy (Lenny Bruce, Mort Sahl, Nichols and May), pointed to seismic eruptions, though no one could have anticipated all that lay ahead. In the Kennedy campaign the new beginning was political—a burst of vigor and optimism, a shift in tone. With the civil rights movement and the growing antinuclear campaign, political activity also became a form of witness. They relied on nonviolent means not simply to alter policy but as expressions of conscience and personal resistance.

But in the arts the thrust was toward the absurd, the irrational, the apocalyptic. A religious fire blazed up in this quest for renewal, alongside a profane libertarian yearning. New Bergman films like *The Seventh Seal*, where a medieval knight plays chess with Death, enacted grave encounters over ultimate issues—pure manna for undergraduate minds. Censorship crumbled under repeated assaults on the sexual hypocrisy of the 1950s, and many banned books like *Lady Chatterley's Lover* and Henry Miller's *Tropic* novels were published openly for the first time. The French New Wave, kicked off by films like Jean-Luc Godard's *Breathless* and François Truffaut's *The 400 Blows*, exalted spontaneity and improvisation, as did many theatrical experiments. They fostered rebellion: personal rebellion (like the Beats), not the old political style of organized protest.

The new off-Broadway theater made Broadway's commercial offerings seem tepid. I was excited by my first experiences of seeing Ibsen, Chekhov, and Pirandello, those wildly contrasting pillars of the modern theater, as well as young American playwrights like Edward Albee and Jack Gelber. I reviewed late Ibsen and early Albee for *Spectator* and soon began auditing lectures on modern drama by Eric Bentley and Robert Brustein. Brustein was just starting out as a drama critic, but Bentley's wit and insight were already legendary, as when he described Chekhov's *Three Sisters* as a play about an eviction. His appearance, even his haircut, was modeled on his idol, Bert Brecht, whom he had helped introduce to American audiences. I rarely missed a production by the inspired anarchists at the Living Theatre. In their grungy performance space a flight up on West Fourteenth Street, Pirandello and Sophocles were in repertory with Gelber and Paul Goodman. New York was catching up with the most turbulent currents of modern drama, and the world felt in flux, shedding its old skin. In Wordsworth's words about the hope and agitation of the 1790s, when all the old ways had come unstuck, "Bliss was it in that dawn to be alive, / But to be young was very heaven."

THIS GATHERING STORM added a new push to what we expected from our formal education. In a college full of brilliant teachers and ravenous students, my friends and I were determined to turn our senior year into an intellectual feast. Since we were majoring in different subjects—English, history, politics—we had never taken a course together. For our collective blowout, we settled on the senior seminar by the historian Peter Gay, who had been working for years on a book on the Enlightenment. This sober subject was hardly in keeping with our Nietzschean and Romantic leanings. For us it was utopia or bust. Nothing less then Brown's mysterious but compelling "resurrection of the body," where sex, visionary thinking, and apocalypse crossed paths, could satisfy us. The eminently sane spirit of the Enlightenment went against the grain, for it was a humane movement of rational thinkers with a strongly empirical cast of mind—men who were friends of science, enemies of autocracy and superstition. They prepared a blueprint for a secular morality, probing social criticism, and popular democracy, undermining the absolute power of church and state. To our little group of impatient young visionaries this temperate company looked, from the outside at least, as exciting as the good gray fathers of our nation, themselves figures of the Enlightenment. But Gay also promised to spend the whole second semester on Jean-Jacques Rousseau, a sometimes hysterical confessional writer with protean literary gifts and a far more idiosyncratic personality. His posthumous *Confessions* had helped ignite the autobiographical fire of the Romantic poets. He was a loner and individualist who feuded bitterly with his colleagues—they came to think him as mad and paranoid—yet his work would exert a tremendous influence in every sphere—politics, culture, education, even fiction.

Gay's seminar, we soon discovered, was played out under a gracious star that distinguished it from the rough-and-tumble classes we were accustomed to at Columbia. To begin with, we met not in a classroom but in the book-lined parlor of his elegantly European apartment on West End Avenue and 103rd Street. Wine was served, his wife, Ruth, attended, and he took notes on everything we said, as if doing fieldwork for his upcoming book. Soon afterward we heard he boasted to his colleagues that this was the most brilliant class he had taught at Columbia, a flattering assessment that set us up for a severe blowback later in the year. Nimble readers all, we lit into each book like dogs with a bone, chewing our way through some of the best group discussions of my college years. We kept learning from each other, while Gay, who knew so much more than we did, seemed to be taking it all in. After the awesome lectures of Chiappe and Zito, where we were positioned as stunned auditors, this course made a strong case for the small advanced seminar as a form of participatory learning.

But the readings themselves were also discoveries. They had little truck with the apocalyptic extremes we had come to expect from modern literature and politics. I came to appreciate the urbane tone and wickedly playful social criticism of works like Montesquieu's *Persian Letters*, which criticized European mores from the point of view of fictional Persian sojourners, and Diderot's sparkling, mischievously satirical dialogues *Rameau's Nephew* and *Supplement to Bougainville's "Voyage,"* where incendiary social and sexual views were disguised as comparative anthropology. If the French philosophes did not invent cultural relativism, especially the ability to see ourselves as others see us, they made ingenious use of it. I wrote an essay for Gay on Diderot's send-up of a novel, *Jacques the Fatalist and His Master*, conceived in the spirit of a great English eccentric, the novelist and cleric Laurence Sterne. It became clear to us that if life was not exactly sweeter before the revolution, certainly the satire was wittier, driven underground by censorship yet full of literate and high-spirited criticism.

Another seminar I took on was even more demanding than Gay's, though it worked out less well. The crown jewel of general education at Columbia was a "Colloquium on Important Books," essentially a two-year ramble through the great books of the Western tradition for fifteen selected juniors and seniors. For decades it had met on Wednesday evenings, overseen by two faculty members from different fields, with admission by application and personal interview. Trilling and Barzun had taught it together before moving on to teach a famous graduate seminar on the nineteenth century. I had passed up the first year, with its Greek, Roman, medieval, and early modern works, but set my sights on the sequel offered that year by the literary critic F. W. Dupee and the legendary (but largely unpublished) philosopher Sidney Morgenbesser, an old family friend with whom I'd first studied, not very happily, in Contemporary Civilization. The colloquium proved to be an impossible course, with a huge book to navigate every week, an ill-assorted group of students from too many different fields, and two fine instructors with rapier wits but utterly disparate sensibilities who could agree on almost nothing—they scarcely belonged to the same conversation.

Dupee, a cultivated critic, was all nuance and style; Morgenbesser, a brilliant mind but also a world-class Yiddish jokester, was unshakably devoted to analytic reasoning and argument. No one but Sidney could be quite so funny yet so relentless in pressing students to reason analytically. When students made their clumsy points, he tried to break them down, to rephrase them as propositions that could be proved or disproved. Dupee's exasperation with his colleague's logical approach came to a head when one hapless student made some lame but thoroughly harmless observation. Morgenbesser proceeded to pick it apart and inspect it prismatically from every angle. "Is your thesis that . . . ?" he said, laying out two diametrically opposed positions, both equally remote from what the kid was saying. "That's not a thesis," Dupee fumed, "it's just a remark, an aperçu." The literary section cheered. Sidney looked nonplussed.

For many weeks we were richly entertained by the dueling wit of two instructors, each on his own wavelength, one-upping the other. Finally they called a halt to the war of words and the course settled down, though it never took off in any meaningful way. In later years I came to know and love both these men, dissimilar as they were, but that year it was mostly the spectacle, the verbal fireworks I enjoyed. My happiest literary discovery was Flaubert's disenchanted political novel set during the revolution of 1848, *A Sentimental Education*, almost a parody of a coming-of-age story, centered on an ordinary protagonist to whom nothing much happens, or matters. (At the novel's close he thinks back to an innocent early visit to a brothel—from which he fled—as his happiest experience.) Its pitiless dissection of politics, love, and personal history appealed to me for its modern outlook and surgical technique. In loving detail, without the least commentary, it prefigures the void, the dank disappointment, ingrained in many later novels, such as Samuel Beckett's, where neither education nor illumination seems possible.

I was still an English major, though roaming through other fields, but one course I took that last year had a special reverberation for me. It was a survey of the English Romantic and Victorian eras, and it quickly gave me the feeling that I had landed on a magic island. It had been taught for years by Trilling himself, but he had passed it on to a gifted young protégé, Steven Marcus, who was then still an instructor struggling against a looming deadline to complete his dissertation on Dickens. Marcus was personally remote, stiff beyond the formal manner of those times, but he was passionate about his subject. The Romantic poets, the fiction of Jane Austen, the discursive prose of social critics like Thomas Carlyle and Matthew Arnold—one baroque and Germanic, the other lethally satirical—came alive under his tutelage, set snugly in their times yet vividly connected to the present time. This had always been Trilling's method, to open up a contemporary dialogue with the books he taught, and Marcus pursued this with a burning intensity. He seemed to have ingested and incorporated these books, not simply read them.

I had happened on scattered Romantic lyrics during high school in out-of-date anthologies like *The Golden Treasury*, usually harmless poems like Wordsworth's "Solitary Reaper," and they struck me as blandly traditional. Now, without warning, the poems of Blake and Wordsworth, Coleridge and Keats, reached me with shocking force. The poems of Blake's *Songs of Innocence and of Experience*, despite their simple forms, seemed daringly modern in their explicit sexuality and their stark yet childlike social criticism. Wordsworth's negotiations of time and loss in poems like "Tintern Abbey" and the Immortality ode unfailingly brought tears to my eyes, tapping into a deep well of bittersweet recollection. They composed a dirge for the passing of an idyllic childhood. This triggered memories of my own happiest hours. I felt a premature recoil from aging, the loss of a halo. I was touched by the darker shadings, the deadly forebodings, that accompany the luxurious sense of fruition in Keats's odes. I drafted a paper on Keats's "Ode to a Nightingale" that was really the first mature essay I had yet written. It seemed a poem about the shifting turns of consciousness itself, about grand aspirations coming up against a recognition of human limits. Years later, when another project fell through, this unexpectedly became the germ of a doctoral thesis and then a book on Keats. Without knowing it, I was on my unplanned way to becoming a Romanticist.

Besides these classes I was also auditing Taubes's seminars, filled with readings in European philosophy, and struggling with the German language, hoping to coast through my final semester in college. But this was not to be: Marcus, Trilling, and the sociologist Daniel Bell, then new to Columbia, were set to give a spring course on literature and society in the Victorian era that was too tempting to pass up, and I abandoned German after three semesters to take it on, perhaps a mistake since another term might have left me fluent in the language.

The reading plan was simple but, for that time, highly original. Each week we would examine some facet of Victorian culture, such as religion or politics, on parallel tracks. A major social novel like Anthony Trollope's aptly titled masterpiece, *The Way We Live Now*, would be set beside some key social and historical documents. Fact and fiction were expected to complement each other, serving as reality checks. In this manner the instructors hoped to uncover what they called the "moral temper" of the era, its inmost feelings about love and death, politics and religion, money and power, honor and shame. In this anthropological approach literature would serve as thick description yet also as an index to the life of feeling, the interior life that historians often miss, something too elusive to document or quantify. The high aims of the course and its actual execution never quite came together—like Dupee and Morgenbesser, the stellar teachers were on different frequencies—but the idea behind it held out rich possibilities. I later realized how much this mixture of literature and social history, focused on the dilemmas of individuals within the larger culture, had taken hold of me, outlining an agenda for my own work. Such a cross-pollination of private and public life, of the creative mind and its social matrix, was second nature for most New York intellectuals, including these three instructors, but here it emerged as a conscious program connecting literature with history.

At the time, though, I got little feedback about my own work from these busy mentors, especially the detached and distracted Trilling, whose good opinion meant much to me. Typically, since political issues had always fascinated me, I had chosen Victorian politics for my term paper and oral presentation, which was scheduled for the final meeting of the semester. But the student presenting before me, and the discussion that followed, took up virtually the whole two hours. "But we haven't yet discussed Mr. Dickstein's paper," I heard Trilling say. On that open-ended note, the anticlimax of my college years, the course came to an end, and I never did find out what he or his colleagues had to say, if anything, about what I had worked up for the occasion. I was often prone to grow wistful over missed opportunities, but perhaps this chance omission spared me some grief. In later years the irrepressible Dan Bell, a zestful storyteller, was fond of recalling how I bitched about the sociological side of the course. "I didn't know this would be a class about real estate," he claimed I said, always repeating this with an impish grin and happy chuckle. I had no recollection of making this twerpy remark but I trusted his expansive memory above my own. Besides, I had long since learned how much real estate mattered, along with other hard social facts.

If this ambitious course lacked a satisfying coda, Peter Gay's class ended on a more sour note. After he had widely advertised how special we were, we let him down by turning in our term papers a few days past the deadline, though our graduation was near. This brought out the scolding German pedant in him. "It's not enough to be brilliant," he fumed. "One must also be disciplined, responsible." Perhaps he had a point, for the Columbia ethos exalted brilliance over everything; a facility with ideas always trumped small-minded procedural details. Perhaps my habits had been skewed by doting parents, not very punctual themselves, who tolerated every fault. As a cautionary lesson for the future, Gay awarded us a shadow grade for the paper itself but then a punitive one that subtracted for lateness, not that anyone cared about grades in the final semester. The earnest paper I wrote for him on Rousseau's religion became my first published essay—I sent it to him when it came out in *Yale French Studies*—but its appearance in print did nothing to temper his unshakable disapproval. For years afterward he carried on a low-grade vendetta against members of the class for falling short of his expectations. In later years I tried three or four times to make peace with him, only to be rebuffed with a cutting remark or a frown of disapproval. His book on the Enlightenment was a huge success; it put him and his subject on the academic map, though its impact was soon overtaken by the intellectual clashes of the 1960s.

THOUGH I HAD HOPED to coast through my final semester, I found myself instead trying as usual to squeeze in too many books on too many subjects. This ungovernable appetite rounded off my undergraduate experience. I had arrived at the university drastically unprepared to be on my own, keeping up my ties to the world I came from—my parents, my synagogue duties, those infernal piano lessons—like a lifeline. Eventually the line frayed and snapped and I took off fitfully in new directions. By the end of that first year I had strolled across the deserted campus with a sense of coming home. Now I felt I'd done everything I wanted to do, guided by remarkable mentors to whom I would always be grateful.

Midway through the spring term we turned *Spectator* over to the most promising juniors and passed *The Supplement* on to two brilliant non-*Spec* juniors, Richard Locke and Peter Winn, who would maintain it as a rigorous intellectual review. It kept on publishing throughout the decade but it would never gain the wide readership we had dreamed of. As our final act we conjured up an ambitious lecture series that would bring all our culture heroes to campus, though we had no money to offer them. I still have a charming note from Norman Mailer begging off—he needed to protect his writing time. Evidently, we were not put off by his having stabbed his wife a few months earlier. I can't recall whether Norman Podhoretz, whose radical makeover of *Commentary* we so admired, bothered to reply. The third Norman, Norman O. Brown, came instead to speak to a class at Barnard, and I managed to attend. He was already becoming a more vatic figure, the prophet of a new cultural dispensation. Only Paul Goodman actually showed up and gave a talk, based on notes he seemed to have scribbled on the subway, about Columbia's relation to the community, its default of civic responsibility, a complaint we had hammered home in our editorials. It was typical of Goodman to bring broad values to bear on local issues, to tune his remarks to his actual audience.

With newspaper work and classes winding down, I tried to revive my neglected social life. My college world had grown too monastic, as if only ideas mattered. I went to a weekend retreat of the Student Zionist Organization but the girls I met were zealous pioneer types, dancing the hora and singing campfire songs late into the night. I danced and sang along with them, giving my hard-earned irony a rest, though this was not my idea of romance. By that time I preferred Bergman movies, Italian opera, and off-Broadway theater to campfire songs; still, they were rousing in other ways. Much time that spring was taken up with getting into graduate school and planning for the summer. I had been warned that Columbia's own sink-or-swim graduate program was large and anonymous. It was nothing like the college and was said to offer little sense of direction. Some of my favorite teachers, including Jim Zito, had nearly gotten lost in it.

Eventually I was set for Yale, which had first turned me down, but I had little sense of what might await me there. Meanwhile, Sam and I had decided to go to Europe for the summer. At the time, before air travel became routine, this was a considerable leap. To my surprise my family agreed, and Sam's father proceeded to make all the arrangements, since he had many European contacts. It was the last years of the great ocean liners, those floating versions of grand hotels. We were set to travel by ship to England, make our way through six countries, and finally return by sea from Haifa, Israel. In a sense we would be reversing our own parents' immigration, journeying back to the sources, not to the shtetl but to the Europe that had been the object of so much of our education.

For the graduation I had been elected a class marshal, adding a braided shoulder loop to my blue Columbia gown, inordinately pleased to be chosen by my classmates rather than the faculty. As if to counteract my bookish bent, I'd gotten to know a staggering number of them. Perhaps I had finally interred the kid who had always played to the grown-ups, the yeshiva boy with his nose to the grindstone, whose hand so often shot up in class. In any case, I no longer liked him, for he was too eager to please, too eager to shine; I wanted to put him behind me. As usual the president himself, Grayson Kirk, gave the commencement address, eloquent but forgettable. In his box as his personal guests were General and Mrs. Douglas MacArthur, whose only son was a classmate of ours. The old soldier, still ramrod straight though past eighty, had not yet quite faded away, as he'd predicted after Truman had cashiered him as commander of American forces during the Korean War. Instead he was living a shadow life as a right-wing icon. But it was time for all of us to move on, our green bunch of twenty-one-year-olds as well as the culture at large, which was already rumbling off in unforeseen directions of its own.

Six

The Grand Tour

S INCE MUCH of our college years had been focused on Europe, actually
going there seemed like the logical next step, almost inevitable. I had
seen little of the world outside New York and the Northeast. I had only
talked about it and read about it. Europe was a persistent rumor to me.
It was where our parents came from, though mine, coming from Eastern
Europe, where their lives were constricted by poverty and pogroms, hadn't
the least desire to return, even for a visit. The remnants of the world they
knew as children had been wiped out by the Nazis, with timely help from
the Russians. For all their anxieties about their own lives and their children's welfare, I shouldn't have been surprised that they let me go. I had
already spent the last six summers on my own, and I was traveling with a
friend they knew well. Sam's life had been as sheltered as mine, his parents
just as protective; this voyage would be our modest way of breaking out.

The era of cheap air tickets and mass student travel was still a few years
off. We had planned to sail on a great French liner, the *Liberté*. Sam's father
knew one of the chefs, who promised to entertain us royally on the voyage: "*Apéritifs toute la journée*," he said. But Sam had actually been born in
western France as his parents fled Paris in 1940, and his strenuous effort
to renounce his French citizenship had long been tangled in red tape. Had
he stepped onto the deck of the *Liberté*, which counted legally as French
soil, he could have been drafted and packed off to fight in Algeria, where a

war was still raging between the French army and the FLN, a determined and fierce independence movement. So at the last minute we shifted our tickets to the *Queen Mary*, the former flagship of the Cunard Line, an aging grande dame that had done heavy duty as a stripped-down troop transport in World War II.

Our tourist accommodations offered little of the stuffy elegance that we could observe in first class. The cabins with their double-decker berths were tinier than dorm rooms, and there was barely space to stand up in the washrooms. The toilets were communal, as if in a public accommodation. "'Avin' quite a session in 'ere, Guvnah," said one bluff Brit when I accidentally walked in on him sitting on the can. My main memories are of endless corridors of polished light-brown wood, of burly English passengers hearty in their bonhomie, and of tasteless, overcooked food that made one pine for missed pleasures of the *Liberté*.

The *Queen Mary* was a very large vessel, massive from without, as intricate as a small city or large hotel on the inside, yet so fast that it had often been able to outrun German U-boats during the war. The trip took five days but the North Atlantic happened to be very rough that week, gray and foggy day after day, a good preparation for the dank June weather in England. The good ship was heavily "stabilized," as they said, so that the rocking movement, though incessant, was tamped down—so subtle that our bodies grew accustomed to it. It was only when we set foot on the dock in Southampton that my legs went wobbly and the earth began to spin. Terra firma was suddenly a disorienting experience, and it took some time for the body to get the hang of it.

In London some relations of Sam had found us a room in outlying Golders Green, long home to many lower middle-class Jews, an easy bus or Underground ride into the center of the city. By day we visited tourist sites and haunted the bookstores around Charing Cross Road, where even new hardcover books were incredibly cheap since the dollar was strong. By night we explored the theater, including a new play by one of our idols, Jean-Paul Sartre, *The Condemned of Altona*, dealing in complicated ways with German war guilt. One evening we saw that the D'Oyly Carte Opera Company, devoted to the operettas of Gilbert and Sullivan, was performing in our own neighborhood, at a huge late Victorian theater called the Hippodrome. The show was one we had never seen, *Patience*, a rollicking send-up of the young, not yet scandalous aesthete Oscar Wilde as the garishly affected Bunthorne ("If you're anxious for the shine / in the high aesthetic line / as a man of culture rare, / You must get up all the germs / of the transcendental terms / and plant them everywhere. . . ."). With its precision timing, musty comic turns, and the perfect articulation of the actors, *Patience* left us in fits of ecstasy.

Later in the week they were to put on *The Mikado*. "If this is what they could make of *Patience*," Sam said, "imagine what they might do with *The Mikado*." And they did, they did. We had never seen anything so ritualized, down to every gesture and comic inflection, yet so exuberant. The staging went back to the original productions but didn't feel ossified. The effect was Victorian yet hardly distant since the city around us still felt so Victorian, smoky and gray with age. Modern architecture was as yet unknown, and the brick and stone buildings, with their quaint chimneys and turrets, were covered with the grime of decades. This was the Old World without the charm.

We knew some of G&S because, across the street from Columbia, Barnard had a thriving Gilbert & Sullivan Society that put on, as I recall, two productions each year, in a little postage stamp of a theater called the Minor Latham. Along with triple-decker Victorian novels and tartly witty Alec Guinness movies like *Kind Hearts and Coronets*, *The Lavender Hill Mob*, and *The Ladykillers*, these antique and antic shows had become our hall-of-mirrors introduction to England. I was prepared for a nation of eccentrics, of Dickensian personalities. What I was not prepared for was London's pervasive shabbiness: the dingy colors of the soot-covered buildings, the dull uniformity of the Lyons Corner Houses, the dark hole of the Underground tube lines, with their long, rumbling wooden escalators and rickety prewar trains. It was as if England had never bounced back from the war, from the stoical fortitude of the wartime blitz, the austerity of postwar rationing, the satisfactions of self-denial in which the English took such virtuous pride.

The food was in a class by itself. The soggy breakfast that came with our room featured fried bread and fried eggs swimming in grease, followed by fortifying cups of strong tea. It was a working-class breakfast, including the bacon or sausages we could not eat, since we were vaguely keeping kosher without examining too closely how our food was prepared. Daily rations would be a problem throughout the trip, since we would not eat meat or shellfish and had little inclination to seek out kosher restaurants. They felt like scattered remnants of an earlier era, serving food that was not always as fresh as it could be. (I had two cases of food poisoning from eating in such places.) We were no pub crawlers but I grew fascinated by the sociability of English pubs, where I felt much more comfortable than I ever had in American bars, peopled by hard drinkers and pickup artists.

One London episode stands out for me. My surrogate mother, Esther, now widowed in New York, had virtually no blood relations in the States. But she had two long-lost brothers in London whom she'd not seen since before the war, and I promised her I would visit them. Their places in the old East End, though roomy, were darker, their furniture heavier, than anything I'd seen since my childhood on the Lower East Side. I begged off when they invited us to stay with them. Esther was thrilled that I saw her brothers, but I brooded on the dingy meanness of their homes and the poverty of the neighborhood, so far from the bright lights of the theater district and the nightlife of Soho. This was where the poorer Jews of London had long lived, though they were soon to be joined by art galleries and fashionable boutiques. The swinging London of the 1960s was about to happen, with the East End as a new bohemia, but there was little evidence of it as yet.

Our week in London was really a prologue to a trip to France, Sam's birthplace and his spiritual home. Paradoxically, he could visit without fear of being drafted because the French, at the last minute, had confirmed his renunciation of citizenship. Paris in 1961 seemed almost as poor and run-down as London. De Gaulle had returned to power only two years earlier, and André Malraux, the novelist and adventurer, now his minister of culture, had not yet scrubbed the churches and monuments; it was hard to imagine that they had ever been anything but gray or black and covered with bird shit. The Sélect, our hotel on the Place de la Sorbonne, looked unimaginably time-worn and basic, but unlike its grim equivalents in London it seemed all the more authentic, as if we had been magically set down in Eugène Atget's Paris of the 1920s.

In fact, between wars, depression, and postwar poverty, little had really changed since then. Staying in the heart of the Fifth Arrondissement, literally a stone's throw from the university, we were surrounded by cheap restaurants, cafés that spilled out onto the streets, vest-pocket movie theaters showing exotic fare in many languages, and dozens of storefront bookstores, some of which also published their own books. Only a few blocks away were the irresistible bookstalls along the Seine, a random cornucopia of old books, new books, books with uncut pages, all in their plain yellow paper bindings. The Latin Quarter as a whole was still a bohemian slum and a pocket of academic life. Like the bookstalls, it was not yet geared entirely to tourists—as if we were anything but wandering young Americans, virgin travelers.

Naively, I was shocked to see German tourists in Paris only sixteen years after the war. Little did I know that they had started coming back right afterward. They loved Paris so much they wanted it for themselves. Like so many visitors before me, I fell for Paris at first sight. We set out methodically to canvass the city, from the Gothic arches and flying buttresses of Notre-Dame to the sepulchral white glow of Sacré-Coeur, sitting atop the steep hill of Montmartre, which we could lazily ascend by an old funicular rail line. We rambled aimlessly among artworks of the Louvre, took an obligatory side trip to Versailles, where everything from the luxurious salons to the fastidiously clipped gardens reeked of the loathsome privilege of the Old Regime, and made pilgrimages to the graves of Baudelaire and other writers in the Montparnasse cemetery. Some of these visits, like living slide shows, were really life-size visual extensions of our college courses in literature and art history. We had studied the Amiens cathedral as a specimen of Gothic architecture, so we set out to see similar examples, including Notre-Dame itself. I felt I could "read" these sights; they made sense to me, as the streets and monuments and churches of London did not.

It was one thing to know the architecture academically, another to experience its soaring height and delicacy of detail, the intricately ribbed vaults, the saturated color and complex imagery of its stained glass. But the real excitement of Paris was simply being there, walking the streets, hearing the language I had studied pedantically, immersed in a storybook atmosphere we dreamily associated with art and love and sensory pleasure. Yet to an American steeped in modern styles and creature comforts, Paris, like London, looked poor, unkempt. The Lost Generation mythology still held sway, though signs of the last deadly stages of the Algerian conflict were everywhere. Menacing gendarmes with submachine guns guarded the entrance to many Métro stations.

Both the French forces and the FLN, the Algerian independence movement, had resorted to brutal forms of terrorism. Only a few months earlier, hundreds of Arabs had been found floating in the Seine, "disappeared" by the police or the army. This desperate and vicious conflict had little impact on an American visitor, for whom daily life went on as usual, but the city sometimes seemed like an armed camp. Even in cheap restaurants, the only places we could afford to eat, the wine flowed and the food, though modest by the standards of French cuisine, proved far better than that in London or New York. Darkened by grime though it was, Paris still provided a lesson in the art of living.

The French, it appeared, took pleasure in their lives, even when their lot was meager. We were invited to lunch at the home of some distant relations of Sam's in the leafy suburb of Saint-Cloud. They were an elderly couple, graciously hospitable to us, with time on their hands. It was an exquisite cold lunch of several courses, but what struck me most were the remarks that garnished each course. The husband had received some wound in the First World War, and since then, Sam said, he had been on disability; he never worked another day. Their means were modest but what they had in abundance was a proverbial joie de vivre. With each course he made little impromptu speeches about the wine, the cheese, the bread, the butter, the vegetables, the fruit, and the pastry, making sure that we knew that France produced the best fare the world had ever known. A true patriot of gastronomy, glowing with national pride, he not only spoke about the glories of fine eating but savored each dish in turn. In florid detail he paid tribute to the cafés he frequented, the inexpensive restaurants, the sights of the city. Having grown up among Jews who were suspicious of the least self-indulgence, who worked long hours and were prone to lament their burdensome lot, I had not met anyone who had less of a work ethic or took more pleasure in his daily life. We liked them so much that we saw them again several times, and I looked them up and enjoyed another simple but sumptuous lunch at their home when I was back in the city three years later.

THE NEXT STOP on our trip was less typical, a detour on our route to Italy. I have no recollection of why we chose Interlaken, an Alpine town in Switzerland between two lakes, the Thun and the Brienz. It was surrounded by tremendous snow-covered peaks, especially the Jungfrau and the Eiger, a spectacular open-air respite after two close encounters with world cities. Instead of wandering the busy streets, we were trekking the nicely marked paths around the two lakes, with distances indicated by minutes rather than meters. We wouldn't have dreamed of visiting Germany—or Franco's Spain, for that matter—but "neutral" Switzerland was another matter. We knew nothing about its record of accommodation with the Nazis, especially on banking matters, during the war, or the barriers it erected to Jews and other refugees fleeing for their lives.

Despite my misgivings about things German, the sound of the language was curiously musical and tripped easily off the tongue. We were able to take a small train high up into the mountains, to a station called the Jungfraujoch, where a light snow was falling and there were breathtaking, somewhat terrifying views in every direction. My own mountains, barely bumps on the landscape, were the Catskills and Poconos, the scenes of my late summer follies. I had confronted the Alps only in the poetry of Wordsworth and Shelley, where they appear as landscapes of thrilling sublimity, but I was enthralled and appalled by their craggy otherness, their utter indifference to anything human. The poets had understood and felt challenged by this, felt transported by their encounter with such an inhuman kind of beauty.

Before these Romantic travelers the Alps had been little more than physical obstacles on the route from France to Italy; afterward such sights stimulated an awed feeling for the sublime, what Wordsworth describes as the "beauty, which, as Milton sings, / Hath terror in it." The unimaginable scale of this gray rock flecked with snow was beyond anything I had ever seen, above all the forbidding north face of the Eiger, so sheer it looked impossible to climb, though many had died and a few had succeeded in the attempt. At more than 13,000 feet, I found the cold thin air bracing, cleansing, but it added to my city boy's sense of a place inhospitable to human habitation, yet unforgettable.

Pining for a city again after this exposure to the Alps, we set off for Luzern, on yet another network of lakes, and for Lake Geneva, which gave us some glimpses of French-speaking Switzerland. I recall our stop at a Protestant chapel along the lake, a single large wooden room with a bare crucifix, otherwise graced by no ornament or symbol. After the huge Gothic cathedrals of France, it seemed shockingly spare and unadorned. My background had hardly qualified me for fathoming different strains in Christianity but here the impact of the Reformation became palpable. I was moved to the quick by this church that was no church but simply a site of intimate personal prayer, a physical enactment of unmediated intimacy between man and God. Emblems of communal ritual or ecclesiastical display had been supplanted by introspection. Compared with a Catholic church, this contemplative space enforced a sensory deprivation, stimulating the worshiper to look inward, yet this chapel also looked out on the rare natural beauty of the lake and the wooded shore. Elsewhere on the lake we stopped at the Castle of Chillon, where one of Byron's memorable figures had been imprisoned. So much of Switzerland evoked memories of Romantic poetry for me. Taken by the beauty of the setting, by its stunning variety and picture-postcard perfection, we postponed our departure from day to day; it served as relief from seeing too many of the monuments of civilization.

Though I later learned the Swiss could be quite anti-Semitic, one pleasure of Switzerland in 1961 was that it was easier to be Jewish, since dairy dishes, along with fish from the numerous lakes, took up more space in the Swiss diet than in that of France or England. I wrote home to reassure my parents that we were not on the brink of starvation, telling them, perhaps dubiously, that the Thunersee was the source of the word *tuna fish*, that perpetual staple of my gastronomically deprived childhood. One day in Switzerland I gorged on milk products in so many forms, including whipped cream, that I turned queasy, sick to my stomach, and could barely eat for twenty-four hours. Dairy seemed the definition of bland, the diet of tiny tots; I felt betrayed just when I felt safely on home ground.

From Switzerland we moved on to Italy but my memories of this first encounter with Venice and Florence, with only a few days in each, have been overlaid by too many later visits for me to sort them out. These places meant more to me long afterward than they did at first sight, when they were little more than perfunctory stops on a tourist itinerary. We stayed longer in Rome. What I most recall is the stifling heat and crowds, as if we had passed into a different climate and a more hectic social scene in coming down from Florence. Modern Rome felt too much like New York, and ancient Rome meant little to me; I had never studied Latin, which was soon to perplex me in graduate school, nor had I ever been possessed by the literature, not even by Virgil. Apart from the Sistine Chapel, which was impossible to resist, the splendors of the Vatican were lost on me. Especially after the spare Protestant settings of Switzerland, the place seemed profane and overdecorated, almost pagan in its flaunted luxury. A few years later I would react differently, enthralled by Bernini and the baroque.

Worse still, my days in Rome were wiped out by another culinary episode, an unfortunate meal—in a kosher restaurant, no less—that left me with an attack of dysentery, living on tea and toast between sieges of the runs. Days later I was still weak and unable to eat as we boarded the train to Brindisi, in the heel of the Italian boot, for an overnight ferry to Patras, on the west coast of Greece. Luckily, Sam's father had secured us a real berth, not simply a place on deck, and I slept almost the whole twenty-two hours of the trip, rocked by the rough surf. On the train ride to Athens I was transfixed by the sparse Greek countryside, which seemed so bare, so parched by the summer sun that I felt I could grasp something essential about Greek tragedy. Even more harshly than the gray, misty Alps, this landscape spoke to me of a pitiless universe. An aura of fatality seemed to emanate from it, as if hardship were baked into the dry rock.

Some of my best days in college had been spent on ancient Greek literature, Greek sculpture, classical architecture. This immersion in classical culture led us to the wonders of the Elgin Marbles at the British Museum and now to the Parthenon, from which the marble reliefs had famously been lifted, supposedly to rescue and preserve them, early in the nineteenth century. Like every visitor I was struck by how intact the Parthenon columns looked from one angle, how ruined from every other vantage point. It seemed like a gigantic crime that the greatest damage had been done only in the wars of the late seventeenth century, after this miraculous remnant of the ancient world had survived so long.

Our visit to the Acropolis was like a religious pilgrimage, a search for origins. By then these roots of Western culture had almost biblical authority for me. From Athens we took a trip down the coast to Sounion, a tip of land where we could both swim in the sea and visit the temple of Poseidon, located on a breathtaking site, a high bluff overlooking the Aegean. There a guide explained, no doubt for the thousandth time, that the signature of Byron on one stone could not possibly be authentic, since Byron revered Greek culture too much to deface one of its surviving monuments. (He had denounced the removal of the Elgin Marbles to London as an act of vandalism.) We visited Corinth, an otherwise nondescript place some forty miles from Athens, and stood on the low rise in the central marketplace where Paul had preached. This was a tribute less to Paul and the early Christians than to our old teacher Jacob Taubes, a rabbinic Jew who had lectured unforgettably on Paul's epistles to the Corinthians.

The last thing we did in Greece was in some ways the most memorable. At the age of twenty-one I had never flown, but we were booked on a student charter from Greece to Israel. We climbed into an old propeller-driven plane that held perhaps thirty passengers. It flew at a low altitude, so we could easily make out the seascape below and the large, storied island world of Rhodes, surprisingly lush and green, as we passed over it. I felt a mixture of fear and astonishment throughout the flight, as if we were foolishly defying the laws of nature.

Landing in Israel was another piece of drama. As a yeshiva student the phrase "next year in Jerusalem" was an unthinking part of my catechism. This took on real mileage from the hot-to-trot Zionism of my college years and my summers in Camp Massad, that small annex of Israel near the Delaware Water Gap, a workshop or rehearsal meant to prepare us to settle in the place itself. Yet I was caught unawares seeing airport signs in Hebrew, hearing the language spoken, coming face-to-face with something familiar yet till then unknown. I thought of the old injunction to kneel down and kiss the earth on arriving in the Holy Land but, for the life of me, I can't recall whether I actually did so or held back in embarrassment. Something had touched a wellspring of emotion in me. Though moved beyond tears, I was too cool, too sophisticated to acknowledge it openly.

◞◟

IN A SENSE the whole tour was a prologue to our twelve days in Israel. If my courses had prepared me for England and France and Greece, my whole life had set me on track for the Holy Land. We managed to touch base in every corner of the country except the lower Negev and Eilat, at the southernmost tip. They were too far away and, besides, evoked no biblical associations. Even more than when we traveled south in Italy, the climate changed from mile to mile: it was as muggy as New York in Tel Aviv, cool and crisp in Jerusalem, lush, almost tropical amid fruit trees in parts of the north, stony and dry farther south. But the social landscape fascinated me more. Only thirteen scarcely tranquil years had passed since Israel had declared its statehood and fought its first war, and it remained a spare, hunkered-down society. The Israeli Arabs in Jaffa and the Bedouins in Beersheba seemed desperately poor. In Beersheba, mothers begging in the streets held listless children in their arms, surrounded by flies attracted by the pus oozing from their inflamed eyes. The religious sector of Israel was then very small; a socialist ethic prevailed nearly everywhere, not simply in the kibbutz we visited. Despite this egalitarian ideal, the kibbutzniks themselves were a national elite, the officer class of the armed forces, carriers of the Zionist idea.

We took a bus tour north to the Galilee, since it was the only way we could see it without a car, and as we approached the old Crusader fortress of Acre, hulking stone structures facing the sea north of Haifa, the driver and the tour guide changed places: the guide drove the bus and the driver sat down in back chatting with the passengers. In any other place—we had noticed this in Greece—there was a class divide between the college-educated guide and the driver, a working stiff, but here, as it turned out, both men had been imprisoned in this very fortress by the British during the '48 war. For them the trip was something of a homecoming. The collective élan of the struggle for independence still survived.

You could see the same egalitarian informality everywhere, although it was already beginning to erode. The prime minister, David Ben-Gurion, the canny leader who had steered Israel to independence, was soliciting capital from American businessmen to create industries and build factories;

they were laying down conditions, free-market conditions rare in Israel till then. In this expanding private sector of the economy, some people would be making much more money than others, though there was as yet no way to flaunt this wealth. In the beautiful white deco apartment houses of Tel Aviv, like a distant outpost of the Bauhaus, everyone seemed to live alike, on a modest scale, with few if any luxuries. Hardly anyone owned a car, though we did meet a woman whose German-born parents were both doctors and, miraculously, owned a vintage heap. Many German Jews considered themselves a class apart, wary of sinking into a Levantine morass. They congregated with each other and barely learned the language. Proudly, her parents offered to drive us down to see the old Philistine cities, north of Gaza, along the southern coast, a region memorialized by the biblical story of Samson. We were eager to see the excavations at Ashkelon but they only wanted to show us Ashdod, where a new deepwater port to rival Haifa was being built. Economic development was their mantra, incipient capitalism their religion, and at Ashkelon they remained in the car, in mute protest, as we explored the digs at the ancient site.

My own economic fantasy life centered on the kibbutz; I admired the small-scale communitarian socialism of the chalutzim, the pioneers who had come to work the soil, reversing many centuries of land-poor Jewish history. Once in exile Jews were rarely in a position to own land or work the soil, and this invariably kept them from being self-sustaining. We visited one kibbutz and stayed overnight, learning what we could about its daily life as we were lectured about the utopian ideals that lay behind it. I already knew the sensible socialist formula from my days at Massad: "From each according to his abilities, to each according to his needs." This was before kibbutzim began using hired Arab labor and importing guest workers, a time when the old Zionist ideology about the sanctity of physical labor still held sway, but it was already clear that the collective farm or factory was not a dynamic or expanding sector of Israel's economy. I was troubled to learn that the kibbutz did not encourage their young to seek higher education, for fear of losing them to the cities. This meant that the next generation would be less well educated than the pioneers themselves, who had often been exposed to a rich culture before heading back to the land. Here only those with musical talent, a sacred trust, were singled out and sent off to conservatories.

So much in Israel was new and strange yet I felt a sense of arriving where I started, coming home. This began with the food, with its spicy overlay of the Middle East on the Central European—hummus, baba ghanoush, and falafel, then still exotic, but also the heavy stews and smoked fish I knew from childhood. The cities seemed at once ancient and modern, Jewish and cosmopolitan. Nowhere else, not even in New York, had I ever heard so many languages in the street—English and French, Hebrew and Yiddish, Arabic, German and Russian. It was a cornucopia of oral expression, an auditory reminder of the Zionist ideal of "the ingathering of the exiles (*kibbutz galuyot*)," but also of the devastation of the Jews of Europe and the forced emigration of those from North Africa. After three months the Eichmann trial was just winding up but in the excitement of our travels, cut off from the news, I took little notice of it. I must have been as oblivious of the Holocaust as the young Israelis whom the trial was meant to educate.

I was happy to be speaking Hebrew and to hear it spoken around me. We picked up a girl on the beach in Tel Aviv and had a long conversation. "Where are you coming from?" she asked me. I said we had just flown in from Athens. She looked surprised: "My God, they teach amazing Hebrew in Greece." When we visited some of Sam's relatives I spoke to them in Hebrew, he in Russian, and they happily translated back and forth. At one point they looked puzzled: "Wait, you two are traveling together. What happens when we're not there to translate?" "Well," I pointed out, "we have a little English in common." I thought of a joke about two elderly American women who were astonished, as I was, at first seeing street signs in Hebrew, seeing Hebrew characters even on the manhole covers. "Only in America," one of them said, no doubt in Yiddish.

Surely the old religion of my yeshiva days, always pointed toward Jerusalem, drew me to Israel at least as much as my late romance with Zionism. A distant cousin of my father's, not at all religious, was a policeman in Netanya, a seaside resort between Tel Aviv and Haifa. After we met he invited me to come up for the weekend. But while Sam would be looking up relatives, I had a strong urge to spend Shabbat instead in Jerusalem. The intercity bus arrived at the outskirts of the city just before the Sabbath began, when the city's local buses had already shut down, and I found myself chatting with a young woman as we walked into town. She was incredulous that I'd given up the beaches of Netanya, a veritable playground, for a weekend in the Holy City. "There's no action here," she said, in slangy Hebrew. "They roll up the sidewalks." I was taken aback. Was this the voice of the younger generation, secular, hedonistic, godless? She looked bemused when I insisted I was here perhaps for spiritual reasons—that was the "action" I had in mind. I knew where to look for it too, in the winding streets and low stone buildings of Me'a She'arim ("a hundred gates"), a quaint nineteenth-century neighborhood that was home to a small cohort of strictly observant Jews, some of whom refused to recognize the secular State of Israel. For them it preempted the coming of the Messiah; only God's will could restore the Jewish homeland, not national armies.

Most of older Jerusalem had been lost to Jordan in the '48 war, including the historic Old City, and a largely new Jerusalem had sprung up to the west of it, but Me'a She'arim, which housed several Chassidic sects, was a remnant of an earlier world, an island of steep Orthodox piety. It was closed to traffic on the Sabbath and notoriously hostile to secular Jews. As I wandered its streets Friday evening, I could hear singing from the tiny *shtieblach*, or study halls, that could have belonged to eighteenth-century Poland or the Lower East Side of my childhood. Hesitantly, I walked into one of them and sat at the far end of the room. A Sabbath meal was ending and the zemirot, or Sabbath songs, were in full swing, including some haunting melodies I had always loved. Hearing them in this hot dark Jerusalem nook sent me into a trance of enthusiasm, as if I had truly arrived in the promised land. It brought to mind my short-lived religious fervor during my senior year of high school when, for a few short weeks, I was swept up in a wave of piety that was more emotion than belief. And here I was again, as if transfixed by a need to stay within the fold. Part of me still believed that only strict Orthodoxy could be counted as genuine Judaism, that spiritual ecstasy was the only meaningful form of faith.

Finally they took notice of me and insisted I join them. They explained that their rebbe was dead but they still set a place for him at the table. Hearing where I was from, they pointed with pride to one man at the table. "Your countryman, from New York," they said, though of course in his beard and black garb he looked exactly like the others—they all looked alike to me. I envied the aura of devotion, the traditional way of life I saw in their world, free of doubt and ambivalence, though I could not have tolerated it even for a day. Orthodox Judaism seemed authentic yet stifling to me. Only its uneasy truce with Israel's dominant secularism, the multiple strands of Western-style pluralism, made the country imaginable for me. This unstable compromise was the real promise of the promised land.

The Old City and the Western Wall, under Jordanian control since 1948, were off-limits, but the next day I walked a mile or two south to visit my old Massad friend Shlomo R., who had been studying there that year. Once I was out of the city the border was unmarked, though I knew that no-man's-land was no more than a hundred yards to the left of the road. A young man had strayed off the same road a few weeks earlier and was still being held by the Jordanian authorities. The Israel we visited was in many ways a precarious construct, all the more moving because of its perilous borders and intransigent neighbors. It was still in the hands of its founders, the Eastern European socialists who had arrived before the First World War. We were there during an election campaign in which the left-wing labor parties such as Mapai and Mapam were challenged by a newly formed Liberal Party led by Nahum Goldmann, a world Zionist leader who did not actually live in Israel. I came upon Ben-Gurion campaigning in full throttle on a street corner in Jerusalem, mocking a party that "had no Hebrew name," with a leader who wasn't even a citizen of Israel. He was a natural orator, mesmerizing, even on a city street. His iconic tufts of white hair were like flaps or wings alongside his bald, tanned head. Still in the fray, he was a piece of living history, more than half a century since his emigration to Ottoman-held Palestine.

Years later, Ben-Gurion's Mapai party, with its European roots, would lose its monopoly on power to its "revisionist" foes. Their blunt nationalistic platform proved more attractive to poor, religious Sephardic immigrants from Arab lands, who had felt the brunt of discrimination. The Israel we saw was still threadbare but idealistic, endangered by its aggrieved neighbors and vulnerable borders but not yet corrupted by disparities of wealth or morally compromised, as it would be after the 1967 war, by ruling over another people.

The fifteen-day voyage home from Haifa to New York aboard the SS *Zion* took longer than our stay in Israel itself but it gave us the leisure to assimilate all we had seen: the architectural beauty of the white city of Tel Aviv, the aura of sanctity even in modern Jerusalem, the exotic orange and lemon groves of the north, the Arab poverty of Beersheba, the Roman ruins of Caesarea and the Crusader fortress of Acre, the sixth-century synagogue of Beit Alfa, with its surprising astrological mosaics, the marble and stone blocks of the excavations in Ashkelon, and finally the robust working-class atmosphere of the port city of Haifa, where religion played little role, except for the gleaming Bahai shrine, and the transit system ran even on Shabbat.

What struck me most was the new sensation of being in a place where Jews were on their own, bickering incessantly but not simply living (or dying) on the sufferance of others. The ship itself was an extension of that place, giving us two weeks to decompress from our long journey. It included interesting stops all around the Mediterranean: at one of the Greek islands; in Naples, where we fended off kids in the port whose hands were in our pockets and went touring through the ruins of Pompeii; in the rough city of Marseille and the Crown colony of Gibralter, at the southern tip of Spain, which seemed like one large flea market. There I picked up a rare ten-inch LP of the blacklisted Paul Robeson singing "Songs of Free Men," which his record company, Columbia, in response to our queries, denied it had ever put out. Thanks to the cold war, the left-wing culture of the Popular Front had been flushed down the memory hole. It was nice that a small remnant of it survived in Gibralter, of all places—Europe's attic—at the very moment it was coming alive again in the coffeehouses and folk music clubs of Greenwich Village.

It seemed providential that the weather on the trip was sunny and warm, not only in the Mediterranean but through the whole Atlantic crossing—nothing like our dank, gray voyage on the *Queen Mary*. We returned home with deep tans that looked as though we'd spent a summer at the beach. There was only one storm, a terrific squall, as we passed through the narrow strait between Sardinia and Corsica. Thanks to the heaving of the vessel, far smaller than the *Queen Mary*, few people dared come to dinner that evening, but the turbulence at first seemed not to bother me at all. I missed the fun of translating the waiter's slangy Hebrew for my dinner companions. In the almost deserted dining hall I made light of the tender stomachs of my fellow passengers, until I sat over the soup and watched it shift and roll from side to side like water in a rocking pool. The very sight of that undulating soup, a miniature reflection of the rough waters around us, made me horribly seasick, even more than when I first stepped off the *Queen Mary* on British soil. Lurching from wall to wall, I barely made it back to my cabin, where the same earthquake-like swaying lulled me into a deep, refreshing sleep for the next ten hours.

Aboard the *Zion* I met a young half-Jewish historian, Ronald Sanders, who had not grown up Jewish but had developed an interest in Judaism as an adult. With his wavy reddish-blond hair and light complexion, he scarcely looked Jewish at all. But he was a Jew by choice, returning from a long stay in Israel. In New York he had taught himself Yiddish to write a master's thesis on the *Jewish Daily Forward* and its legendary editor Abraham Cahan. Later he would expand this into a fine book on the cultural world of the Lower East Side, *The Downtown Jews*, and would publish searching books on Israel, on Jewish emigration from Europe, on the Balfour Declaration, which promised a Palestinian homeland to the Jews, as well as a memoir that explored his own idiosyncratic journey.

Ron was very knowledgeable about European intellectual history, especially the history of the Left, at a moment when this was not as yet fashionable. Coming late to Jewish life, he was moving in just the opposite direction from me, pitching his tent on ground I thought I had left behind, yet our interests converged. They suggested that one could remain a Jew without being tribal or parochial and one could become an intellectual, even a disinterested intellectual, without turning wholly academic or abandoning one's native roots, emotional ties, and deeply embedded loyalties. This was a lesson worth knowing during the storms of the decade that followed, tempests more life-shaking than those we'd felt at sea. Our travels through six countries, cursory as they were, had shored up my feeling for Western civilization while giving new shape to my identity as a Jew. Both cultures took on a real presence, a historical reality, from this journey to the sources. My comfort aboard the *Zion* reflected my comfort with Zion, which made me more at ease with where I came from and where I was going, though it gave little intimation of how graduate school might shake my faith in the value of some kinds of advanced and specialized education.

Seven

Flying Solo

Writing about unhappy times is a sure way of living through that unhappiness again, but revisiting them, as therapists know, may tell you something about who you are and were. In my first years in New Haven, as I described in my opening chapter, the adventures of my college years at Columbia and the following summer of travel gave way to the dull throb of professional training. A deadly rigor decked out as discipline and scholarship threatened to imprison the imagination. This stifling of inspiration, even enthusiasm, seemed built into the system. I flirted with departing for Cornell, where a newly arrived but little-known young professor, Paul de Man, was enlivening a handful of students in comparative literature. I came to know him on my visits to my friend Sam, and I began to schedule them so as to catch a few of de Man's classes. An extraordinarily charming yet elusive figure, with a piquant French accent and a welcoming grin—you had to resist chucking him under the chin, said one of my friends—he gave the impression of having been around, though no one knew exactly where. He was already in his forties but had just gotten his degree from Harvard. He had seemingly published very little, though we rummaged up a handful of his earlier essays, brilliant and original takes—on formalist criticism, for example, and on Romantic imagery. After we'd spoken a few times and he realized how discontented I was at Yale, he generously offered to take me into the program but thought I would be foolish to leave a department that had vastly more prestige. A few years later, when I was running a graduate student lecture series, I sent him his first invitation to speak at Yale. After I had left, he himself would become one of Yale's luminaries as well as a highly influential literary theorist. His murky past, including a period of collaboration as a young journalist during the Nazi occupation of Belgium, would come to light only after his death.

In my first year at Yale I had somehow escaped the blues by studying with three of the department's younger, more engaging teachers. The following year these options, few enough, ran out. There was a shortage of new faces since tenure was then a condition for overseeing graduate students. By December of 1962 I wrote to L, "I have no idea what I'm doing here. It has struck me suddenly that I'm not learning a thing this year. Nothing. My classes are practically worthless, and what's more I'm not really interested in them." I mentioned ruefully that de Man was "the best mind I've come across in a long time," but I had neither the languages nor the background to switch to comparative literature. Ithaca seemed a remote outpost, much as I liked the people I met there. Leaving Yale, I felt, would be a failure, a derailment, though one of my friends, Steve Miller, dropped out after the first year, and another, Sam Weber, who was fluent in German, left Yale for Cornell soon afterward. Both would build prolific careers as writers, one outside, the other inside the academy.

In my second year I dealt with the doldrums of Yale by burrowing more deeply into subjects I already cared for—Romantic poetry, Victorian literature—even if I could not expect the most stirring instruction. On a lark, but with my upcoming orals in mind, I also took a yearlong course on the poetry of Edmund Spenser, the Elizabethan author of that rich allegorical epic *The Faerie Queene*, much beloved by the Romantic poets. From what I already knew, I didn't expect to like it—I instinctively preferred a grounded sense of the actual world to most forms of allegory—but it was to be taught by a young professor rumored to be dynamic and provocative, a veritable Roman candle of ideas. This proved to be true in the worst sense imaginable as Spenser became the target of a riot of interpretation. The ideas indeed went off like firecrackers but were only loosely rooted in the poetry.

This literary adventure began in a much more promising way. Before reaching poor Spenser we spent four weeks on the dialogues of Plato, the

The Reitman family on the Lower East Side, 1948. Standing, left to right: Lou Sachs, married to my aunt Fay; my father, Abe Dickstein; Uncle Sam Reitman, who had moved to Miami Beach; myself, half hiding, under the hat; and my look-alike cousin, Avrumi, with his father, Louis Reitman. Seated, left to right: The three sisters, Aunt Lily, Aunt Fay, and my mother, Anne, holding my sister, Doris; Louis's wife, Rebecca, holding her daughter, Dianne; my cousin Dotty, Sam's daughter; and Pauline Krug, Lily's older daughter.

Mom, Dad, and me, before my first haircut, Rocky Point, ca. 1941.

Mom, Dad, Doris, and me, Rocky Point, ca. 1949.

My parents, Anne and Abe Dickstein, Central Park, New York, early 1950s.

Mom, Dad, Doris, and me, Central Park, early 1950s.

The camera buff,
inseparable from his
Argus C-3. Rocky Point,
mid-1950s.

Punting on the Cam, to Grantchester. Cambridge, England, June 1964.

Young love. With L on the ferry from Bridgeport to Long Island, summer 1965.

The infamous bikini: L on the beach in Rocky Point, 1965.

Strumming my guitar, exploring folk music, keeping my thesis at bay. New Haven, 1966.

At last, getting my Ph.D. Yale graduation, with mother and son Jeremy, New Haven, 1967.

With L in Riverside Park, Upper West Side, 1967.

Jeremy in Gigondas, France,
summer 1969.

Jeremy and our daughter Rachel, 1970.

The hippie couple, L and me with long hair and beard, early 1970s.

With L, Jeremy, and Rachel, Rocky Point, summer 1972

most seductive and literary of all philosophers. This turned out to be the highlight of the course: how could it go wrong? But go wrong we certainly did, for once the poetry was before us, the grandiose theories and the lines on the page simply failed to mesh. This brought out the worst in me, an adamant resistance, a stubborn appeal to principle, bordering on rebellion. It was like my last years of high school all over again, except that my resistance was provoked by the murk of literary theory, not the drone of Talmudical debate.

Close, patient reading—"reading in slow motion," as Reuben Brower called it—was relatively new for me, but getting it right, understanding the words on the page, had become almost a religion, a calling. What were we there for, to build castles in the air, as my instructor seemed to do? I didn't anticipate the theory years, when this would become common practice; he was simply ahead of the curve and I was destined to be a holdout. His annoyance at my needling questions became so palpable that he eventually threw a fit. "You *must* go along with me," he shouted, his voice rising with anger and frustration. "I can't teach unless you go along with me." Word must have spread through the department that he had wigged out, lost it in public. I took no pride in my obstinate contrariness. I can barely make sense of it today except as stubborn arrogance but it seemed then that I had no choice. My undergraduate teachers had relished the give-and-take, often rewarding me for talking back to them. They encouraged students to speak up, even to be rude and uncivil. Here instead I had provoked a young scholar, as cocksure as I was, to the verge of a breakdown. If his tack was misconceived, my response was hard to excuse, yet I took pride in it. No one was going to tell me that black was white, that a blurry picture was in sharp focus. I made his life a misery, perhaps because I too was miserable, strenuously trying to argue my way out of it.

Around us, meanwhile, the world was on the verge of crashing in flames. One day in October 1962 we learned that President Kennedy would be making an urgent address to the nation. There were rumors of an international crisis. At the small eating club of the Yale kosher kitchen a radio was brought in so that we could tune in to the president over dinner, though the dinner itself, with dire rumors flying, would prove as hard to get down as Kennedy's speech. He announced that Soviet missiles had been installed in Cuba, ninety miles offshore, proclaimed a blockade of ships to and from the island, and warned ominously of a nuclear confrontation. Over the years students have asked me about the level of anxiety for people living under the shadow of annihilation during the cold war years. I've told them that we lived bifocally, in compartments, casually going about our daily lives while remaining under the gun, never quite forgetting that a cold peace, occasionally punctuated by hot wars, was built on the threat of mutual destruction. The situation was so surreal that its mood could be captured only through bizarre comedy, in the black humor of Stanley Kubrick's *Dr. Strangelove*, the novel and film versions of *The Manchurian Candidate*, or the poker-faced fantasies of Kurt Vonnegut— all so characteristic of the early 1960s. On that night in October and for a week afterward that fear of the ultimate war, kept under wraps in a dim region of the mind, burst up to the surface. My protracted struggle with Latin, those nasty arguments with my teacher, the contested readings of Spenser's ripe, luxurious poetry, even my newfound happiness with L—all that seemed to pale as the future suddenly seemed in question.

Like everyone else I breathed a sigh of relief when the crisis was resolved with improbable speed toward the end of the month. Years later we learned how close we had come to a nuclear exchange. Though it shortly became clear that some of the president's advisers had pushed for bombing Cuba or even invading the island, we've since learned that one of the Soviet submarines thwarted by the blockade almost fired a device with a nuclear warhead. This could have led to an American attack on the Soviet Union, as Kennedy had warned. Still, we were frightened enough; the long postwar standoff had come to a deadly crisis, a high-stakes game of chicken. Balancing defiance with caution, the president restrained his hawks, pursued deft diplomacy, and made quiet concessions, enabling the Soviets to back down. The president came of age as a strategic player but the cold war also effectively ended at that moment, though it would drag on less threateningly for three more decades. We could all go back a touch less complacently to our private lives, even as other pressing issues soon came up—civil rights at home, a war in Asia—that would make any real retreat from politics untenable.

In my case private life was a mixed blessing; the tensions in my little world were on the rise. Though I felt happily in love, I was not at all ready for the kind of permanent commitment L needed. It was my first serious relationship; I was too immature to think about settling down, taking on real responsibilities, becoming a husband and father, as some of my classmates had already done. (My biophysicist friend and onetime roommate, Bob, no more grown-up than I was, had gotten married the preceding December, under the eye of the same venerable rabbi who had presided over my bar mitzvah, and I served as his best man.) This was a time when kids were still marrying young, as they had in the 1950s, especially when their college girlfriends had gotten knocked up. I was twenty-two, going on twenty-three, but emotionally years younger, still something of the brainy nerd who always piped up in class, though I was learning to be more restrained, less forward and aggressive about what I thought I knew. The closer L and I grew, the more our intimacy raised questions I was unable to deal with. Sex and love were an adventure; engagement and marriage were for settled adults, not a footloose graduate student. I had somehow sidestepped total disaster at Yale, meeting the minimum demands of my courses, assimilating a bit of Latin I would soon forget, but my academic life seemed to be going nowhere. Still, I never doubted I wanted to teach and write—if they would let me.

Alongside my love affair, which had transformed my world, I felt a growing sense of strain, not consciously but through my body, just as I had in my freshman year when I had come close to a breakdown. This time it came on more subtly. For months I had chronic dull headaches whenever I sat down to work. Finally I began to wonder whether I had some kind of brain tumor, a nagging worry eventually dispelled by an x-ray and a soothing lecture from my cousin Bernie, now a neurosurgeon, who served as medical consultant for everyone in the family. But I had little insight into how the mind could exert pressure on the body, how ingenious it could be in singling out a physical weak point, an aperture of insecurity. Without much warning I would respond to an emotional quandary by becoming ill, or imagining I was ill, which seemed a way of trumping my problems— shaky health, zero responsibilities. Psychoanalysis would eventually help, since it would take me back again and again to where these psychic stresses had first cut their grooves, in childhood, amid family life. But the easiest

solution that came up that year was simply to get away, leave everything—
beloved L, confounding Yale, enchanting Spenser—behind.

I received a letter from my old Shakespeare professor and faculty adviser,
Andrew Chiappe, asking whether I'd consider spending the following year
in Cambridge. Since the 1930s Columbia had offered Kellett Fellowships
for study at Oxford or Cambridge to a few graduating seniors. Chiappe
himself had been one of the first recipients, along with the future poet John
Berryman, who would one day surprise the world with a wacky series of
syncopated riffs he called Dream Songs. My most ferocious and brilliant
teacher, Jim Zito, had followed them to Clare College, Cambridge, where
the Kelletts in English usually went. I had been disappointed, yet perhaps
secretly relieved, at being passed over in my senior year, and the exhilarating
trip through Europe that summer was my reward—a way of going abroad
without having to stay on. Chiappe informed me that the endowment had
grown, so they could now offer a research fellowship to students who were
already a year or two into graduate school. At the very least, I thought, this
would be sweet vindication for having first been rejected.

I knew even less about Oxford and Cambridge than I had known
about Yale. For a poor kid from the Lower East Side those names meant
distinction, membership in an exclusive club, a vague sense of having arrived.
Yale and Cambridge sounded more like accolades, badges of achievement,
than places to live and learn. This is an exaggeration but I thought little
about what being there might actually mean, especially for someone who
had scarcely ever lived on his own. The academic timing could not have
been better. I would complete my course work, prepare for my orals over
the summer, and take them just before leaving, since the British fall term
didn't begin until early October. I could spend the year abroad in complete
freedom working up the right subject for my Yale thesis.

But how would that time abroad, that long separation, affect my future
with L? When I called to tell her I'd been offered the fellowship I sensed her
distress. I was asking her advice, giving at least the appearance of a decision
we would make together. Her life as much as mine was at a turning point
yet she didn't feel she could object. We had conflicting needs; she longed
for assurance, I needed to hang loose, perhaps even break free—an old
story between the sexes. Torn but determined, half-consciously hell-bent

on going, I sent queries to eminent critics at Oxbridge colleges. Applying was remarkably informal; a word from them, a nod from Columbia, was all that was needed.

L and I chewed through it again and again, deep into the night. Some of these overwrought conversations, as we mulled over our future, ended with both of us in tears. We were upset at the prospect of a long separation. Halfheartedly, she thought of going along and even wrote to Cambridge University Press to see whether it had an opening, only to be brusquely rebuffed. The press hired no women in editorial positions, she was informed. Well, it's only for a year, we reassured each other, nine months really, as if that were not an eternity in one's early twenties. I settled on Clare, knowing nothing about it except that it was venerably old yet reputedly liberal, and had a fabled history, year after year, with Columbia graduates in literature. Norman Podhoretz, the *Commentary* editor who was now the young pretender of the *Partisan Review* set, was one of them. He had gotten his start as a critic there, studying with the cantankerous critic and editor F. R. Leavis, staying on for three years.

My orals loomed on the calendar. With two amigos from Yale I sublet a faculty apartment for the summer near the Columbia campus—from L's former Russian professor, Bob Belknap—while actually intending to live with her, twenty blocks south on Riverside Drive. In June we took a test drive in living together, an advance honeymoon in idyllic Ithaca visiting friends who were subletting Paul de Man's ramshackle house. The place felt transient and unassuming, as if he and his family might soon decamp. The severed leg of the sofa was supported by a pile of books, among the relatively few books in the house. Supposedly he had lost two libraries in his postwar peregrinations, though no one knew exactly where he had been.

Soon after my father helped me move my things into town I came down with a mysterious, enervating illness that landed me back home in Flushing. I remained there under the care of our clueless family doctor, who had rescued me from my over-busy life as a freshman. He tried various antibiotics, all to no effect. He guessed I had a virus, perhaps mononucleosis, something he could not confirm. After a few days of fever I was left nursing a sore throat but otherwise feeling fine, just so long as I did next to nothing. Even half a block of walking left me exhausted, utterly depleted.

Since I'd been a child, any kind of illness had always freed me from obligations—this was how children were raised in a family in which duty was otherwise absolute, any form of shirking inconceivable. Instead of living in sin with L in the city, I settled into a suspiciously pleasant routine of lounging in bed and reading for my orals. I still recall a blissful time, ten days at least, that I spent entirely with George Eliot's *Middlemarch*, reading a hundred pages a day, really living inside that book. Eliot's grave, intelligent sentences, her subtle sympathy for her characters, kept me under a spell day in and day out. I felt as if I'd never encountered such a fully re-created world, or characters explored with such delicacy and penetration. With my sister away in camp, my mother waiting on her fallen son, and my mind in a state of literary exaltation, this was a reasonably happy place to be, though not at all where I had planned. I was reading a novel centering on two people, a brilliant young doctor and a thoughtful, idealistic young woman, who make quietly disastrous marriages to the wrong people for the wrong reasons. As if it were taking my measure, the book unfolded with just the emotional insight about love and marriage that I couldn't summon for my own life.

My illness was real but also a way out, since it allowed me to regress to the condition of a sick but clever child, safely under the maternal wing, stretching my mind but freed from the choices of a grown-up life. Puzzled by our phone conversations, sensing that I was hanging back, L came to Flushing to visit, though she knew my mother was leery, perhaps jealous of her. She found me in pajamas, surprisingly content as a pampered invalid babbling about the wonderful books he was reading. She shrewdly sized up the situation and gave me the name of a doctor in the city who, after seeing me, quickly diagnosed a strep infection and prescribed the right antibiotic. My mother was shocked as usual by L's forwardness—utterly unimpressed with my convenient illness, skeptical of the supposed comforts of home, she had announced matter-of-factly that she wouldn't visit me again— but even my mother could hardly argue with a cure. My condition soon improved, and after a single night in my supposed apartment I was living covertly with L, my would-be roommates having promised to let me know whenever my parents tried to reach me. We were keeping up appearances— that still seemed important in those buttoned-up years—and by now I felt little guilt about this recourse to deception. For all my hesitations I knew this was where I wanted to be, and I was awed by how nicely she had brought it about.

Against all odds the summer turned idyllic as I read my way through English literature by day, often in Riverside Park, and we made love at night after seeing free Shakespeare in Central Park, or taking in a concert at Lewisohn Stadium, near City College, or simply playing house, which seemed best of all. New York became our playground, and trial marriage was our way of making the most of it. Preparing for my exams, I sometimes sat in on Quentin Anderson's lectures on the English novel at Columbia, listening to his austere, resonant sentences punctuated by long pauses, as if he had bravely rescued them from a vast silence. One night, before a packed audience in Earl Hall, which housed Columbia's campus ministries, we heard Hannah Arendt take on the harsh criticism of her controversial report on the Eichmann trial in Israel, her voice quavering with anger. Her resemblance to L's imperious mother—both of them thin, gray-haired German Jewish ladies who spoke in heavily accented English—was striking, even disquieting.

I was due to depart for Cambridge two days after my orals. I still had to send off a large metal trunk full of books and winter clothes, foolishly leaving that for the last minute. This was a lifelong habit—I did everything at the last minute—but it also indicated some resistance to leaving. As the summer ended I was already going though pangs of nostalgia for its carefree pleasures, and when the time came for the orals I felt hardly ready for either the ordeal at Yale or the upcoming journey. Returning to New Haven for last-minute cramming, I made my way through astounding quantities of material that needed to be at the tip of my mind, rereading five hundred pages of Spenser's *Faerie Queene* in one sixteen-hour sitting the day before the exam, then waking up before dawn to read a slew of poems by Tennyson and Pope, neither of them favorites of mine—their work had languished on the back burner of my preparation.

I was keyed up for a grilling on anything at all in English or American literature, especially where my record showed obvious gaps, such as the medieval period. It looked like any small seminar room except that the student was on the hot seat, the faculty grouped around the table. My tense expectations were soon deflated. The questioning proved insultingly simple, the perfect capstone of my rocky Yale experience. Keyed up to stand and deliver, I was almost affronted to be asked to *name* as many of Chaucer's pilgrims as I could, and then to name as many of Shakespeare's history plays that came to mind. "Name?" I asked, with a slightly curdled intonation, as if my hearing had failed me. After all, I had a whole theory about those plays—I had notions about everything—but hardly got the chance to vent it. My last-minute Tennyson came in handy, though I was asked about the part I'd skipped in Pope's apocalyptic satire *The Dunciad*, not the three other sections I had crammed that morning. Still, I had "passed" an exam that hardly tested anything I knew. The only real drama came as I was leaving the room. There stood the next platoon of faculty examiners, including my theory-laden Spenser professor, who flashed his teeth in Brechtian style like Mack the Knife and said, "Oh, I'm *so* sorry I missed you." I'll bet he did. That was one spectacle I could do without, bound to be more bloody than the history plays. Somehow my guardian angel had spared me, though I was to be spared little else in the coming months.

There was an omen of trouble on the day of my departure as I was driving from Queens into Manhattan to buy another suitcase and pick up L, who would be joining my obviously miserable parents to see me off. As I passed LaGuardia Airport on the Grand Central Parkway, I caught sight in the rearview mirror of a huge car, traveling in the opposite direction, as it jumped the metal barrier and bore down on the tiny VW Beetle some two hundred yards behind me. It was a Lincoln or a Caddy, perhaps a limo, which had reared its front end up like a furious animal or killer whale. It seemed to be stalking the smaller car that veered wildly in one direction and then another to escape the predator. A moment later the road curved and I lost sight of them. Framed by the mirror like a composed image, it was both frightening and unreal, especially since I had passed through that point of the road not ten seconds earlier. It could have been me, I thought, with a strange cold detachment. Had my eyes played tricks on me? Had I imagined the scene, hallucinated it, simply conjured it up? Had the two cars, so unevenly balanced, collided head-on? I would never know, for I wasn't around the next day to read about it in the tabloids or see the story, if there was one, on the local news. An incident without closure, a distant glimpse, an omen of uncertainty, it haunted me on the flight that evening and for months afterward. In my mind the truncated scene came to stand for the insecurities of my English year and the way they would disrupt my ongoing life.

I HAD FLOWN only once before, on that charter flight from Greece to Israel two years earlier, so the flight itself felt slightly nerve-racking yet also like the first lap of a great adventure. London seemed even dingier than it had two years earlier, still a soot-covered Victorian city, and after a few days I went up to Cambridge to settle in. The picturesque town and its ancient colleges were so beautiful I gasped with amazement. Clare, which went back to the fourteenth century, was at the heart of the old university, its entrance close to the town's main square, with vast landholdings along the picturesque river Cam, the so-called Backs. On one flank was the even wealthier King's College, founded by Henry VI, a college strongly associ-ated with the Apostles, a secret society of the elect, and more recently with the fashionable Bloomsbury group of Virginia Woolf, Lytton Strachey, and E. M. Forster; on the other side were the small Trinity Hall and vener-able old colleges like Trinity, St. John's, and Magdalene, a row of hoary tradition, where poets like Milton, Wordsworth, and Tennyson had once lived. The faux-Gothic of the Yale campus, dating mainly from the 1930s, had not prepared me for the soaring delicacy of King's College Chapel—it looked its best from the Clare side—or the austere elegance of the rectan-gular Old Court at Clare, designed in the neoclassical style of the seven-teenth century. My rooms were across the river in Memorial Court, built in the 1920s, connected by a path that took me past the lushly green fellows' garden and over the graceful Clare Bridge, which rose above the modest Cam, a crescent of weathered gray stone.

In this enchanted setting, so charged with history, class, and style, it was not clear why things went quickly wrong for me. I was meeting many people but they seemed guarded, unreachable. The memory of my summer with L was my only consolation, as if I'd been expelled from paradise, looking back longingly at my last happy times. "I've been thinking about you constantly since we last saw each other," I wrote in one of my first letters, "and the

image of you has helped me feel spiritually secure in alien surroundings."
"Perhaps alien is a bad word," I added self-consciously, for what was only
"a slight dissonance." By the following week this sense of being out of place
had worsened. "I'm unhappy and terribly lonely," I wrote. "I miss you more
and more, no matter how many people I get to know. I can't get over this
feeling of strangeness."

Some of this dislocation was physical. The weather was already chilly
and wet when I arrived, and the cold seemed to penetrate everything. My
rooms were commodious yet stubbornly uncomfortable, as if discomfort
were the norm, the very point. I had an unheated bedroom with little more
than an iron bedstead and dresser, a sitting room with a flat gas burner set
into a fake fireplace, and a tiny galley kitchen that held a small cupboard, a
sink, and a gas burner. The only refrigeration was provided by the kitchen
window sill, wide and flat, a surface so drafty that food left there could
freeze unexpectedly. The carpentry ("joinery," as they called it) was at
best haphazard. When the wind was up it howled through the ill-fitted
windows, which didn't quite close, up the stairwell, and under the thin door
that came nowhere near reaching the floor. The miniature gas fire, whose
range extended about eighteen inches into the room, was the sole source of
heat; if you sat up close to read, it practically singed your eyebrows, even
put you to sleep, while your back remained in deepest chill, as if you were
being barbecued at the wrong temperature.

I soon came down with a brutal cold and began wondering how I could
endure the coming winter. The preceding winter—the winter Sylvia Plath
had turned on the gas—had been the coldest of the century. The river
froze, the water and gas lines froze, and it was hard to imagine how anyone
in Cambridge, with its woefully inadequate heating, had gotten through it.
"Line your bed with newspaper," one Clare student was told, as if this were
an ideal form of insulation. Layers and layers of clothing and bedding were
the more typical solution.

Even more than the cold and damp, the food quickly became a major
theme of my time there. Much of what I ate was strange, literally foreign,
much of it deep-fried or overcooked; my stomach, a sensitive barometer of
my overall mood, began to rebel. Within two weeks I was beset by what
I took to be ulcer symptoms, and this offered an outlet for anxieties that

had no better release. As a research student, more or less on my own, I was obliged to eat in the college dining hall only one night a week. The room, with its high table for faculty fellows, was like a cathedral choir, furnished with every shade of dark wood paneling. To get by I could usually skip the main dish and stick with soup, some soggy vegetables, and dessert. I noticed that English cooking had not improved in the two years I'd been away. Cambridge had a Jewish Society, like the Yale kosher kitchen, that served robust kosher lunches five or six days a week, as well as Shabbat dinners on Friday evenings. It made up for my own rudimentary cooking, limited to scrambling eggs and other basic dishes that reminded me of home, fare I knew I could trust. If you are what you eat, I should have turned into a banana. Some evenings I treated myself to a fish dinner at a fine local restaurant, but never took on the Scottish dishes that were its specialty, notably the unspeakable haggis—a pudding confected from a sheep's heart, liver, and lungs.

As I threw myself into Cambridge life, my digestive tract soon became my weak link, a persistent reminder that I was out of my native habitat. Living on the edge of low-grade anxiety, I felt like someone negotiating a high wire without a net. My parents had lived their lives in a very narrow round, between the store, the children, their extended family, and the synagogue. My mother's cooking was confined to a few staples but they were reassuringly familiar to me, a meat-and-potatoes diet that seemed in its very blandness to cushion my life and shield me from outside threats. Beyond the warm family circle lurked the great unknown, a hostile or indifferent world. So my parents had often warned me—it was how they themselves lived— and, unconsciously, I must have taken that message to heart.

The regime of keeping kosher hardened this mistrust into a commandment, but even while hewing to its demands I felt at risk. Once I dreamed that I was three thousand miles away, as indeed I was, but with a long umbilical cord, like an undersea telephone cable, that linked me to home. Yet it was stretched to the breaking point and could snap at any time. I was amused that dream symbolism could be so obvious, almost kitschy. I began seeing a sympathetic young doctor from the National Health Service who gave me some pills and said that my mild stomach irritation was a long way from becoming an ulcer. Periodic visits would calm my fears for a time but before too long I would begin to fret, as if the anxiety itself were a sentinel, a way of keeping one's guard up, remaining alert for dangers that might skulk around any corner.

All the while I was taking advantage of something I'd never before enjoyed, a year without courses, cramming, or exams, a time when I could do as I pleased. I threw myself into what became a yearlong arts banquet. I could read what I wanted, go where and when I chose, make my life up as I went along. Cambridge had a peculiarly partitioned academic system—lectures that no one actually had to attend, and one-on-one academic supervisions, including written essays, that prepared undergraduates for the "papers" that made up their ultimate exams, the so-called tripos, taken at the end of their second and third years. University lecturers were fellows of colleges but college fellows were not necessarily invited to lecture. A professorship was a rare and culminating honor; there was usually only one in each field, like the honorary chair of the department. The most distinguished literary presence in Cambridge was F. R. Leavis of Downing College, who had recently retired. Though he had helped create the study of English at the university in the twenties and thirties, he'd never been named a professor. Leavis had been a burr in the side of the literary establishment for decades, and this contributed to his chronic complaints of neglect bordering on persecution. Leavis also claimed—boasted, really—that none of his students had ever been appointed to the Cambridge English faculty, but this claim was undercut by the inroads of several gifted young acolytes at Clare, especially John Newton, who supervised many undergraduate literature students.

Newton was said to have been an amateur boxer before he became an English scholar; his compact, muscular physique seemed to bear it out. His soft-spoken, extremely diffident manner and instinctive reserve did little to mask his strong literary views, only partly inherited from his pugnacious mentor. If Leavis in his provocative book *The Great Tradition* had boiled down the core of English fiction to only five novelists, from Jane Austen to D. H. Lawrence, Newton wrote exacting essays showing where even these stellar figures, including Henry James, sometimes fell short. For me this could be bewildering. I had come from a culture of appreciation, directed above all toward the Western classics, and now I'd landed in a culture of exclusion in which even the masters were scrutinized for their flaws, their faults of imagination or execution. Leavis had once written harshly about one of the books I lived by, Conrad's chilling omen of modern corruption, *Heart of Darkness*. When I was a freshman freshly in love with Conrad, that had infuriated me. In a public lecture Newton performed a similar operation on my favorite James novel, *The Portrait of a Lady*. I argued with him in vain, and even produced a copy of the paper I'd written on it for Charles Feidelson at Yale, perhaps the best work I had ever done. Since it was a reading of James's way of imagining his world, with little emphasis on literary evaluation, no carefully parsed verdict, it cut no ice. His was a take-no-prisoners account of where the book worked and where he thought it stumbled, and we agreed to disagree.

Still, I admired his literary mind, his relentless seriousness, and especially his sense, rare in Cambridge, that these judgments, these writers, really mattered. Looking for the kind of intellectual community I'd known at home, I sometimes joined his informal sessions devoted to reading texts with undergraduates. One of the papers set for the tripos that year was on Dickens, a writer Leavis had once devalued as an undisciplined entertainer but then had gradually annexed to his Great Tradition without ever admitting his views had changed. Newton was preparing a small knot of Clare undergraduates to write on Dickens, and I asked to join the reading group, which included Richard Locke, a Kellett fellow in his second year, whom I'd known distantly at Columbia. Thus began my most bracing literary campaign of the year, a long march through nearly all of Dickens's major novels at a clip exhilarating for the slow reader I still was. The feverish pace matched the intensity of Dickens's own writing, so incandescent and richly mannered that it sometimes seemed closer to hallucination than to conventional storytelling. (Not for nothing was Dickens a great favorite of Dostoevsky's.) I could feel desperate about other matters but Dickens held me spellbound for months at a time. The novel of the week became a highlight of *my* week. *Dombey and Son*, the breakthrough into the late Dickens, *Great Expectations*, the most disciplined and affecting of his novels, and *Little Dorrit*, his dark masterpiece, became my special favorites. Step by step we tracked how Dickens transformed himself from the crowd-pleasing popular entertainer of *The Pickwick Papers* to the feverish social critic of the late novels without losing his audience along the way.

Officially I was studying not with Newton but with my formal supervisor, Raymond Williams, preparing to write a Yale thesis on politics in the Victorian novel. The project was a distant offshoot of the Victorian seminar I had undertaken as my swan song in college. My work with Trilling and Marcus had completely undercut the reigning clichés about the stuffy, reactionary Victorians. Instead, I had come to see the period as a laboratory of modern life—in science, politics, religion, but especially in industrial development. This in turn had given rise to a vibrant social criticism, in novels but also in brilliant prose tracts by Carlyle, Arnold, Ruskin, and others. Schooled in the arts, not politics, they were keenly attuned to the dehumanizing effects of these social changes, and I was drawn to the radical edge I found in their criticism. It paralleled the work of Marx and Engels, who themselves admired the ornery and implacable Carlyle.

I had been a great fan of Williams's recent work, especially *Culture and Society* and *The Long Revolution*, which traced a critical path through the whole line of British cultural criticism from Burke and Carlyle to Leavis himself. Williams's knotty books—history-minded, socially concerned, subtly humane—exemplified the virtues of that tradition. Williams was a recovering Marxist whose view of art and culture had been broadened by these conservative yet caustic critics. His own background was Welsh and working class, and he could write about it from the inside. His resonant autobiographical novel *Border Country* finely explored his relation to his father as it evoked the epochal British General Strike of 1926.

But Williams as a writer and Williams as a supervisor were different matters. From the first I learned a great deal; the other, preoccupied by his own work, I scarcely got to see, and he rarely said much when I did see him. Though I was officially working on the politics of Victorian fiction, I had yet to read many Victorian novels. He got me to write about George Eliot's scarcely known *Felix Holt, the Radical*. A line from that book, "there is no private life that has not been determined by a wider public life," could have served as a motto for the thesis I had in mind. But the politics of the novel itself proved anything but radical, and only the marriage plot, reminiscent of *Middlemarch* at its best, took fire. I began to wonder how much the political novel really interested me and how competent I was to write about it. Williams's university lectures on the novel were always worth hearing, but his relative inaccessibility threw me back on Newton and Leavis as my strongest links to the Cambridge faculty.

Though recently retired, Leavis had been invited by Clare to help prepare a handful of undergraduates for the "dating" paper on the tripos. On the exam they would be handed some specimens of English prose or poetry and would be asked to date it purely on the elements of its style. Leavis and his contemporaries, including I. A. Richards and Clare's own Mansfield Forbes, had introduced this ambitious exercise close to four decades earlier, and he, the survivor from another era, was the only one left who could truly prepare students for it. Though I was not taking these exams, or any exams, I attached myself to a small group simply to see a master critic at work; this soon became a highlight of my week. Every Tuesday morning in Downing College he would bring in graying stacks of quotations he had once used in lecturing, and each week we would be thoroughly confounded by these examples. He would then demonstrate, as if by magic, how much about a writer's mind and surrounding world was reflected in his use of language, its diction, rhythm, and imagery.

Physically, Leavis was an impressive figure with his bald, tanned head, penetrating eyes, and craggy profile. His collar was always open, not a Byronic affectation, it was said, but because he had been gassed during the Great War and could not abide a tie. Though he was in his sixty-ninth year, he could often be seen running with a rucksack along Queen's Road, not exercising but hurrying off impatiently to his next destination. His personality was as rough-hewn as his appearance. An inimitable storyteller who loved to ventilate his pet peeves, Leavis was especially hard on onetime friends and allies who lacked his stomach for cultural warfare. Once he reminisced about the young I. A. Richards, whose early work had helped inspire modern methods of close reading. According to Leavis, he had been an embattled rebel at Magdalene, one of Cambridge's most hidebound colleges. One day, encountering the elderly Master on the lawn reserved for college fellows, Richards fumed, "My only consolation in this place is that every day an old man dies." To which the Master was said to respond, "Yes, but every day a young man turns into an old man." With a mischievous gleam, Leavis added, "Yes, and that's *just* what happened to Richards."

On another occasion Leavis recalled how a celebrated critic, William

Empson, had stopped by his home to pay a call. Once Richards's prize scholarship student at Magdalene, Empson had been expelled from Cambridge under mysterious circumstances—supposedly because a servant had discovered a woman in his room, though we then knew nothing of this. Working in the garden, Leavis's hands were covered with mud and, as he told us, he was pleased to excuse himself from shaking hands, as if Empson himself was unclean to him. I had relished some of Leavis's razor-sharp polemics, most recently against the overrated novelist C. P. Snow, but many people had evidently disappointed him, and he could not resist drawing a younger generation into his ancient and current feuds, always trying to discredit his perceived enemies and, in effect, to vindicate his place in literary history. He felt he had rarely received his due from either the university or the glib metropolitan literary culture, represented by Sunday papers like the *Observer* and weekly magazines of opinion like the left-leaning *New Statesman*.

His longest-standing target was Bloomsbury, which he saw as a smug upper-class coterie that expertly wielded the levers of literary power—in the universities, the Arts Council, the Sunday papers—to vilify him and exclude his students. But his acolytes, passed over by the universities, found their way instead into the schools, where their impact was enormous. There they trained more than one generation in close reading and in the moral seriousness and social urgency of great literature. From 1932 to 1953 in his legendary little magazine, *Scrutiny*, he and his contributors had waged a guerrilla campaign against the Bloomsbury writers and their influence, though they carved out large exceptions. The magazine repeatedly attacked Virginia Woolf but was almost reverential toward her father, Sir Leslie Stephen, the late Victorian man of letters. Leavis himself, in 1939, had published a discriminating essay on Woolf's friend E. M. Forster, whose novels I had been reading to capture the spirit of old Cambridge. Back then he had subtly threaded his way through Forster's strengths and faults. Now, twenty-five years later, it pained me to hear Leavis roundly dismissing his work, and I pulled the mean trick of quoting his own essay against him, much to his amusement. A Brit to the core, he never took Americans all that seriously.

Either Leavis's critical faculty had coarsened, perhaps overtaken by personal animus, or his opinion had simply changed for the worse. But Forster's novels, some now sixty years behind him, seemed to have weathered the decades at least as well as the man himself. Now an octogenarian, he lived next door in King's College, a frail monument of the Edwardian era. His prewar novels, especially *The Longest Journey*, spoke of an earlier Cambridge to me as much as Leavis and *Scrutiny* did. I had one of his novels in my back pocket one day, later in the year, as I crossed the Clare Bridge with Richard Locke. Walking past the fellows' garden toward the main court, I scarcely noticed the old man who passed us in the other direction. "That was Forster, you know," Richard remarked. I turned around to see him standing on the bridge, peering pensively down into the Cam as if contemplating the flow of time itself. With a brashness that astonishes me today, I walked back and introduced myself, and even whipped out my copy of the novel for his inspection. As if nothing could surprise him, he began chatting about some of the adaptations of his work then playing on the West End, novels published not long after the turn of the century. Since I hadn't seen the plays I grew tongue-tied. I could barely connect those books to the whimsical old gentleman before me; having just read them, I was convinced I remembered them better than he could. Old age was a total mystery to me, and I had my doubts he could remember them at all, as if written by a different man in another life. Finally, he examined my copy of *A Room with a View*—he may never have seen the Vintage paperback—took out a pen, crossed out his name on the title page and signed it just below. As we parted he invited me to call on him at his rooms in King's, but by then my time in Cambridge was nearly over and I didn't take him up on it. Years later I saw him interviewed there for a documentary film, and he complained afterward, "My chamber pot rather let me down." I suppose it was not meant to have put in an appearance.

One fellow at King's whose invitation I did take up was a young London journalist in Cambridge on a three-year appointment, John Gross. Coming from New York, I was surprised to see how British Jews kept a low profile as Jews. I never met Harold Pinter, whose stark early plays beguiled me, but on the basis of his work I would have been astonished to learn that he was the son of an East End tailor, or was Jewish at all. Gross, on the other hand, like Isaiah Berlin, was quite up-front, seemingly unembarrassed by who he was and where he came from. A prolific reviewer with impeccable mainstream credentials, totally connected, he published as much in the weekly *Jewish Chronicle* as in the *New Statesman.* In Cambridge he was the closest thing to a New York intellectual, writing as a generalist with wide learning but little academic baggage. I introduced myself after one of his lectures, and it turned out that he knew many of the same people I had already met in the *Partisan Review* crowd. We hit it off immediately and, as we parted, he invited me to drop in on him in King's, adding, more than once, "Do come. I really mean it." This last bit puzzled me. I couldn't imagine why he would bother to say it if he *hadn't* meant it. Surely he didn't owe me an invitation.

A week or two later I knocked on his door one evening and encountered a harried-looking man, perhaps working on a deadline, who turned me away quite brusquely. He seemed shocked that I *had* taken him up on it. Gross appeared even more nonplussed a few weeks later when I cut him on the street with barely a nod, a deft British slight I had just learned to pull off. It was a trivial but eye-opening malentendu. I was coming to understand the rules of the social game but it poisoned the well for me. Having mistaken mere politeness for friendship, I sometimes turned aside overtures of friendship as mere politeness. I was getting wised up about English manners yet the intricacies of the code escaped me, and always would. When Gross kept insisting on the sincerity of his invitation, it was a sign for me to be wary of accepting it. Once I realized this, too late, it seemed little more than outright hypocrisy.

Perhaps I should have understood this dance, these crossed signals, more intuitively. I had fallen in love with English literature—it was the chief reason I was there. Part of the power of the English novel flowed from how writers explored the gaps between what people felt or thought or meant and what they actually said, plumbing their reticences and silences, their conscious and unconscious motives, the discretion and indirection that oiled the gears of many social encounters. An ingrained virtuosity at role-playing, not Method-like sincerity, was at the heart of the great British acting tradition, a reserve lit up by hints of emotion largely concealed, fleetingly revealed. The English, as I should long since have grasped, could be people of deep feeling yet maddeningly oblique expression, though this differed according to class. I stemmed from a more operatic culture, Jewish as well as American, where emotions usually rang out fortissimo. My family and friends were just a generation or two from the shtetl; our schooling in manners and social decorum, in cultivating restraint, was far more limited, and I found it hard to apply my literary insight to the world that now enfolded me.

Another part of the code that perplexed me had to do precisely with class, particularly as it concerned the servants who kept life in the Cambridge colleges humming. Every batch of rooms at Clare had a "bedder," always a woman of a certain age, who made the bed and cleaned up, and a "gyp," usually an elderly man with decades of service behind him. He was a general factotum with obscure responsibilities, a throwback to a time when the young aristocrat would come up to Oxford or Cambridge with his own manservant. But now he also served as a spy charged with reporting any infraction of the rules to the college authorities, especially an after-hours visit by someone of the opposite sex. This last was a rarity since all but a few of the colleges were still all-male, and the three women's colleges, located at a considerable distance from the center of the university, were segregated by sex as well.

One stumbling block was that I could never adapt to being addressed as "master" or as "the young gentleman" by a taut, hardworking man in his sixties. I stubbornly balked at putting my shoes outside my door each night so that they could be polished by morning. I rarely shined my shoes at all, let alone had them done for me. But no matter where I left my shoes, even when I deliberately hid them, the gyp would steal in and search them out before I woke up, then buff them to a bright glow. I realized that instead of sparing him menial labor I was making his life more difficult, keeping him from doing his job, and I grudgingly let go of my virtuous, pseudo-egalitarian resistance. The whole system would soon collapse under the onslaught of the sixties—the obsequious yet vaguely threatening servants, the obligatory black scholars' gowns with their clerical cut, the nightly curfew when the college gates would lock down, the sexual segregation and parietal rules—but in 1963 they were still in place, calcified remnants of an earlier era, sustained by sheer inertia.

I felt out of place, off-kilter, but somehow that began to matter less.

Despite my loneliness and longing for L, my errant stomach and my bouts of cross-cultural misunderstanding, against all odds I began having a good time. Cambridge was a marvelous film town, thanks to a number of local art cinemas and the Cambridge Film Society, chaired that year by Richard, who was becoming my closest friend at Clare. Blond, blue-eyed, and unusually intense, Richard had already spent a year in Cambridge by the time I got there. At Columbia he had been an early member of the Taubes circle, having encountered the elfin sage as a freshman and taken virtually all his courses thereafter. A graduate of Lawrenceville, where he was taunted as a Jew, he could have passed for a preppie but chose otherwise, having passed up a gentleman's life at Princeton for the intellectual stimulation of Columbia. Once in Cambridge, he took warmly to the cultural mix that kept the university abuzz, especially the very active film scene.

Between Europe, Japan, and India we were in the midst of a spirited renewal of film as art, a period of experimentation and personal expression the likes of which had not been seen since the freewheeling days of the 1920s when the Russians, inspired by the Bolshevik Revolution, the Germans, depressed by war and inflation, along with the French and the Americans, were all developing the new medium in thrilling directions. Cambridge was giving me a film education I hadn't sought or expected. I also began going to London at least once a week, usually staying in the Hillel House, where bed and breakfast could be had for little more than half a pound (about $1.47). I took to walking the streets, haunting the museums and bookstores, listening to parliamentary debates, going to the theater.

My fellowship stipend was meager, only two thousand dollars for the whole year, but the dollar was strong and the cost of living ridiculously low. Books, plays, meals, travel cost next to nothing by American standards. At the museums I fell in love with the British Romantic painters, with the rich Constable collection at the Victoria and Albert, where his oil sketches seemed to anticipate impressionism, with the tempestuous Turners at the Tate Gallery, teeming with a wild energy, virtual explosions of color and form, and even with minor nineteenth-century landscape painters like Richard Bonington, dead of consumption (like his contemporary Keats) before the age of twenty-six. I witnessed the birth pangs of Laurence Olivier's National Theatre in its inaugural season at the Old Vic, doing classic repertory theater as I'd never seen it done in New York, always in freshly conceived productions, utterly compelling thanks to virtuoso acting.

I was soon making good friends in Cambridge, though I realized only later that they were all distinctly oddballs, or at least outsiders in some fashion. David S., the most conventional of the lot, was an animated undergraduate, not especially literary, who reminded me of some of my earliest Columbia friends, before I fell in among the intellectuals. His Jewish background resonated with mine, and once or twice I stayed at his parents' flat in London, where the family was warm but the bedroom so chilly that I needed a hot-water bottle to heat the sheets before crawling into bed. David G., on the other hand, was a budding young Leavisite gravely serious about literature but so reserved, so given to mumble offhandedly, that he made the shy Newton, his tutor, seem demonstrative. Jules L., an avid student of art and architecture, helped educate my eye. Once in London, as we gazed at the House of Commons, he memorably pointed out the disparities between Victorian Gothic, all decorative surface, and the genuine medieval style. The voluble Frank S. was a brilliant student of Near Eastern history and languages with an unusual background. His mother was a Jewish refugee from Hitler's Germany; his father, a tenth-generation descendant of a Scottish clan. On ceremonial occasions Frank sometimes donned a kilt with his dad but his interests tilted markedly to the maternal side, which provided me with another small Jewish connection that helped my little world feel more like home.

By late November of 1963 I was increasingly happy, in part because I had decided to go home for the monthlong Christmas break if I could find a cheap enough charter flight. I wrote to L, "My stomach is the last holdout against the new reign of serenity and order (comparatively)." Having escaped any firm commitment to our being together by leaving the country, I was now desperately eager to see her again; we had somehow grown even closer by being apart. Then disaster struck, not for me alone but for the world at large. It took place as I was enjoying the festive Shabbat dinner at the Jewish Society, with soup, noodle pudding, chicken, and red wine on a white tablecloth, almost a home-cooked meal. A rumor spread around the table that the American president had been shot though no one knew anything definite. I walked across the road into the courtyard of St.

John's and saw two undergraduates deep in conversation in a ground-floor room. I asked if they'd heard anything about an attack on Kennedy. One of the boys looked mystified and said he knew nothing. The other piped up, "Oh yes, he's dead."

This intelligence was doubly chilling, first for the shocking news itself, then because the young man had not found it worth mentioning to his friend, whatever urgent matter they were chewing over. As an American in a foreign land, I had never felt more alone, more displaced. I spent the rest of the evening and much of the next day with Richard and Peter Winn, who was also in Cambridge on a Kellett. For hours we talked about nothing special, nothing I can remember. We felt helpless, as if the moorings of our world had been shaken loose, even more helpless for being so far away. Like them I was miserably depressed, incapable of getting my mind around the wretched turn of events. Our form of mourning was to create a little outpost of home, like émigrés huddling together to hear a bit of their own language. We needed each other desperately to help absorb the blow.

The weekend passed as if in a bad dream, partly because I felt so removed from what took place in the States, unable to share what must have been a collective national trauma. There was only one TV set in Clare, in the common room, and there I saw a few disjointed bits of that grim weekend, including LBJ making a brief speech after the plane carrying the body landed in Washington, and finally the shooting of Lee Harvey Oswald two days later. It all seemed remote and indecipherable. I was unnerved to hear Johnson's solemn Texas drawl after those years of Kennedy's patrician New England tones, the high voltage charge of his youth and energy. Seeing life, as I often did, through the prism of poetry, I wrote to L that Coleridge's Dejection ode came to mind: "For hope grew round me, like a twining vine, / And fruits and foliage, not my own, seemed mine. / But now afflictions bow me down to earth." Recalling such bathos embarrasses me; amid the national calamity I let myself indulge in a spasm of self-pity. I felt orphaned, as if the country I came from had mysteriously vanished. I grew even more determined to go home for the holidays, perhaps to stay for good.

The year abroad seemed like a gigantic mistake, a luckless roll of the dice. My bruised psyche was aching but I worried instead about my tender gut, as if an ulcer might prove to be my Achilles' heel, the chink in my armor I had always feared and sought, the little point of weakness that would bring me down. The doctor ordered a set of x-rays, an upper-GI series, more to reassure me, I suspect, than because he was concerned. It was scheduled for the second week of December, which gave me three or four days to spend in London after the term ended. For the first time since I'd arrived in England I became an avid tourist again, revisiting some of the sites I'd first seen in 1961, such as St. Paul's Cathedral, more monumental than I remembered, and the ineffable Elgin Marbles in the British Museum. I took in a handful of plays, movies, and art exhibitions, including Camus's overstuffed adaptation of Dostoevsky's *The Possessed* and Luchino Visconti's ravishing film version of another great novel, Giuseppe di Lampedusa's *The Leopard*, which became my new standard for transferring fiction to film. I was still somewhat lost in that vast metropolis, not a great walking city like Paris, since everything was so spread out. The size and anonymity of London made me realize how much at home I now felt in Cambridge, where everything had grown familiar, even welcoming. In the long run, though, I might have been happier spending that year in cosmopolitan London.

I returned uneasily to Cambridge to see whether the exam would bear out my nagging fears of an ulcer. It involved swallowing a chalky white fluid containing barium. The equipment in the room was something out of a *Flash Gordon* serial; it was the size of a cyclotron, perhaps thirty years out of date, and as the technician kept urging me to drink faster, swallow faster, I felt the dim beginnings of a new bugaboo, wondering whether I was being zapped by too much radiation. Even today it is humiliating to recall my irreducible attachment to these shifting, cunning fears, a free-floating anxiety looking for an inlet in the mind or the body. In the history of literature, from Molière's *Le Malade Imaginaire* to Joseph Heller's *Catch-22*, hypochondria has usually served as a subject for farce rather than a serious matter. We're amused by Mr. Woodhouse, the father of Jane Austen's *Emma*, supping on a basin of thin gruel and urging everyone to avoid drafts. I was stuck in a comedy that felt like the preview of a tragedy. "The future seems like such a question mark," I wrote to L. "Somehow I must solve my own problems before we can be happy together." Today this sounds like a patent excuse for keeping my life on hold. Still, I was much relieved by the negative test results. My vague symptoms soon cleared up, as they usually did after tests like this, and I could head home with a clean bill of health.

I learned that my charter flight was canceled, and I found another, for a negligible cost, that would leave a few days later. It was a propeller-driven flight from Gatwick to Toronto with stops along the way in Ireland and Newfoundland, followed by a commercial flight to New York. The whole trip would take as long as a jet flight to Australia today but it seemed well worth it, if only to break the pattern of my English exile and reconnect with those I loved and missed. The delay meant additional days to kill in Cambridge, where most of the undergraduates had already headed home. Richard too was stranded at Clare for a few days before leaving for London, and I sometimes sat reading in his rooms, soaking up both the literal warmth and the warmth of human company in the deserted college. I relished those tranquil hours; I had always loved the quiet grandeur of old university campuses emptied of students. Guidebook in hand—the Cambridgeshire volume in Nikolaus Pevsner's mammoth Buildings of England series—I explored some of the colleges I had not yet seen, one of them with a court from the fourteenth century, still largely preserved, as well as a church dating from the eleventh century, before the Norman invasion. I was overwhelmed by these great vistas of time, by structures that had survived so many centuries, but appalled by the spartan living conditions they still imposed. The Old Court of Clare had installed hot running water and bathtubs for each stairwell only a few years earlier, over the objections of one of the older fellows, who saw hot baths as a decadent luxury, bound to sap the strength of the younger generation. "And after all," he was reported to have said, "it's only an eight-week term." One of the largest, most venerable colleges, Trinity, still had not gone in for such advanced plumbing; its hardy denizens kept their kettles at a boil. Americans in Cambridge were always accused, with joshing indulgence, of being soft—habituated to their creature comforts, especially hot water and central heating—while a good number of the English felt supremely virtuous at not being spoiled, living an austere way of life.

Like most charter flights in those days, my plane left many hours late and took so long that we developed a strong sense of camaraderie with the crew. The markings on the plane said Trans-Canada Airlines, which I had confused with Air Canada, the national carrier. Trans-Canada turned out to be a smaller operation; I learned belatedly from one of the crew that this was their only aircraft. To a novice (and nervous) flier this was strangely reassuring; it meant that they would take good care of it (and of us), as they did. Of course I missed my connection in Toronto and had to take a later flight, yet L somehow was there to greet me at the airport when I arrived in New York, beaming with pleasure but shocked at how much weight I had lost. Beanpole thin to begin with, I was down to 125 pounds. She observed that I looked like a Holocaust survivor, an appearance enhanced by exhaustion from the long flight. My mother, though overjoyed to see me, acted as if her worst fears had been realized: I had foolishly left the shelter of home and was slowly dying of starvation.

The month in the city passed as if in a dream, a renewal of the happy summer that now seemed years behind us. L and I, like orphans in the storm, were keeping house again, making love every night, trying to make up for lost time, though I staggered back to Queens at three or four in the morning to keep my parents at bay. Some kind of propriety still needed to be kept up; had I stayed with L overnight, the quarrels with them would have poisoned my whole time in New York. From Ithaca, New Haven, and Cambridge our friends converged on the city for the holidays, a scattered troupe finding its way home.

On my last night before returning to England in January, L and I climbed into bed in her apartment on Riverside Drive and simply looked at one another, wondering what the next few months would bring. She had resolved to quit her job and join me in Cambridge in May or early June. We decided that we would travel through England and Europe together, whatever the appearances, but could we be sure our bond was strong enough to endure five more months of separation? We lived in hope and anticipation, rekindled by our monthlong reunion. For the first time since I returned, instead of having sex we simply held each other for hours, awake and asleep, before I took the subway home. The next day I resumed the struggle to show I had finally grown up, left the nest, and was rugged enough to survive on my own.

Eight

BACK TO CAMBRIDGE

THE CHARTER FLIGHT back to England was as drawn out as my interminable trip home a month earlier. Concerned about missing my connection, I flew up from New York to Toronto four hours early, only to find that the charter flight would leave at least four hours late, well past midnight. After all the time we'd spent together, the passengers and crew greeted each other like old friends. Thanks to the delayed departure we arrived for our stopover in Gander, Newfoundland, in the middle of the night. There I wandered around the huge, empty airport, built only a few years earlier, dedicated by Queen Elizabeth herself but soon rendered obsolete by nonstop jet travel. In this hollow, almost abandoned setting I had a strong sense of what Dr. Johnson called the vanity of human wishes. The world had speeded up but I was still traveling by go-cart, on a propeller-driven flight a decade out of date.

We didn't arrive at Gatwick Airport till late the next night, where I caught the last train to London and wandered the streets looking for a room. My bags were heavy with winter supplies, warmer clothes I knew I'd need, and the streets were sloppy with slush—the first winter snow, I was told. At my wit's end, I hailed a cab, which directed me to modest lodgings not yet closed for the night. I snagged a room barely larger than the bed, popped a shilling in the gas meter for an hour's warmth, and fell into a comatose sleep for twelve hours. The next thing I knew the grumpy landlady was rapping loudly at the door. It was noon and I had to vacate the premises.

Back in Cambridge I continued sleeping till noon all week, jet-lagged without having taken a jet, until I forced myself awake for a morning lecture. Until then I saw little daylight, for it was quite dark by four in the afternoon. The damp, penetrating cold was like nothing I'd experienced. I wasn't sure how I'd get through the next few months but I was determined they'd be different—less anxious and fretful, more gratifying—and so they proved to be. It was partly the movies that saved my life. Richard suggested I try writing film reviews for an undergrad broadsheet called, well, *Broadsheet*, sloppily edited, badly mimeographed, on sale for sixpence and covering the Cambridge arts scene quite fully. Thanks in part to the French New Wave and to Italian directors like Michelangelo Antonioni, Federico Fellini, and Luchino Visconti, it was an extraordinary moment in film history, and I was swept up by it. I had been intrigued yet taken aback by Antonioni since *L'Avventura*, a film in which a central character disappears halfway through and is never found. The rerelease of *La Notte*, another tale of upper-class ennui but with stars (Jeanne Moreau, Marcello Mastroianni), along with his disappointing new film, *L'Eclisse*, gave me a chance to make sense of what he was doing and why it mattered. Where the postwar Italian neorealists had focused on the travail of the poor, Antonioni zeroed in on the hollow, bored lives of the newly rich, portraying their world less through plot and character than by way of mood, glacial pacing, and richly suggestive visual imagery. It became clear that *L'Avventura* was as much about the barren rocks on a Mediterranean island and the waves that lap around them as about the woman who vanishes in this remote setting. Untangling my feelings about this new kind of work proved deeply satisfying.

I followed up over the next few months with articles on Orson Welles (*The Trial*), Luis Buñuel (*Nazarin*), Sergei Eisenstein (the belated release of *Ivan the Terrible, Part Two*, long suppressed by the Soviets), and, most unlikely of all, westerns (Raoul Walsh's last film, *A Distant Trumpet*). Rereading these pieces after almost half a century, I'm surprised and amused by their elevated tone, as if Leavis himself had improbably begun writing about movies. Perhaps I was compensating for dipping my toe into popular culture, stuff typically ignored or patronized by critics I admired.

Or was I simply feeling uncertain about dealing with a visual medium? I wrote earnestly about how Welles, whose work I liked, had betrayed and misunderstood Kafka. When the Welles piece was attacked by another contributor, Tony Palmer, I responded with an article so grandiose it sounded as though Matthew Arnold had risen from the dead to pronounce again on the function of criticism. Reaching for the moon, I compared westerns to Aeschylus's Oresteia trilogy as myths of the birth of culture, in which the law of revenge, or the law of the gun, was succeeded by an organized social and legal order. I hadn't seen all that many westerns but the few I knew and loved, among them *High Noon*, *Shane*, and John Ford's late masterpiece, *The Man Who Shot Liberty Valance*, had told me all I needed to know.

The simple truth was that I was enjoying myself, exercising my critical muscles on something other than literature. It would be more than a decade before I started teaching film and writing about it again, but this student adventure anticipated a signal turn in my life, a new awareness that popular culture and high art were not so far from each other as I had been taught. Part of this recognition came from reading a big novel of Dickens alongside three or four talkative undergraduates each week, since Dickens had been both wildly popular and dead serious, an unparalleled comic artist who doubled as the Victorian social conscience. This immersion in Dickens spilled over into our weekly meetings with Leavis, who had been Dickens's most notorious modern detractor. It was rumored that his views had since changed, a momentous bit of intelligence in those days. He had already published an essay on *Dombey and Son*, a neglected novel that marked the writer's turn toward the trenchant social criticism that would power his late work. In December, Leavis had asked us to suggest a subject for our final meeting before the holiday, and we proposed Dickens's *Little Dorrit*. We had heard it was now his favorite Dickens. If Leavis were to execute a full reversal of his damning view of Dickens as an undisciplined popular entertainer, *Little Dorrit* would be the steep slope he would have to climb. We were determined to speed this move along, if we could. It's hard to explain today how much this mattered to us, but the very substance of our feeling for literature seemed to hang in the balance.

When the day came, Leavis arrived with the usual stack of passages, which he distributed to us, since his method was to build directly on the words of the text. He tried one, then another, then another, but the session stubbornly refused to take wing. He seemed for once inarticulate. There was a noticeable gap between the words on the page and the significance he tried to attach to them, and by the end he looked downcast and defeated, even apologetic. With a persuasive show of humility, he begged our indulgence for another crack at the book, after the holidays. At our first meeting in January he arrived with a pile of excerpts twice as thick; still, no tack he tried seemed to work. He was old, perhaps no longer at the top of his game. His little magazine, *Scrutiny*, hugely influential despite its tiny circulation, had been defunct for a decade, though its entire twenty-year run was just then being reprinted in hard covers by Cambridge University Press. Almost a decade had passed since his last book, a study of D. H. Lawrence, sometimes strained and excessive in the case he made for the writer. Far from being methodical like most academics, he waited like Trilling for inspiration, a magical moment of connection that had not as yet arrived with Dickens. In a fit of exasperation he offered to take one last shot at it, as if we could have said no, and the following week came in with an even larger pile of quotations, which must have taken him a good part of the week to ferret out. Of what he said that morning I recall nothing, only the sense that it clicked from the first moment and never let up. Like an actor in synch with his audience, he felt the connection and so did we. A few years later, when he and his wife, Q. D. Leavis, herself a formidable scholar and critic, published a book on Dickens, the long chapter on *Little Dorrit* was the pièce de résistance. It made the book, and I felt we had a hand in it. By then *Little Dorrit*, with its somber mood, its great galaxy of characters and subplots, and its potent echoes of Dickens's own father's time in debtor's prison, had become my own favorite Dickens novel as well.

But this was only one moment, a powerful one, in my exhilarating Dickens year. I was overwhelmed by the Shakespearean range of his language, the satiric energy and humor, the preternatural vitality of the characters, the shameless melodramatic intensity, the piercing social observation. Our little study group's current assignment, beginning with early works like *Pickwick Papers*, *Oliver Twist*, and *Martin Chuzzlewitt*, became my most enthralling preoccupation. *Dombey and Son*, *David*

Copperfield, *Hard Times*, *Great Expectations*, and *Our Mutual Friend* soon followed, all but *Bleak House*—the undergraduates had all read it in school. It was an education in itself, another England from the world around me, and I feasted on these books with an unappeasable hunger, a warm rush of discovery. It expanded the compass of fiction writing as I knew it.

Soon after Leavis's stirring encounter with *Little Dorrit* he repeated the feat in public on an unlikely subject, reading a paper on Tolstoy's *Anna Karenina* before Cambridge's Slavonic Society. Again he needed a point of departure from which to engage the book, some comparison that would set it off. He tried working from Matthew Arnold's late essay on Tolstoy's novel but came up short, as he had stumbled at first with *Little Dorrit*. Oriented toward poetry, Arnold had rarely written about prose fiction. His approach was dated, simply not consequential enough to serve as a foil, let alone any kind of critical guide. Leavis moved on to some jeering comments by D. H. Lawrence on Anna's adultery with Vronsky but this too went nowhere. Finally he fixed on an unlikely comparison between Tolstoy's subtle treatment of marriage and the embattled real-life marriage of Lawrence and his wife, Frieda, a Prussian aristocrat who was prone to breaking dishes over his head when they fought, which was nearly all the time. Here was Leavis, touchingly protective of Lawrence, a man already dead more than thirty years, yet using the writer's mundane conflicts, along with his flippant jibes, to bring out Tolstoy's delicate insight, which the Russian himself could not bring to bear on his own tempestuous marriage.

The whole lecture was unexpected since Leavis, who approached novels as he approached poetry, through their language, had virtually never engaged with a translated work. I was surprised the old man would extend himself this far, setting aside the pet peeves and personal rancor that often diverted his attention. He told our Tuesday group that his wife had encouraged him. "Oh, go ahead and do it," she said bluntly. "You've read the book." That was the difference between them, according to him. "If she's read the book, she wouldn't hesitate to do it." Feigning diffidence, he appealed to a more exacting standard, a wary critical restraint; the contrast between them became clear only later, when I met her.

My film year and my Dickens year was also turning into my Leavis year as I bought all his earlier books, just out in new Penguin editions, and threw myself into the writers he'd singled out, especially Conrad, James, and Lawrence. I was particularly taken with the brilliant social comedy of a neglected James novella to which Leavis had devoted a shrewd essay, *The Europeans*. Here, instead of Americans in Europe, James portrays Europeanized Americans in stodgy New England, with a gossamer touch reminiscent of Jane Austen yet also an underlying moral gravity that looks ahead to Edith Wharton. I was engrossed by the way James (and Leavis) worked out these relationships, highlighting the subtle ways the characters reflected the culture—in this case, New England—from which they took their values.

In the end I learned much of value from Leavis, a critic whose slash-and-burn attack I had at first resisted. For him the moral import of a work was not simply an idea, the striking of an attitude, certainly not any kind of preaching or message, but something fully realized in form and language. Unlike most academics, whose criticism was a catchall of a writer's themes, Leavis could be brutally selective and discriminating. The importance he gave to literary judgment, his almost missionary seriousness, appealed to me enormously, though it sidelined more playful comic novelists from Fielding and Sterne to Thackeray. Their work, as he saw it, lacked the moral weight and formal control he found in Jane Austen, George Eliot, and Henry James. Time vindicated his choices; his main line of English fiction holds up well. My Jewish moral education, reinforced by working with Trilling and his colleagues at Columbia, drew me strongly to the same writers. It was a pity that Leavis's fine sensibility closed down after his appreciation of T. S. Eliot and Lawrence; he had virtually nothing good to say about the writers who followed them, let alone any of our contemporaries.

Much has been made of a puritan strain in both Leavis and Lawrence. There was no way I could idolize Lawrence as Leavis did, but his book pointed to what was best in the writer—not *Lady Chatterley's Lover*, though it certainly struck a mighty blow for sexual frankness and tenderness, not his preachy and mythmaking later books, with their invocation of the dark gods, not even the delicately autobiographical but conventional *Sons and Lovers*, but *The Rainbow*, especially, and *Women in Love*; his extraordinary short stories and novellas; and his wonderfully sharp, opinionated critical writings. Some of these I wouldn't fully appreciate till I taught a course on

Lawrence a decade later, at the height of feminism, when his work became a battleground. But already Lawrence, along with Kafka, spoke to me most personally of all the modern writers, partly because of the deeply implanted repressions of my upbringing, when sex was such a taboo subject. In the late 1950s, long after his death, Lawrence helped shatter those cultural taboos, not only by his explicit treatment of sex but by the personal intensity of his work, his harsh demands on his characters and his readers. And Lawrence's cruel, capricious intelligence seemed as liberating as his sexual gospel, while his peripatetic life and prickly personality made him as fascinating to read about as to read.

The same could be said about Conrad's restless life and mind, though his wanderings on sea and land came well before his literary career. His Polish upbringing, his adventurous career as a seaman, made him the most worldly and traveled of English writers. But as I read his books and stories I balked at Leavis's promotion of late, ironic works like *The Secret Agent*. I much preferred the lush sensory language, exotic milieu, and metaphysical quest of *The Nigger of the "Narcissus," Lord Jim*, and *Nostromo*, as well as novellas like *Heart of Darkness*, *Typhoon*, and *The Secret Sharer*. The prose alone of these short novels, along with their lofty themes, had inflamed me as a college freshman. Intellectually, I was still a child of fifties existentialism. Conrad's Melvillean brooding about questions of honor, courage, and moral responsibility, his willingness to confront some ultimate nullity at the heart of human existence, set my late adolescent mind on fire. Even more than Melville he turned the adventure story into a richly elaborated interior journey. For a time I was taken with the idea of writing my thesis on him, looking ahead to the sheer pleasure of reading and rereading his work, at least until I explored the university library and saw how much had already been done—only a fraction of the criticism that would later appear. I also balked at the politics of later books like *The Secret Agent* and *Under Western Eyes*, with their caricatures of radicals and anarchists as clumsy, self-defeating terrorists and double agents. Conrad's Polish background, including his father's romantic nationalism, and his passionate love of English life seemed to have left him with a terrific fear of change and an all-consuming investment in the established order. This fear and resistance would never work for me.

I got only an occasional look at conservative, class-bound England while

I was there, but that sampling was hard to forget. At Frank S.'s rooms for drinks one afternoon I had a pleasant chat with a lively, cultivated young man, then ran into him again next morning as we both waited for the London train. It took me a while to realize that his plummy accent, clipped articulation, and air of privilege were not simply an English manner but were easily read as distinctly upper class. As he spoke of jaunts around the Continent and compared skiing in Gstaad with other Alpine sites, a working-class youth standing nearby began making satiric faces and faintly mocking sounds, as if jeering at one ludicrous performance. I grew more and more uncomfortable, caught in a crossfire between a twit and a hooligan, and would have dearly loved to move away, but my preening new acquaintance simply carried on. He was either oblivious to the young man's reaction or else delighted to be provoking him. I caught his sense that the kid was simply a nonperson, completely beneath his notice, the way someone might undress before a servant. The surprising thing, hard to explain, was how ill at ease I became, shrinking back as if, simply by talking to him, I felt implicated in these class attitudes. This vague sense of guilt, proverbially Jewish, brought to mind my futile struggles with the college servants over their small but demeaning chores. I couldn't imagine how I would ever fit in or feel remotely comfortable in such a class-bound world, even installed in a privileged position.

Cambridge had stirred up conflicts I didn't know I felt. Some self-tormenting side of me came to the surface, and I was at sea about how to loosen its grip. Returning from New York, I tried to arrange for psychotherapy, first in London through the respected Tavistock Clinic, then, when that didn't work out, with a doctor in Cambridge who was part of the National Health Service. I saw him a few times but he showed little interest and even less insight into what I was telling him. His solution was mild tranquilizers for the psyche, antacids (if necessary) for the tummy, and, basically, a stiff upper lip. The rumor of talk therapy had not yet reached him—or if it had, he dismissed it. This was too English for me. Freud had found refuge in England but the culture of psychoanalysis had as yet made few inroads into British psychiatry. I did some digging and soon found the only Freudian analyst in Cambridge, Dr. B. B. Zeitlyn, who I guessed was a Jew (true), perhaps Viennese to boot (not in the least). After an initial consult he managed to schedule me for one session a week. Thus began a saving turn in my British adventure.

As a therapist Dr. Z. was anything but the classical Freudian blank screen, the neutral canvas on which to project one's feelings and fantasies. A large, bespectacled, balding man in his early forties, not at all taciturn, he was bitingly open and direct in a way I had yet to encounter with anyone in England. He had a quicker, sharper mind than my previous therapist, and he warmly agreed with my preference for talk over any drug regimen. He encouraged me to speak about the relationships that had formed me, however far back, and to imagine how they might still affect my life. Why had I grown so anxious in cozy Cambridge? Dr. Z. soon prodded me to some speculative conclusions. My mother, though reckless with her own health, had fretted over me since childhood, warning me repeatedly that the world was a dangerous place. She had actually come from a dangerous place, a Ukrainian shtetl in an unsettled time, during the civil war that followed the Russian revolution. She had childhood memories of murderous pogroms in the years just before she left. Away from her sheltering anxiety, I had created a built-in mother to fuss over me, to monitor what I ate and what I wore, to worry about imagined threats and dire consequences. "It shouldn't develop," she would say if I caught a cold, which meant it might *well* develop, into God knows what. All this was at once foolish and obvious, unseemly for a grown man, but this did not mean I could easily relax its grip on me. If I could come to understand it, really take it in, that might prove to be a first step.

If I accepted this take on my predicament as novel and astute, on other points I fought the good doctor to a draw. Since I was no longer much of a believer, and he was for sure devoutly secular, he saw no rational sense in my leftover religious observance, especially the adamant need to keep kosher. Away from home it put me to all sorts of inconveniences. Clearly, he wanted me to see it as an atavistic remnant, an inert unwillingness to stand up to my father, or break with my past, perhaps even a kind of cowardice. Much of this was said not directly—that would have been against the rules—but through the pressure he put on how I justified myself. His tone was skeptical, even sarcastic, yet the more he challenged me, the more I resisted. He wanted me to strike out on my own course. But I had little desire to break sharply with my parents' way of life or with the Jewish world in which I'd been a cosseted young star when I was growing up. These attachments still meant the world to me, even if I couldn't fully say why. As a freethinking intelligence yet a child of the ghetto, a vagrant offshoot of a venerable tradition, I would either learn to live with contradictions or perish under their weight. Still, as Freud had reasoned, just talking about these conflicts made it easier for me to live with them.

With an exchange rate heavily weighted in my favor, I was buying secondhand hardcover books and cheap new Penguins by the armful, abuzz with all the reading I was doing. I managed to explore Dickens with Leavis and Newton, write about movies as a growing passion, send letters to L that were full of love and sexual longing, but also run off to services to make a minyan when I was needed. Turning twenty-four in February left me momentarily depressed, as if old age were just around the corner. I had the feeling that my life was slipping inexorably through an hourglass. Yet in early March I read my bar mitzvah portion aloud in the makeshift synagogue with a purr of satisfaction. "I chanted like an angel," I wrote to L, "and was a great hit, not least (as you can see) with myself." It would have been hard to separate this ego stroking from my undying love of those Hebrew melodies. I was showing off, preening, but also felt warmed to a glow by reenacting these familiar rituals in an unfamiliar setting.

A day or two later I went off to London with Richard to hear one of our idols, François Truffaut, talk about his films at the British Film Institute. He showed excerpts from his feature films along with a recent short called "Antoine and Colette," from *Love at Twenty*, a delightful resumption of the autobiographical Antoine Doinel saga he had begun with *The 400 Blows*. He looked surprisingly like his on-camera surrogate, Jean-Pierre Léaud, who had stood in for his younger self in those films. His talk was restrained, bland, not very forthcoming. I was new to the defenses artists built up around their work, the unease they felt in commenting on its meaning or their intentions. Before the discussion ended I stood up and asked whether he would expand upon his view of Catherine, the enigmatic femme fatale incarnated by Jeanne Moreau in *Jules and Jim*. L and I had seen this movie again and again, spellbound by this woman who loves and is loved by two men who are close friends. In his response he opened up for the first time, talked about the source novel as the autobiographical work of a sixty-seven-year-old man, Henri-Pierre Roché, summing up the mystery and allure not simply of women he had known but of womanhood itself. It was a revealing reply, not only about the film but about Truffaut himself, his reverence for an older generation, his own womanizing, his ingenuity and fidelity as an adapter, using an evocative narration to convey the rhythm and feeling of the original novel. But later I wondered how I'd had the nerve to stand up before a large audience to question a film director I so admired. Evidently, the anxieties that set me spinning coexisted with a confidence bordering on arrogance.

Hearing Truffaut and seeing his work again made me long for Paris, where I planned to spend some of the Easter break. I thought I'd go from there to Milan, Florence, Rome, perhaps even as far as Sicily, re-creating some of my trip with Sam nearly three years before. "That's too much of an itinerary, I know," I wrote to L. "I may never get beyond Paris," which was precisely what happened. I fell in love with the city all over again, in part because it was so *not* England. What appealed to me in England I already knew: the centuries-old architecture, the endlessly resourceful theater scene, the unbroken literary tradition, the wry, understated humor, the echoing sense of the past. I saw these things in the uplifting lines of King's College Chapel, in the stellar productions at Olivier's new National Theatre, in the moral urgency of Leavis's criticism. In Paris I encountered—or constructed—something utterly different, a world that valued pleasure, intellect, fine art, and beauty in ways the English seemed incapable of doing. Much of this was sheer projection since I engaged the French so superficially, but it was just the elixir I needed as an antidote to my English experience, the saving parenthesis within this troubled year.

The first good omen was the Channel crossing, as calm and clear as my crossing three years earlier had been tempestuous, foggy, and vertigo-inducing. On the train to Paris I was shocked that everyone, even the children, was perversely speaking a foreign language, rapidly, colloquially, as if they'd hatched a conspiracy to make me feel excluded. Gradually my ear began picking out phrases I understood, though they bore little resemblance to the schoolroom French I'd once learned. In Paris I went to a Left Bank hotel someone had recommended, didn't like it, went to another that had no rooms, then finally back to the place on the Place de la Sorbonne where Sam and I had stayed in 1961. They had only an attic room, a genuine bohemian garret on the seventh floor, reached with some difficulty by a combination of elevators, hallways, and steep flights of stairs. The bed itself—narrow, lumpy—was under the eaves and I could stand up straight only in half the room, but it was cheap, six and a half francs (about $1.30) a night. Summoning up my French I asked whether they didn't perhaps have "une chambre un peu plus chère," but that was all they had, and I grabbed it. To my great surprise, this became my rabbit warren for the next month—or should I say my eagle's nest, since the one narrow window looked out on many rooftops and chimneys.

Passover was coming and I wondered how I'd manage the holiday, especially the trick of finding food I would allow myself to eat. I couldn't imagine that matzoh was a French staple but Paris was a more Jewish city than I imagined. Even outside the Marais, Paris's Lower East Side, Sephardic, observant Jews had been streaming in from North Africa, feeling threatened by the surge of militant Arab nationalism. I was in the heart of the Latin Quarter, just a stone's throw from the Sorbonne. There were student restaurants, including the Foyer Israélite, where the kosher menu, albeit extremely limited, was just what I needed, though far from what this gastronomic city had to offer. I could snag a filling meal for about seventy cents while keeping my religious scruples intact. Geoffrey Hartman, whose friendship had helped me through my first year at Yale, was in town with his gracious wife, Renée, whom I first met when I'd shown them around Cambridge a month or two earlier. Living in Paris for a few months, they invited me to dinner, knowing well what I could eat and couldn't, and I asked them back to a little Russian restaurant off the Place de la Sorbonne where I ate frequently. I prized the borscht, which must have reminded me of Jewish cooking; Geoffrey, who had a finer palate, thought it tasted like a decent vegetable soup. About how and what to eat, certainly, I saw again I had a lot to learn.

GEOFFREY WAS a comparatist, as comfortable in French and German as in English literature, and he was just then finishing the book on Wordsworth that would make his reputation. Both Geoffrey and Renée had narrowly survived the Holocaust, she in Bergen-Belsen with her younger sister, then as a foster child in New Haven after the war, he as part of a *Kindertransport* that took him to England, where he was separated from his mother until the war ended. Both had slight but colorful Central European accents. At home and at ease in Europe, they seemed very worldly to me. Besides cuisine I had a good deal to learn from him about literary criticism, one of his specialties. In the intellectual hothouse at Columbia the overwhelming emphasis was on themes and ideas. My Yale classes, colored by the New Criticism, had focused more strictly on forms and techniques. But Roberto, my Brazilian friend at Yale, had also introduced me to the unorthodox Marxist criticism of Lukács, Adorno, and the Frankfurt school, and I marveled at their dia-lectical ingenuity and their way of embedding literature in social history. This work was still largely unknown in the States but newly available in French, which I could read much more easily than the original, with my halting German.

Geoffrey directed me in yet another direction, toward the pheno-menological criticism of idiosyncratic men of letters like Maurice Blanchot and Gaston Bachelard. Along with younger scholars such as Georges Poulet and Jean Starobinski, they were not simply critics but dazzling essayists in their own right. Instead of analyzing discrete poems and novels the way more formal critics did, they took the whole body of a writer's work as a unit, dismantling and reassembling it to locate its angle of vision. They looked for the particular lens that colored the way the writer perceived the world. This seemed at once alien and absorbing, and I began buying critical works in French at a frantic clip, including all of Roland Barthes's books to date, Benjamin's selected essays, only one of which had come out in English, Lukács's once-suppressed early books, such as his seminal *Theory of the Novel* and *History and Class Consciousness*, and Blanchot's 1949 collection of essays, *La Part du feu*, which I liked so much I set about translating its brilliant opening essay on Kafka into English. I didn't always get as far as I hoped into these books—their abstractions often eluded me—but they showed me a world elsewhere, a less empirical, more speculative criticism closely allied to philosophy and psychology. Cheaper editions of their work I mailed to friends at home as if to announce my new discoveries.

My month in Paris, like the whole year in England, was one long immersion in the arts. The city was bursting with museums, films, plays, and concerts. Though I had little money with me, barely a hundred dollars that needed to last the full month, I gorged myself on art and performance, taking advantage of cheap student tickets and free admissions. (A "student" in Paris then could be anyone under sixty with an ID card.) At the venerable Comédie Française the actors performed Molière's *Tartuffe* in a staging so fusty they took bows after major speeches, like opera divas. I snapped up cheap seats at the Opéra to see Berlioz's *Damnation of Faust* and at the Opéra Comique for Mozart's *Figaro*, and took in many newish movies, from Godard's *Contempt* and Bergman's *Silence* to Buñuel's *Viridiana* and *Diary of a Chambermaid*. Though Cambridge was a splendid film town, Paris was incomparable, especially just then, with dozens of tiny theaters showing old movies. It was the heyday of the Hitchcocko-Hawksians, as they called themselves at the *Cahiers du Cinéma*. Where else could I have seen Howard Hawks's heroic *Sergeant York*, with Gary Cooper doing a patriotic turn, or Nicholas Ray's *Party Girl*, a *Cahiers* favorite, both of them long out of circulation back home? They were no masterpieces—they'd been forgotten for good reason—but well worth a look, especially with good French subtitles.

Painting added another cubit to my ongoing education. As I had been overwhelmed by the Turners and Constables in London, I fell upon the paintings of Georges de La Tour at the Louvre, with their mysterious pools of light at the center of a contemplative scene of darkness and shadows. They reminded me more of the chiaroscuro of noir cinematography than of any paintings except Rembrandt's, and they radiated a spiritual glow I could not explain. Meanwhile, as in one of those casually eventful New Wave films I was seeing, I met a woman, I'll call her Irene, whose company I enjoyed especially at museums and over modest student dinners. I was too loyal to L—or too shy or guilty-feeling—to sleep with her, though we made out like sweaty teenagers a few times. Paris, with its fabled aura of romance, was a bad place to be alone, but this was more a flirtation and a lark than a relationship. I was attracted to Irene and really liked spending time with her. L and I had told each other before I left that we were free, but our separation, our many letters, had bolstered our feeling for each other, or so I hoped.

My old teacher Jacob Taubes had been separated from his wife, Susan, and she was living in Paris. Richard, who had taken courses with both of them, urged me to look her up, though we had never really met. Still, I always felt freer, more forward in foreign cities, unhampered by social inhibitions that would have held me back at home. I had idealized their marriage as the perfect union of two smart, beautiful people with two attractive children, and when I called her she invited me to visit. The dark, heavy furniture in her apartment seemed to match her sad, pensive mood. Columbia, unlike colleges in isolated towns, offered little social contact between students and faculty, but Richard had gotten to know her, as he'd gotten to know her close friend Susan Sontag, Jacob's brilliant protégée. I didn't know whether I was paying a call as a friend of a friend or an admiring student of her husband, but whatever it was I soon began pouring out my tale—the world I came from, my Columbia experience, my unhappy year in England, the woman I had carelessly left behind. As we spoke, she seemed to grow more fragile and iridescent, almost an apparition, yet I left with a sense of having made real contact. Her dark, reddish hair, pale skin, and plaintive air haunted me. I would think about this day with a sense of desolation five years later as I listened to an eloquent eulogy by a Harvard dean and hugged Jacob at her funeral. She had walked into the ocean off Long Island the same week she published an autobiographical novel about their lives together called *Divorcing*.

Seeing Susan Taubes living alone on the Left Bank only added to my uncertainties about marriage. She and her husband had been more like mythic constructs than real people to me, and I was stunned to see their marriage fail, although I knew nothing of the circumstances and could not ask. There had never been a divorce in my extended family, though there were couples who lived together in a state of permanent hostility. My loneliness in Cambridge made me long to be with someone, with L especially, but still I remained wary of any binding attachment and threw myself into activity to keep my indecision at bay. My last week in Paris was busier than ever. I reported to L with excitement that I'd seen my first Wagner at the Opéra (*Tannhäuser*), heard three Mozart piano concertos, and gone to my first concert of atonal music, in which works by Arnold Schoenberg and Anton Webern were played off against Claude Debussy and Charles Ives, all pieces I was hearing for the first time. I was at the age when life was full of discoveries, when every new thing seemed fresh and exhilarating, even time-worn novelties decades or centuries old. Western culture lay before me like a banquet, and I made little distinction between tradition and the new.

French university classes had begun again. I haphazardly sampled some courses in English and American literature, which proved to be deadly, at least two generations behind the curve. At a class on Jane Austen I heard one student report on doing a quantitative study of the most commonly used words in one of her novels, which turned out—no surprise—to be "a" and "the." No conclusions were drawn. Academe, the Sorbonne, had spoken, and it had nothing to say. As a few amused students, laughing in the balcony, tried cutting out, the instructor began screeching at them, "*Partez! Partez avec vos camarades.*" I took this diversion as a cover for slipping out quietly, but as I headed for the exit my *strapontin*, a hinged wooden seat, snapped back up with a tremendous crash and I ran up the Rue de l'Ecole de Médecine as if pursued by a bear. So much for academic life in Paris.

I was completely out of funds as I left for England but still managed to buy one last book I'd been coveting, the compact two-volume Pléiade edition of Molière's plays. This required a small loan from Irene, which really became a parting gift since to this day I can't recall ever paying her back. This time I bounded across the Channel in a low-flying aircraft, the *Flèche d'argent*, a neat rail and air connection, rather than trusting to one of the rocking steamers. But a few days in London depressed me all over again. "London is hateful, the weather miserable," I wrote to L, discovering that I was much more at home in Paris. Seeing a production of Edward Albee's *Who's Afraid of Virginia Woolf*, which had been a big hit in New York, dispirited me even more. The incessant rancor between the characters added up to one of the most sour portraits of a marriage that I had ever encountered, though in the end the couple stays together. Still, marriage was in the air. Back in Cambridge, Peter Winn and I threw a little champagne party for Richard, who had gotten engaged to his American girlfriend, Sonja, over the Easter break.

Soon the weather improved, and so did the mental weather as L and I began planning our summer together in Europe. She made the mistake of telling my parents she was going to meet me, and this inspired letter after letter from my mother urging me to come home after the semester ended. May in Cambridge unexpectedly turned out to be a beautiful month, with the only good weather we'd had all year, and I spent much of it reading in the Clare garden, where everything was in bloom and the carpet of grass had remained thick and green all through the winter, thanks to the never-ending slow drizzle. I began to feel I had pissed away my time abroad, enjoying myself, tormenting myself, reading up a storm but making little academic progress.

I had come to Cambridge to develop a thesis topic and now I had only five weeks left to do so. I got a whiff of the odor of failure, the sense of being at a dead end. The politics of Victorian fiction slipped to the back burner as I realized, after reading George Eliot, Dickens, and Benjamin Disraeli, how massive and elusive the topic would be. I eagerly consumed Walter Jackson Bate's new biography of Keats, the poet who had lit up my senior year in college, but as with Conrad I wondered whether I had something new to add. Instead, I zeroed in on Thomas Carlyle, the half-forgotten Victorian sage, once touted as a model of style but now largely out of fashion for his dyspeptic temperament, his baroque Germanic eccentricities, his faith in heroes and hero worship, as well as his putative kinship with fascism. He had ended his life as a Prussian-style reactionary, writing a multivolume biography of Frederick the Great and attacking the progressive Reform Bill of 1867, which widened suffrage, in the most apocalyptic terms. But his earlier work, from an essay called "Signs of the Times" to his book *Past and Present*, had appealed to radical thinkers from Marx and Engels to my own supervisor, Raymond Williams, who had devoted a sympathetic chapter to him in his *Culture and Society*. Working with Williams closely for the first time all year, I sketched plans for a thesis that would focus on Carlyle's influence on other Victorian social critics, all deeply indebted to him, especially John Ruskin and Matthew Arnold. They were conservative radicals, humanist critics of the new industrial order, of a peculiar stripe that distinguished them from both left and right. With this worked out I could return to Yale with a plan of action and a virtuous sense of having ended the year on a constructive note, finding a path forward. But what mattered more were all the seemingly irrelevant things I'd read and written and seen all year, the people I'd met, the emotional quandaries that had beset me, the education I had waywardly pursued.

The Leavis sessions had not continued into the spring term but Leavis wanted to round off the year and wish his charges well for their upcoming exams. A natural teacher, he obviously cherished his informal work with Clare students. It cushioned his retirement, perhaps made him feel less neglected. He invited them to tea at his home on a Sunday afternoon for a small gathering. As an auditor I was not formally invited, in fact not invited at all, but Richard convinced me that as a regular participant in the group I should come along. Since this would likely be my last encounter with him, I couldn't pass it up. At the door Leavis greeted me with elaborate courtesy, perhaps signaling that I'd made a grave faux pas simply by showing up, but I was American and couldn't be expected to have proper manners.

As the four or five of us sat around the parlor a little seminar evolved, with Mrs. Leavis—Queenie, as everyone referred to her—forcefully in charge. A thin woman with graying dark hair and hawklike features, she had her own real achievements more as a scholar than a critic. Her doctoral thesis, published in 1932 as *Fiction and the Reading Public*, was a piece of literary sociology that served as one of the founding texts for the *Scrutiny* group, and she had contributed many articles to the magazine itself, notably a pioneering sequence of essays that reconstructed the intricate steps of Jane Austen's literary career. But though she had done some supervisions at one of the women's colleges, Cambridge, a male bastion then, had made little use of her gifts, and her resentment at being disregarded was rumored to be even stronger than her husband's. Indeed, it was he who often spoke about it on her behalf. Without doubt it was an egregious example, typical of the times, of an accomplished woman forced to take a backseat to her husband's career.

It soon became obvious that she had no reluctance to broadcast her sweeping, self-assured literary opinions. Disconcertingly, she had the habit of speaking for both of them, sometimes turning to him for confirmation as he sat back and gravely smiled or nodded. Her way of holding forth was clearly nothing new to him and he'd developed a form of passive but sibylline acquiescence that could be read in different ways. With Americans in the room, she looked around for something provocative to say. The con-

versation turned to *The Great Gatsby*. It was not yet the inescapable classic
it later became; I had read it only a few months earlier among the raft of
Penguins I'd devoured. She had no use for the book and came out with both
guns blazing. Gatsby was a sham, she pronounced, and there was nothing about him to be admired. "As far as *we're* concerned," she said with
finality, "Gatsby is just a thug, *just a thug*," repeating her words for special
emphasis. This was catnip to me and I tried fumblingly to defend the book,
but I couldn't get my head around this kind of indictment, which seemed
more personal, more ad hominem than literary. The moral dimension in
criticism meant much to me, but this sounded almost comically moralistic
and obtuse. The book was ravishingly nebulous to me, and I felt inept in
making a case for it. Gatsby, after all, is an elusive and mysterious figure,
surrounded by just the romantic aura she was trying to dispel. It would
take two or three more readings for me to grasp his shadowy presence in
the book, which I eventually came to love as a finely wrought work of prose
poetry, not strictly as a novel.

The conversation turned somehow to Ludwig Wittgenstein. We were
surprised to learn that he and Leavis had been quite close as young men
in Cambridge more than three decades earlier. I would never have thought
of connecting them, though Leavis had mentioned his name once or twice.
Leavis had long ago written a stern polemical essay, one of his best, dis-
tinguishing literature and criticism from philosophy, the former holistic
and experiential, the latter abstract, conceptual. But Wittgenstein too was
a critic of philosophy as it was usually practiced, and both he and Leavis
became known for their minute, sensitive attention to language. Mrs. Leavis, however, took a far more personal tack. She began telling stories of
his strange behavior, how he frightened, even terrified some of his friends.
Soon he became another Gatsby, a man outside the pale, a freakish oddity,
not really one of us. "As far as *we* could tell, he was mad, simply *mad*." She
turned to Leavis for confirmation: "Isn't that so, dear?" As usual he gave
just the slightest nod, but this time it didn't carry enough conviction and
she insisted. "Isn't that *so*, dear?" Cornered, he paused a moment and then
said something that defined him for me. "Well, to say that he was sane
would certainly be a false emphasis." "Just so, just so," she said with a satisfied look, as if he had merely agreed with her. It was a fascinating glimpse

into the dynamics of their marriage. Much later I was surprised to learn that as Queenie Roth she was from a Jewish family that had objected to the match and written her off. She never spoke to her parents again.

Leavis was a pioneer in the close attention to the text, an approach we identify with the New Criticism, but in certain key essays he also pursued a social approach to literature. Though we now consider this recourse to history essential, his work is completely out of fashion today. His Bloomsbury antagonists made a great comeback, some of it altogether justified, some of it mere gossip about unconventional modern lives. Leavis's reputation was overtaken by waves of Continental theory, by the revival of historical criticism, and by postmodernism. His unexpected foray into *Anna Karenina* did not make him seem any less insular and English. His remark about Wittgenstein was no more than a wry attempt to placate his demanding spouse even as he satirized her bluntness, a trait he also admired, as when he told us how readily she might have tackled Tolstoy. But his amusing comment was also an implied warning against being glib and reductive, an insistence on precision, and even a modest tribute to silence, very much in the spirit of the famous conclusion of Wittgenstein's *Tractatus: Wovon man nicht sprechen kann, darüber muss man schweigen.* I saw that he tended to keep silent about things—ideas, recollections, critical views—until he arrived at precisely the words that fully satisfied him. Then he could repeat them many times over, always with the same gusto. His rigor laid down a challenge. It was no accident that the chattering classes despised him, as he despised them.

L WAS PLANNING to come first to Cambridge; from there we would begin our summer travels. When her charter flight was canceled—no surprise there—she had to ask for two hundred dollars from her parents to book a regular flight—a difficult proposition. Though comfortably well off, they had never been very generous with either money or praise. They complained repeatedly about her tuition bills at Barnard, after urging her to go to secretarial school instead. Now they made her wait and wait for the money. As the date of her arrival approached, I went though a cycle of elation and apprehension. Where were we as a couple after not seeing each other for five months? I had written her many letters laying bare my mood swings, spasms of depression and moments of exhilaration, my exchanges with my therapist. I had been completely open, self-lacerating to a fault, yet somehow had not pushed her away. She kept me posted on everything she felt and everyone we knew, especially their complicated love affairs, one or two of them resembling the triangle in our favorite movie, *Jules and Jim*.

I later discovered that she too had met someone else and seriously thought of not coming, someone who turned bitter when she decided to go. Perhaps she was losing hope for us as a couple, losing patience with my indecision. I had a foolish confidence that things would work out, yet I was completely unable to think beyond the summer. Just as I'd planned for my Easter break, I made some highly unrealistic plans for where we might travel. We would go to Wales, where she had some family; Stratford, to see the plays; the Lake District, where my beloved poets had tramped the hills; the fabled Scottish Highlands. Meanwhile, I luxuriated in the beautiful May weather as the undergraduates crammed for their exams.

L's arrival was set for the second day of June 1964. A day earlier the May sun disappeared, and England reverted to familiar weather, cold, gray, and rainy. The temperature was in the low forties when I met her at the airport. We had been apart so long she seemed like a figure from another world but I couldn't have been more pleased to see her. Eager to show her around, I blithely suggested we do some touring in London since she had never been to Europe. She dismissed this with a pained laugh. Exhausted from the overnight flight, she preferred to go directly to Cambridge to get some much-needed sleep.

Under the college's strict rules, she was allowed to set foot in my rooms only in daytime, so I had found her an inexpensive, slightly depressing room on Jesus Lane, a bit out of the way, in lodgings overseen by a forbidding land-lady. There we would manage to spend very little time, since the grumpy lady warned her darkly against male company. Instead, we made love by day on my hard, unforgiving bed as the months that separated us, the anxieties that bedeviled me, were quickly dissipated. It was not clear where the next months would lead but I felt like a survivor, slightly battered, overjoyed that we were reunited. For a week, until the term ended, I showed her around Cambridge as though it were the loveliest place I had ever lived, and in a sense it really was. She had more feeling for the art and architecture of the colleges than I did, with little need for a guide in hand to tell her what she was seeing. Summoning up some muscle and pluck, I took her punting on the Cam, sinking a long pole into the shallow rover bed to propel the almost rectangular skiff. We went as far as picturesque Grantchester, a village forever associated with the fallen poet Rupert Brooke, who had died of blood poisoning aboard a troopship early in the Great War. Sometimes she borrowed Richard's bicycle and crisscrossed Cambridge on her own. Helping me pack my large metal trunk, now overstuffed, she sat on it while I tried to get it closed. In this way we sealed up my Cambridge year. Despite all my hesitations, I knew in my bones that we belonged together. Two months later, in the south of France, we were engaged.

Nine

THE LONG VOYAGE HOME

I T WAS QUITE another Cambridge, another England with L at my side. We spent that week in Cambridge getting to know each other again, then took off for London, a city that had now grown on me, where I could proudly show her the sights. She was delighted to be abroad for the first time, happy that we were back together, though no more enamored of the country than I had been. The weather remained raw—could this be June?—and she vehemently disliked the cuisine, which renewed my sense of how bad it was. Always alive to her senses, she took deep pleasure in good food, hardly to be searched out then in England, certainly not on the cheap. Staying on a student budget, along with keeping to the dietary laws on which we'd both grown up, made it all the more problematic. Being together, though, and on our own, we hardly cared. We took pleasure in our freedom and in each other's company, as if we had just met.

Showing her through museums brought the art alive for me, and I directed her to my favorites as if I had discovered them: the Turners at the Tate and the National Gallery, the Constables at the Victoria and Albert, the inevitable Elgin Marbles at the British Museum, the efflorescence of American Pop Art at galleries in the East End, where we earnestly debated whether a sink attached to a wall or a bed covered with paint was still a sink or a bed, or was it Art? It depended, I said, on whether you could actually get water out of the tap. What did it mean to put a frame around it, or even simply to exhibit it? Pop Art, we decided, was more attractive conceptually than visually, since it stimulated just this kind of earnest exchange. I missed the vivid, splashy fun of it, little realizing that pop culture would soon be the sea in which we'd all be swimming. The East End was still something of a Jewish neighborhood, as scruffy as the Marais in Paris or the Lower East Side of my New York childhood, so we continued the conversation over a delicatessen lunch, sampling the British equivalent of New York corned beef.

We set off to Stratford to see the Henry IV cycle, with an electrifying young actor named Ian Holm playing young Hal and Henry V in the last three plays. Exuding physical energy but also biting intelligence, he stole the plays from the incomparable Falstaff and his riotous crew, no mean feat. For years these performances would remain my gold standard for Shakespeare production. I had already seen a great deal of Shakespeare at home, much of it in ragtag productions that exaggerated the comedy into farce and defaulted on the poetry. Americans rarely knew how to speak Shakespeare's lines as natural speech, poetically cadenced yet sounding spontaneous, even intimate. My countrymen recited the verse as if it were a foreign language, rarely knowing how to thrust the weight of their bodies and the jolt of real emotions into it. British actors, with their love of impersonation, seem to have been schooled in poetic speech and Elizabethan diction from a tender age. It simply rolled off their tongues, as if they were still embedded in that early culture.

L's aunt Selma, her father's only sister, lived in South Wales, and we geared up for a visit by checking most of our belongings at a London railway station. We were determined to travel light, to see as much of Wales as we could. Selma and her husband, Jack, along with their young son, Claude, had escaped from Germany with L's widowed grandmother at the last possible moment, in August 1939. The old woman's furniture and personal effects followed on a separate boat. When the war broke out it returned to Germany, leaving her with little more than the clothes on her back. The family was admitted because Jack was bringing equipment to set up a factory, and they were sent off to a town near Cardiff targeted for industrial development. This had been a major coal-producing region but the mines were now exhausted; all that remained were small mountains of black and gray slag that pockmarked the landscape—D. H. Lawrence territory, or so it seemed to my literary mind. L's father had come to see his mother just once, in 1950, a few years before she died, and her five grown children had bickered endlessly about supporting her. L, to her regret, had never met her grandmother at all.

Selma, a strong-minded woman, showed us around, took us to swim at her favorite pool, but, not surprisingly, wouldn't let us sleep in the same room. "I don't care what you do elsewhere," she said, "but not in my house." Very little of L's family had escaped the Holocaust. Her mother's parents had first gone into an old-age home, assuming the Nazis would leave the elderly alone. When this proved optimistic, they bought their way into Theresienstadt, which masqueraded as a "model" camp but for many was little more than a way station to the camps in the East, or a place to die of malnutrition and disease rather than Zyklon B. L's grandfather, older and ailing, died within the year. His wife survived for several years before being sent off to the death factory at Auschwitz in 1944 on one of the last transports.

L's uncle Ludwig, the oldest of four brothers and the most stiffly religious, had been deported to the Riga ghetto before being shunted around to half a dozen concentration camps, where he managed to keep kosher and never lost track of the holy days on the Jewish calendar. He somehow escaped a death march from Buchenwald that finished off many of the remaining prisoners. His wife and three young children, one of whom looked remarkably like L, had been shot in a mass killing soon after their deportation. Selma and her family were among L's few living blood relations; the fate of those left behind and killed had haunted L's childhood. This legacy of grief, guilt, and loss was new to me, since my family had all arrived in America in the early 1920s, just before the immigration pipeline was shut off. We liked Selma and Jack, both of them welcoming and convivial, and it was a pleasure to find stray family in a remote corner of the world where history had deposited them.

Once we realized that it would be too ambitious to tour the Lake District, let alone Scotland, we decided to spend our remaining time in Britain crisscrossing Wales. We must have looked like perfect innocents, for it proved surprisingly easy for us to hitch rides. So we made our way north with the goal of reaching Caernarvon Castle, in the northwest corner of Wales, where the heir to the British throne was formally invested as Prince of Wales. No sooner did we leave Cardiff than the landscape began to change, as did the whole social landscape. South Wales was flat, industrial, and entirely English-speaking, essentially a pocket of greater England. In central and northern Wales the grim industrial terrain turned lush and green. The picturesque towns and cities had unpronounceable Celtic names full of consecutive consonants unrelieved by vowels. The towns were situated on beautiful streams crossed by quaint bridges; they were nestled among picture-book hills and mountain scenes. The Welsh mountains and nearby towns reminded me of the green lowlands of the dramatic Swiss landscape that had enchanted me three years earlier. We began hearing much more of the Welsh language without knowing whether it was a deliberate modern revival, like Gaelic in Ireland, or simply the enduring spoken tongue of these rural regions. A new nationalism had begun roiling the supposedly united kingdom, but even in England I was amazed by the differences in regional as well as class accents. I should have known as much from the language games of *My Fair Lady*, evoking Hertford, Hereford, and Hampshire, where hurricanes hardly happen.

Few specific memories remain of these exotically named towns, though we quickly learned the guttural sounds needed to pronounce them: Llangollen, a walker's delight, where they were preparing for an annual singing competition, the Eisteddfod; Llanrwst and the irresistible Betws-y-Coed, the gateway to Snowdonia, an almost Alpine mountain region; Llandudno, from which we took a rickety mountain railway to the summit of Mount Snowdon, one of the tallest peaks in the British Isles. Since we would not make it to the Lake District, Snowdon would have to fill in as our homage to Wordsworth, for it serves as the memorable setting for the last book of his autobiographical poem, *The Prelude*. I didn't see exactly what he saw—he climbed the mountain at night, with the cloudless landscape illuminated by moonlight—but like him I felt up above the world, looking down at a sea of mist in which other peaks floated like humpbacked islands:

> *. . . at my feet*
> *Rested a silent sea of hoary mist.*
> *A hundred hills their dusky backs upheaved*
> *All over this still ocean; and beyond,*
> *Far, far beyond, the solid vapours stretched,*
> *In headlands, tongues, and promontory shapes,*
> *Into the main Atlantic.*

This was at once awesome and terrifyingly inhuman, like what I'd felt near the summit of the Jungfrau. For Wordsworth it appeared as "a fixed, abysmal, gloomy breathing-place" where he heard "the roar of waters, torrents, streams / Innumerable, roaring with one voice!"

Nothing else we saw could quite match the stark sublimity of Snowdon but Richard had urged us to visit Bodnant Gardens, a wonder of horticulture, some eighty acres of formal and more natural gardens in a northern corner of Wales. The sweeping banks of flowers were in their own way almost as impressive as the craggy mountain. Here the British love of gardening was carried out with impeccable taste on a grand scale, as I had already observed in the more modest gardens of the Cambridge colleges. We made it as far as the courtyard of Caernarvon Castle to see where the royal princes were crowned, though this seemingly hallowed custom was little more than a modern invention, perhaps designed to bind rebellious Wales—the Wales of Shakespeare's sonorous blowhard Owen Glendower, whom we had just seen at Stratford—to the British crown.

The other thrill of Wales was more personal: we were traveling as a couple, footloose and carefree in our little adventure far from home. Since we were together all the time, it was also another trial marriage, the intimate tie that had once kept me in a turmoil of indecision. To my surprise we were challenged only once, by a bed-and-breakfast lady in Llangollen. "Would ye be married folks then?" I was slightly abashed to shake my head and say no, but I would have made a poor liar. We were turned away. L had bought a fake wedding band in a variety store for such an occasion but honesty demanded something more. For just that moment the good Jewish boy in me felt we were doing something illicit, living in sin, which made it all the more satisfying.

My sense of adventure might seem hard to credit today, when cheap travel by young people, cohabiting or not, has long been routine. It was less common then, though also far less expensive. At the time, "Europe on five dollars a day," as promised by a popular guidebook, seemed profligate; we regularly managed to live on less. My hardworking parents had pressed me to come home but were footing the bill, though they themselves, after making that one long journey to America, never went anywhere. L was paying her own way with money she had saved from her job as a writer and editor that year, but her parents would have been outraged—and later *were* outraged—to learn that we were in Europe together. She had told them she'd be traveling with a woman friend but might connect with me somewhere along the way. Instead, our two lives were merging unpredictably, often in romantic settings far from everyone we knew.

After Caernarvon we set about to return to London, hoping to head straight for the Continent. After a few short rides we were picked up by a lorry driver who took us all the way from central Wales to London, depositing us at a tube station on the outskirts of the city. Fitting into this vehicle was no small feat since the cab had only one passenger seat. I gallantly insisted on sitting on the gear box, where I could keep the driver from groping my girlfriend—he had encouraged her to sit beside him. The problem turned out to be something else. Our burly benefactor had a thick accent—Hertfordshire or Herefordshire, I thought—and L could not make out a word he said. After a year in England, though, I could pick up perhaps every third word, so I was able to translate. He was piqued by the idea that we were off to France, which inspired rants against the French as pleasure-loving, cheese-eating, wine-drinking, French-speaking people who never did a stitch of work. The appeal of working-class solidarity had not crossed his mind; he saw English workers as thrifty, hardworking, and productive, nothing like their lazy French counterparts. This was not the kind of man I had ever encountered in tony Cambridge but he was adding considerably to my education. Even his accent, so hard to penetrate, taught me something about the diversity of the country, yet also its insularity. Evidently the English Channel was a wider body of water than the map suggested.

Without lingering in London we recovered our belongings and took the train to Gatwick Airport, followed by a twenty-five-minute flight across the treacherous waters of the Channel to Le Touquet, then another train to the Gare du Nord in Paris, the reverse of my trip in April. An unexpected incident marred the last leg of the trip. Something must have spun off a train whizzing by in the opposite direction and it crashed through one of the windows of our car, where two English couples sat facing each other. To my astonishment they stood up, expressed surprise in barely ruffled tones, and began brushing off hundreds of shards of plate glass. "Oh, dear," one of the women said, "what a lot of glass," as if it were but a minor inconvenience, a spot of bother. I thought of the hysteria with which members of my family would have greeted such an untoward event, as if the universe were conspiring against them, as it threatened at times to do. It was the last of many lessons I learned that year about the English, their glacial stoicism and admirable fortitude, so foreign to me. It shed a curious light on my fugitive but insidious anxieties.

Everything about France was a revelation to L: the food, the art, the architecture, the joie de vivre, the sensory magic I'd first encountered three years earlier. The waiters, like everyone else in service positions, were invariably surly, as if they loathed foreigners, detested each other, and found their work demeaning, but the physical settings, though often shabby, radiated storybook charm to an American eye. Like London, Paris had not yet fully emerged from the war. There was as yet no building boom and little renovation or modernization; we might have been in the fabled Paris of an earlier era, the refuge for artists and expatriates of every stripe. The houses and public buildings were still dark with layers of industrial soot. We took a room at the Sélect once more, on the Place de la Sorbonne, where I had spent a happy month in April, a hotel still grungy but ideally situated. By now this was *my* neighborhood, I knew it intimately, though L was aghast at the places where I'd been eating, especially the Foyer Israélite. One modest meal there, knockwurst and beans, was more than enough for her, especially because she was set on breaking out of the culinary ghetto once and for all.

Despite her strictly Orthodox background, or perhaps because of it, L had come to Europe determined to sample everything new and different, including forbidden foods she'd never eaten. I envied her spirit but my mixed feelings kept me from following her; my links to the world I came from were too strong, or else some food taboos were too deeply entrenched in me, as my life in Cambridge had already shown. British food had offered no temptation to L but the French menu was quite another matter. So there we were, having lunch in a café at the foot of Sacré-Coeur. L was staring at a sandwich of *viande froide* as I was staring at her, not saying a word, posing as a completely neutral observer, riveted by the little drama being played out in front of me but trying to appear indifferent, anything but censorious. Though it was served on a baguette with butter and mustard, it looked enough like American cold cuts, but to both of us the difference was enormous. This was one leap I could not yet take, would not take for years afterward. For L it was a river that needed to be crossed if she was ever to feel free of her rule-bound childhood and overbearing German parents. I understood that for her it needed to be crossed without any judgment from me, since I had no wish to be her parents' finger-wagging surrogate, her superego. Having lost the belief system instilled in her as a child, she thought it hypocritical to follow its commandments out of habit or inertia. For me it was still interwoven with a way of life that had nurtured and sustained me, and I could not bear to let it go.

It was no accident that we were in the vicinity of Sacré-Coeur for L had developed a strong attraction to churches and cathedrals, not only for their glorious art and architecture, the complex rose windows and stained glass biblical scenes, saturated with color, but also for the solemn Mass, the rich vestments, the waving censers—everything that appealed directly to the senses. I loved to tease her about this, since the pomp of Catholic ritual felt utterly foreign to me, as did the sound of Latin, then still its lingua franca. The art was another matter; I had long since learned to separate art from belief, to pry it loose from its religious moorings. I'd been exposed to late medieval and early Renaissance art in college but came to grasp it far better through L's attentive eyes. She had been studying sculpture at the New School when I met her and had done some impressive pieces in clay and plaster, graceful figures of male and female nudes, effectively realistic yet touched with abstraction. Her supple fingers could re-create the mold and mass of the human body. Of one of these pieces, a reclining woman with a winglike arm uplifted, her teacher that year, Seymour Lipton, said with tactless enthusiasm, "If you never do another thing it won't matter," a remark she took as the kiss of death. L was ecstatic at seeing so much art in Europe—the rich lode of sculpture at the Musée Rodin, for example—but it didn't soften her tough estimate of her own work.

L taught me to examine sculpture from every angle, as I said earlier: to explore it with my hands whenever I could—a tactile appreciation that even the most lackadaisical museum guards were quick to discourage. L was always trying hard to get *into* what she saw, to get the actual feel of it, with an unfettered curiosity I soon came to admire. Once, in a venerable cathedral, she stole up the circular marble steps to the high lectern to get the cleric's-eye view of the space and the congregation. Spotting her from below, her eyes pointed downward as she turned the pages of some ancient missal, I felt a moment of sheer rapture at a personality so unlike my own, rule-bending, slightly anarchic, endlessly curious. If I didn't yet know how much I loved her, I knew it then. That day in church we inwardly tied the knot, though I did not yet realize it.

After exhausting the museums, the churches, the parks, the neighborhoods, the side trips to Chartres and elsewhere, we left Paris and made our way south toward Nice for a respite from touring, a beachy week of rest and recreation. Dumping our stuff in a cheap hotel room near the train station, we set off for our first look at the Mediterranean. It couldn't be far, I supposed, yet it was nowhere in sight and we had no idea in which direction to walk. Feeling incredibly stupid and American, I buttonholed someone on the street. "*Pardon, monsieur,*" I stuttered, "*mais où est la mer?*" With a look of disgust or disbelief, he pointed the way, and after ten or fifteen blocks we were in another world, a long strip of seaside resorts with posh hotels, stylish cabanas, an azure sea, and a beach unlike any I had ever seen, a narrow strip covered with rocks and pebbles rather than sand. L and I had grown up on opposite sides of the Long Island Sound, not far from the most plebeian beaches imaginable, but they were mostly sandy and inviting. We had gone swimming near Bear Mountain on the first day we met and gone swimming again every chance we could. The beach was part of our story and this beach would add another chapter, though we also took day trips on the coastal rail line to the beaches at Saint-Tropez, made famous by Brigitte Bardot, and Cannes, which boasted the only strip of sand beach we found along the coast, perhaps carted in from somewhere else.

Nice then was less classy than these resorts. Behind the Promenade des Anglais lay a real city, a destination for pensioners and lower middle-class vacationers who also, especially in August, flocked to the innumerable camping grounds that dotted the Côte d'Azur. We also discovered a separate world in the *vieille ville*, the old city of Nice, built into a mountainside overlooking the city and the shore. The streets were sloped and narrow, the restaurants cheaper yet better, and the culture more Italian than French. Though the common language of international tourism was making inroads, many local inhabitants still spoke a Niçois dialect. It brought to mind our puzzled encounters with the Welsh language.

We were led to old Nice by a voluble young man, seemingly gay, wearing the briefest bathing suit I had ever seen. He attached himself to us on the beach, spent the day with us, and joined us for dinner at a very good restaurant he knew in the old town. L, always alert to sexual motives, was sure he had his eye on me but I found that hard to imagine and guessed he was simply starved for company. The Mediterranean sun and all the exposed flesh created a delicious aura of sensuality, especially for us pale northerners. One night, as we lay in bed bleached from the sun but not too tired to make love, I felt possessed with everything I'd ever wanted, and afterward, on a spontaneous impulse, I said, "Why don't we get engaged?" L had long since stopped raising the question of marriage, which meant that I had to raise it, and so I did. Once before I had almost taken the leap but she was in a bad mood and the moment passed. Now I had at last proposed, only by doing an end run around the fraught notion of marriage itself, avoiding the very word. Getting engaged, though, had its inexorable consequences, which she was prepared to contemplate, though later she sometimes recalled I'd never actually asked her to marry me.

The rest of our trip flowed from this moment, since it all became yet another honeymoon, as it had unspokenly been all along. We took the train from Nice to Venice by way of Milan, expecting to stay only a couple of days in each city before moving on to Florence. We never reserved anything in advance, which left us at the mercy of spotters at the railroad stations, mostly old folk who promised to lead us to good hotel rooms. When we arrived in grimy-looking Milan the hour was late; the walk to the hotel, carrying our things, seemed interminable. Surprisingly, there was still a man behind the narrow desk who asked us all sorts of questions. "*Matrimoniale?*" he asked. As in Wales I gritted my teeth and said no. "*Matrimoniale?*" he said again, incredulously, as I shook my head. "*Letto, letto matrimoniale,*" he shouted in exasperation, unable to believe—or accept—that a young couple would willingly turn down a double bed. We were in Milan so briefly we saw little more than the obvious: the overwrought late Gothic of the Duomo, so darkened by weather and pollution it was more black than gray, and Leonardo's *Last Supper*, which lived up to its reproductions.

If the real life of Milan eluded us—we were not unhappy to leave—Venice was another story. The city was a walker's paradise once we learned to stay away from the legion of tourists in St. Mark's Square. Instead we explored the back streets—the real city—with its narrow canals, arched stone bridges, crooked alleys, and innumerable churches, postponing our departure from day to day. One day, exhausted from a stomach virus, L decided to sleep in. I walked the streets all morning, determined to cram in as many sights as possible, bursting to tell her how much she'd foolishly missed. But when I got back she was still contentedly asleep, leaving me indignant and deflated. I wanted to do everything, see everything, but even as a traveler I had to learn to ease up. A high point of our stay was the 1964 Biennale, especially the adventurous American pavilion featuring the new Pop Art. I could reconnect to the work of Robert Rauschenberg that had already intrigued me in London earlier in the year, though I still appreciated it less as art than as a challenge to one's notions of what art was. We took a jaunt from Venice to Ravenna to see its extraordinary Byzantine mosaics, some of them dating from the sixth century. Though we knew little about the period, we loved their glittering, gemlike workmanship and stylized iconic imagery, altogether new and strange to me. As a rich and powerful maritime culture, Venice had had close links to the eastern Mediterranean, and the Byzantine art and architecture in Venice, especially in St. Mark's Basilica, whetted our appetite for more. Moving back so far in time, we felt that the whole history of art was unrolling before our eyes.

Having been seduced by Venice, we went on to fall in love with Florence, using Mary McCarthy's crisply intelligent *Stones of Florence* as an elegant, informative guide. It was like a course in Florentine history and art. Her pages on artists like Paolo Uccello, who fell deliriously in love with perspective, would stay with me for a long time. One book we kept close by all through our journey was Nikolaus Pevsner's *Outline of European Architecture*. Its chapters tracked our itinerary as we progressed from Romanesque to Gothic to the Florentine Renaissance, with Rome and its baroque masterpieces still ahead of us.

In Florence we landed not in a hotel but in a pensione, part of a woman's cavernous flat. She provided us with yet another introduction to Italy and the Italian language. Brandishing two keys, one to the building's front door, the other to the apartment, she acted out a vigorous little monologue to explain which was which. "*Questa di su*," she said with extraordinary emphasis on each syllable, all the while jamming the key upwards four or five times, "*e questa di giù*," she articulated, jabbing it downward, toward the floor, as if we were quite retarded. Never had I seen a more theatrical piece of practical instruction, acted out with broad gestures and a fierce determination to leap the language barrier.

In the days that followed we lost ourselves in the paintings at the Uffizi Gallery and the Pitti Palace, the sculpture in the Bargello, the beauty of the churches beginning with the Duomo and the Baptistry, the bridges across the Arno, the piazzas and gardens and Renaissance palaces. For days we breathed in the sculpture of Michelangelo and Donatello, the spirituality of Saint Francis, the designs of Brunelleschi. The hordes of summer tourists were not yet as suffocating as they later became, and we were not as jaded as we might have been, since everything was so fresh to us. My brief stay three years earlier had simply whetted my appetite for what Florence had to offer. Nice and Venice had put us in a celebratory mood and Florence was where we celebrated—perhaps too much, as it turned out.

In France I had at times had trouble finding what I could eat. *Sole meunière* was sometimes the only bit of fish on the menu. In Italy, thanks to the great pasta and abundant variety of fish, this problem evaporated. But one night we splurged on a festive dinner, putting away several courses, a great deal of wine, and a rich dessert in a really nice restaurant. As the meal ended I began to feel my heart pounding in my throat and chest. My breath grew shallow. As with the panicky feeling that engulfed me as a college freshman six years earlier, I thought I was having a heart attack. We made our way to the curiously relaxed emergency room, the *pronto soccorso*, of a nearby hospital, where I was casually but amiably examined. All I could make out in the chatter of the interns around me were words that sounded like Italian for "heart attack." No doubt they were simply saying I hadn't had one, since they sent us home with the injunction to take it easy for a day or two. After so many days of intense touring, this had to be welcome advice.

There were no aftereffects—I felt as energetic as ever—but the episode brought back the vulnerability I'd felt through much of my English year, the anxieties that psychotherapy had defused and L's presence had dispelled. As a Freudian I wondered whether I was unconsciously making a last stand against marriage, commitment, and adult responsibility, against the sheer fact of growing up, a resistance expressed as usual through my body and the fears it triggered. ("Or maybe just heartburn," an astute editor writes in the margin.) I had never been more sure of what I was doing, yet a voice from the chorus was murmuring its dissent. I sensed that these conflicts might haunt me for some time to come. L was signing on for something she couldn't fully grasp, something intractable perhaps, and neither could I.

It was a jolt to move on from Renaissance Florence to Rome, where the heat and sprawl of the city again reminded me of New York. Moving from the almost illegible classical ruins of the Forum to the obscenely showy baroque splendors of the Vatican, we felt lost, even with Pevsner to provide a context for what we were seeing. Yet we were drawn in by the architecture and sculpture of Bernini, especially the famous *Apollo and Daphne*, in which the young woman, caught by the god, gradually turns into the bark of a tree as one circles the statue. I had never imagined that sculpture could not only tell a story but prove dynamic enough to express motion and sequence. We were a long way from the resplendent stillness of Michelangelo's *Moses* or *David* or his sculpture for Lorenzo de' Medici's tomb. Yet here in Rome, pulsing with vitality, were his masterworks for the Sistine Chapel: the panorama of biblical scenes for the intricate ceiling and the anguished apocalyptic vision of his *Last Judgment*, painted nearly thirty years later. No crowds of gaping tourists could take anything away from these works; they humbled and uplifted us.

Uncomfortable as we had become in Rome, one more tourist attraction was impossible to avoid, the plein air performance of Verdi's *Aïda*, complete with live elephants, amid the ruins of the old Roman Baths of Caracalla.

With its pomp and grandeur, the performance was as spectacular as promised. During the intermission I was approached by a polite American student. "Excuse me, sir," he said, looking puzzled and curious. "Is this a new play?" It was nice to know that there were still innocents abroad, wide-eyed and blankly inquisitive, though I think we may have been almost as dewy-eyed in our rapture for art and culture. But we reserved our final week in Italy, like our last week in France, to unwind and relax. We settled on the island of Ischia, in the Bay of Naples, mainly because it was off the beaten track, much less expensive than its tony neighbor, Capri, with fewer tourists and no Americans. We were charmed by the island and the surrounding waters, the bluest, most crystalline waters I had ever seen.

One day we took a ferry to explore its sister island, Capri, with its spectacular rocky coastline, sculpted into the sea, and its even bluer waters. Three years earlier I had been surprised to find Germans in Paris so soon after the war, but Germans had been drawn to Italy, and especially to Capri, for a long time. We found ourselves exploring the views from the zigzagging pedestrian walkway of the Via Krupp, built into the side of the rocky coast, named after the German munitions maker, a longtime patron of the island. My sharpest memory from this excursion is of a young Italian on board ship, thumping his stomach and claiming he had indigestion from skipping lunch. Although we were beguiled by everything we encountered in Italy, we guessed that only Italians could get indigestion from *not* eating, a nice twist on my own gustatory problems.

After Ischia we made our way north. L had to get back to London for her return flight to New York but I was leaving three days earlier from Milan. Richard was getting married outside Boston the last weekend of August and he'd asked me to "stand up" for him as his best man, which was beginning to look like a dress rehearsal for my own wedding. He would be doing graduate work in English at Harvard, though he felt conflicted about committing himself to academic life. I would be returning to Yale to propose the thesis on Victorian cultural criticism that I had worked out with Raymond Williams. L and I would look for an apartment in New Haven, though we recognized the awkwardness of our situation. Earlier in the trip she had written to her parents, casually, that we were traveling together. After weeks of silence her mother had sent her an angry, accusatory letter, telling her she had shamed them and the family, but with a postscript from her father, straight out of *Goodbye, Columbus*, saying, "I know my baby would not do anything wrong." When they met her at the airport in New York, she thought she could disarm them before they attacked her. "Mom, I'm engaged," she said happily. "I don't care," her mother shot back. "You've ruined your life." I learned from L that her mother had disapproved even more harshly twenty-five years earlier when her only sister, emigrating to New York from Palestine, told her she'd been living with a man there who had now dumped her. "You've disgraced the memory of our parents," she told her, showing her the door.

Since L's parents lived in New Haven—something of a small town— there was no way we could live together there before we got married. Instead we found an unassuming five-room flat on Beers Street, only a few blocks from where I had lived on Sherman Avenue, and we would have dinner and spend evenings together before she returned to her parents' home to sleep. By this fiction we preserved the appearance of respectability that mattered to them. It was a shock enough—a real token of love—for her to come back with me to the New Haven she had left behind six years earlier. Thanks to her science background L was able to get lab jobs, first in the medical school, then at Yale's biology department, where she assisted a professor whose research was on blind fish who lived in caves. The job bored her no end and her boss was mean and dull; it was little more than a holding action till I could get my degree.

I approached a former teacher of mine who specialized in the Victorian era in the hope that he would take on the supervision of my thesis. To my surprise he was skeptical, finding it a tad too ambitious. "The professors of English would never approve a joint dissertation on Carlyle, Ruskin, and Arnold," he said, with finality. Perhaps he meant to save me from hardship, since the collected works of these writers, titans of creative stamina, were voluminous. Or perhaps, since his own affinity for Victorian prose writers ran more to Cardinal Newman, he had no liking for the fiery social criticism Williams had already excavated in these conservative yet paradoxically radical prophets. Like Dickens, they belonged to the restless, angry conscience of Victorian England. They had attacked the new industrial society and the complacencies of the middle class as sharply as Marx and Engels, but had done so as outraged humanists, grounded in art and religion, not as radical firebrands. In any case I knew what he said wasn't exactly true, since the faculty would sign off on anything he saw fit to sponsor, and this convinced me that we were not well suited to work well together.

As my backup plan I turned to Keats, one of the poets I most loved, and went to see Fred Pottle, a venerable scholar, flinty editor of the newly published Boswell papers, with whom I'd studied the Romantic period. He felt he was too close to retirement and sent me to his own student, Harold Bloom, who had squeaked through to tenure while I'd been away, over fierce objections from a few of the department's leading lights, including some of his own teachers. Already in 1964 Bloom was an eccentric figure at preppie Yale, doleful, disheveled, courtly, with an impish wit and a poetic turn of phrase. His literary memory was phenomenal, but his sallow complexion suggested that he had never seen the sun. His resemblance to the ample-girthed, Falstaffian Zero Mostel was uncanny. Above all he was himself a Romantic, a votary of the sublime, anchored in the visionary poetry of Blake and Shelley, no favorites of the reigning modern criticism that descended from T. S. Eliot and Ezra Pound, whose work he detested with a passion.

With Bloom's arrival the department's genteel (and gentile) Anglo-classicism and its academic version of the New Criticism hung in the balance. But with three large, brilliant books on the Romantic poets already to his credit, it proved hard for the university to turn the upstart down, though some senior figures in English tried hard to do so. They may have grasped how influential he might become, seeing how prolific he already was. The field itself was in bad odor in a conservative department more oriented toward the medieval era and the eighteenth century. Now, with tenure in hand, he would be allowed to supervise graduate students, and I think I was the first to approach him with a project. I dug out two papers I'd written on Keats, the first as a college senior, the second for Mr. Pottle, and asked Bloom whether he saw the makings of a thesis, since the critical commentary on Keats had already filled countless volumes. Keats had written poetry for hardly more than four years, and had only *become* the Keats we knew in the last year or two, before dying in Rome of consumption at the age of twenty-five—an age I myself was fast approaching. (He had also died on my birthday, February 23, a slightly eerie connection I put out of mind.)

My angle of vision on Keats was very much the expression of whom I had become and the critical paths I had already been tracing. Keats had a wonderfully ingratiating personality, always fully alive on the page, but this was not what most drew me in, though it would enrich my life. Instead, I came to him under the influence of existentialism, with its focus on both mortality—we're all death-haunted, time-haunted creatures—and on moral choice, the decisions we make in the face of our condition. Touched by a cursory reading of Hegel and European phenomenology, I set about to study the supple and subtle forms of consciousness that radiate through Keats's poems and letters. In the fresh, eager, sometimes tormented self-awareness that appears everywhere in his work, we are caught up in a sensuality tempered yet also heightened by a consciousness of death.

To me Keats seemed very close to his chosen model, Wordsworth, ever a student of the shifting currents of his own mind, but also a darker, more tragic poet than most readers had allowed. Bloom suggested that if I concentrated on his early poems, especially his improvised 4,000-line would-be epic, *Endymion*, I might have an opening, since these dreamy, sensuous works, some of them structured only by free association, had eluded or confounded modern criticism. As my reward for scoping out these neglected poems, I could then take a shot at his more mature work, especially his 1819 odes, among a handful of the most remarkable lyrics in English. I took this Solomonic advice as a stroke of unbelievable luck and was off and running.

With the kind of gusto Keats himself savored in his inimitable letters, I set out to read everything written by and about him. Eager for teaching experience, I also signed on as assistant lecturer in John Hollander's undergraduate course in modern poetry, partly to repair my own patchwork knowledge of those difficult poets. To fulfill one last language requirement, I petitioned to take an undergraduate course in nineteenth-century German drama, since it would let me concentrate on literature while beefing up my shaky German. As with some of Hollander's elusive poets, I was barely acquainted with a few of the playwrights: Heinrich von Kleist, whose surprisingly modern stories (such as *Michael Kohlhaas*) reminded me of Kafka's, and Georg Büchner, whose *Woyzeck* had been transformed into a dissonant and dramatic opera by Alban Berg. Both Kleist and Büchner were extreme, self-destructive characters who had died absurdly young, like Keats, with their work unfinished, and I was attracted as much by the suicidal intensity of their lives as by the uncanny modernity of what they wrote.

WHATEVER COURSES I was teaching and taking, it was hard in the fall of 1964 not to be swept up in a larger world, even in provincial New Haven, which could be so self-enclosed. It felt like a different country from the one I'd left behind a year earlier, before Kennedy's assassination. Like so many on that fateful weekend, I'd felt traumatized and helpless, and cut off by being far away. The very sound of Lyndon Johnson's southern drawl had been unsettling, as if the country had fallen back into the old politics, from which the vibrant young president had seemed to rescue us. Once in office Johnson had proved to be anything but the redneck I feared. Much of what happened in America the year I was away remained a blur to me, but by the time I returned Johnson had effectively channeled the grief and guilt of the nation into support for Kennedy's stalled programs, especially civil rights.

Kennedy himself, elected by a razor-thin margin, politically cautious, had unconscionably dragged his feet on civil rights. But when Bull Connor's Birmingham cops had set their dogs on black schoolgirls in June 1963, in full view of the television cameras, Kennedy made a stunning about-face. Riding a sense of national outrage, seizing the moral high ground in an electrifying message, he made an eloquent and forceful case for civil rights legislation. Watching him speak, I was moved and heartened by his turnabout, which radiated a moral urgency I had not seen in him before. Caught up in preparing to take my orals and leave for England, I had missed the great March on Washington at the end of August, which Kennedy at first resisted and tried to derail, just as FDR had responded to the threat of a similar march by A. Philip Randolph twenty years earlier.

Like the lunch counter sit-ins that preceded it, the 1963 march proved to be a prologue to a decade of protests that pulled us right in as it shifted some of the political action from the halls of Congress to the streets. Martin Luther King's silver oratory and organizing skill, his heroic adherence to nonviolence, helped bring the civil rights issue to the top of the nation's agenda. But at the time of Kennedy's death his proposals remained locked up in a Congress still dominated by southern Democrats and other conservatives. With astonishing political skills—and an unabashed moral passion that outweighed Kennedy's—Johnson and his new liberal allies in Congress had broken the deadlock and put through much of Kennedy's program as a tribute to the slain president. The ultimate congressional insider, Johnson had improbably become the standard-bearer of a resurgent liberalism. Now he was running for president as a peace candidate against the tribune of the new conservatism, Barry Goldwater, whom he portrayed as a loose cannon who might lead the nation into a ground war in Vietnam, perhaps even into nuclear war. Few could know that the escalation of the war was already being discussed, even actively planned. The whole nation, starting with the universities, was about to implode and we would be inexorably caught up in the turmoil.

With little sense of the coming maelstrom, our private lives moved on as L and I began planning our wedding. She had been more than willing to tie the knot in Europe, but I felt I wouldn't be truly married without a grand Jewish wedding. These had always been special occasions in my childhood—staying up late, watching the family dress up, rejoice, quarrel, take pictures and take sides. I wanted what my older cousins had had, a moment of pomp and ritual passage, a Jewish moment under the chuppah, stomping on the glass as a breakthrough into a new life. One complication: this match was a virtual intermarriage. Getting L's uptight German family and my boisterous Eastern European family to concur on anything would require unusual diplomacy. It was agreed that the wedding would take place in New York, since most of both families lived there. Because my extended clan was so much larger, L's parents resented paying for it; they were marrying off their daughter, their only child, and could hardly object, yet object they did. They grumbled about the cost—a waste of money, they said—and didn't invite any of their New Haven friends. Without their input we planned everything, spent weekends in the city listening to different bands, looking for a photographer, and checking out garish catering facilities like Leonard's, a *simcha* factory in Great Neck, where several weddings were proceeding at once, one more loud and tasteless than the other.

To avoid such horrors we settled on my parents' modest synagogue in Flushing, where the rabbi had known me for years and the caterer was decent and kosher enough for L's exacting parents and my father's *frum* family. But the menu itself ignited a protracted (and absurd) quarrel. L's father insisted on roast chicken, a basic dish no caterer could spoil, he claimed. My parents, always sensitive to appearances, preferred "prime ribs of beef," since the alternative looked mean and ungenerous. A professional chef with a choleric disposition, L's father countered that it wasn't worth the money, since Jews didn't really know how to make roast beef without turning it into overcooked pot roast. As intermediaries—they never communicated directly—we managed to negotiate a solution: L's parents would pay for chicken, my parents would fork over the difference for prime ribs. The whole contretemps could have been staged as farce, the Prime Ribs Follies, but if not peace there was at least a truce; the real business of the wedding could proceed. We set a date for the last Sunday in December, then postponed it a week since the Christmas rush was the busiest season in my parents' store, a time when they worked fifteen hours a day.

Like our summer travels, the fall months became a rehearsal for living together. My relation to Yale shifted dramatically from my first two years there, when the stultifying demands of my courses made it almost impossible to have a real life. Now, burrowing into subjects close to our hearts, we all felt on our own, able to breathe again. Some of my best friends had left, including Roberto, who had returned to Brazil but would soon be in political exile in Paris, and Jim and Adele Dalsimer, who had gone off to Boston, where he would complete his psychoanalytic training. Precociously, they already had their first child, Jenny, born that spring while I was away. At once perky, bright, and self-effacing, adept at putting herself down, Adele was perhaps my favorite among all the women in the graduate program. She too was working with Bloom, studying the influence of Shelley on the poetry of Yeats, though she felt that Bloom did not take her seriously. In Boston she would finish her thesis and begin teaching, good Jewish girl that she was, among the Jesuits at Boston College. Incongruously, she would persuade them to start an Irish studies program, and her own life would grow completely enmeshed with Irish culture.

Those who remained were enjoying their new freedom, discovering each other as if for the first time. Some were fellow Romanticists who would one day make a great name in the field, including Jerry McGann, working on Byron, and Ken Johnston, who would eventually do landmark work on Wordsworth. Both were slightly older than me; both were already married, with backgrounds that had little resemblance to mine but were in some ways oddly similar since they each had strong religious roots. Jerry had gone to a Catholic college in Syracuse, where even Kant was still on the Index of forbidden books; becoming a secular scholar and intellectual was a serious adventure for him. He was wry and ironic but had a genuine Romantic temperament, a gift for showmanship, that provoked him to identify intensely with his great subject. He once gave a paper at the Modern Language Association dressed in period costume and wrote a book on Swinburne, a neglected late Romantic, in the form of a dialogue. Ken was big, affably boyish, and fair-skinned, looking a little like a Scandinavian farmer's son. His stories about his taciturn Swedish American family, so different from mine, given to long silences, always fascinated me. He and his animated, dark-haired wife, Betty, soon became our closest Yale friends, though they were so discreet that we had no sense of the tensions in their marriage.

Ken had grown up in Minnesota, had gone to a small church-related college, and from there to the Divinity School of the University of Chicago, not to be ordained but to take a master's degree in religion and the arts. For Jerry and Ken, to a surprising degree, literature had become a religion, as it had in part become for me as my religious observance waned. This was true even for Jerry's good friend John Gerber, a Catholic priest who also became a close friend of ours. Handsome, athletic, attractive to women, visibly conflicted over his vows of celibacy, he had been sent by his order to Cambridge to do advanced work in literature. There he'd been bitten by the bug called F. R. Leavis, and was now trying, with little success, to write a thesis on the poetry of D. H. Lawrence, of all people, just at the moment when the church itself, under the liberating hand of Pope John XXIII, was undergoing a signal transformation. His conflicts eventually proved insoluble—though, unlike many of his closest friends, he never left the priesthood.

Thanks to our freedom from onerous course work, all of us found ourselves doing much that we had no time for in our first years of graduate training. One of them was an informal book group that pulled us out of our fields to discuss books that were being hotly debated in the broader culture, such as Erik Erikson's luminous collection of psychoanalytic essays, *Childhood and Society*, and Henry Roth's Lower East Side novel *Call It Sleep*, just published in paperback thirty years after it had first appeared. Though set soon after the turn of the century, Roth's novel triggered my own memories of growing up on the Lower East Side. Writing from the half understanding of a young child's point of view, he evoked his early memories with an astonishing emotional intimacy.

There was an endless stream of old and new movies at the Yale Film Society and in local art cinemas like the Lincoln, a converted barn. We could catch plays like Beckett's *Endgame* at the Yale colleges, makeshift settings for unconventional theater, and kept up with musical events such as visiting string quartets that filled Woolsey Hall. At the New Haven Arena we first encountered Bob Dylan, a slight, shy figure tagging along with the singer we had come to hear, Joan Baez. His voice was something between a snarl and a plaintive drawl, nothing like her ringing, mellifluous sound, and she sometimes patted him on the rear end as if for encouragement. Meanwhile, political protests grew more frequent and more heated as the war in Vietnam became an American war and the reassuring peace candidate of 1964 became the dour, bellicose war president of 1965. In early February, only weeks after being inaugurated, he ordered daily bombing runs over North Vietnam. The turbulence of the sixties was already in the air; what seemed to us a brutal and unnecessary war ensured that we would be pulled into it, though I myself—as a student, and married—would never be drafted. My new mentor, Bloom, turning thirty-five, was briefly alarmed when reclassified 5-A instead of 4-F. He liked the 5 but found the A disquieting. One of his students reassured him: "It means that when they draft my grandmother they'll draft you."

Scenes of vulgar, noisy Jewish weddings have become so stereotyped that it would be hard for me to give a freshly observed account of our own nuptials. With only a hundred and fifty guests it was comparatively small and the setting itself was unusually spare and tasteful. The Flushing Jewish Center had started out in a loft above the stationery store in the 1930s, then moved to what had once been a sizable private home. Eventually some larger structures were added: a basement gym in which my Boy Scout troop had met, where I had played innumerable games of dodgeball, and a new sanctuary that opened up into a large synagogue on the high holidays or a party space for weddings and bar mitzvah receptions. It was plain enough, with warm wood paneling and high windows that looked out on lush greenery. The congregation was not wealthy or ostentatious; it had few pretensions, and this unassuming location suited us just fine.

The religious branches of our extended families were not so happy. L had already upset several of my father's nephews, all of them rabbis, when she had refused to sign the engagement contract (the *Tena'im*) because of its medieval provisions favoring the groom and his family. Among other things, it spelled out the terms of a broken engagement: if the bride was responsible, the groom was still entitled to her dowry; if the groom ended it, the bride got nothing. It was all moot, as L had no dowry to speak of, other than some books and recycled furniture; still, even in those prefeminist days, the language offended her. I was embarrassed by her resistance to what I saw as a mere formality, yet not surprised. I loved L's gumption and independence. But when her father announced—indirectly, through her mother—that he wouldn't attend the wedding unless she first went to the mikvah, the ritual bath, she went along, to forestall his wrath and his threatened boycott.

The rabbinical cousins in my father's family were also on hand for the wedding, though it was taking place in the alien setting of a Conservative synagogue. Yet they seemed to be bickering about the details even as the ceremony unfolded. Ignoring the affable rabbi, Paul Hait, who was actually marrying us, they squabbled about the exact order of the *Sheva B'rachot*, the seven Hebrew blessings that were recited under the chuppah. As strict Orthodox Jews they were at pains to get the ritual exactly right, but no one could agree on what "exactly right" required. L's uncle Ludwig, a survivor of the death camps, was determined to show that he was more Orthodox than anyone else, so he personally checked out the kitchen and the caterer, then stood alone, rigidly at attention, throughout the proceedings, something that neither law nor custom required. This must have seemed odd to my friends from Columbia and Yale, mostly assimilated Jews, but also to our Yale friend Father Gerber, whose clerical collar added an especially lively note to the affair. "Who's *that*?" L's mother whispered, as if alarmed.

Waiting my turn to walk down the aisle, I found myself surprisingly relaxed as friends preceded me: Marshall, my best man, with whom I'd stayed in close touch since college, though we'd rarely been in the same city; L's friend Naomi as maid of honor; my sister, Doris, now a junior in college, as bridesmaid; and several other friends, none of them the least bit religious, all wickedly pleased to see me getting hooked up, who would serve as ushers. I joked, perhaps a bit hysterically, with each of them as they set off to assume their positions along the center aisle. Soon all eyes were turned on us as my parents got ready to accompany me to the bimah, and I was genuinely shocked. "What, me?" I recall the feeling of being taken unawares, as if I'd somehow forgotten that I was no supernumerary, no spear-carrier, but was slated for a starring role. My legs turned watery as I walked past my beaming friends, who seemed altogether delighted that it was my wedding, not theirs.

Once planted up front, I turned to see L, flanked by her parents, coming down the aisle. In the svelte silk wedding gown she'd borrowed from a friend, she looked radiant, happy, and suddenly it was alright, the months, the years of indecision, the fears of commitment, of taking on responsibility, the sexual delirium, the future that lay before us like a blank canvas, ready to be filled in. She made a beeline for the altar without pausing for the photographer to take the obligatory snap, and I had never been more elated to see a living soul. It was our story after all; the hubbub around us—the quarreling rabbis, the ancient rituals, the family and friends—no longer mattered except as the backdrop to this privileged moment in our lives. We had something huge to celebrate, and they were all here in suburban Flushing to savor it with us.

And celebrate we did, hopping from table to table: the three tables of our friends, strategically placed to separate a few who weren't talking to each other; the single table that held the remnants of L's decimated family; the table full of dark hats and dark suits for my father's brothers, nieces, and nephews; the tables for my mother's family, one for her eldest brother and his large clan, others for the younger siblings and their families. Had any of these people been accidentally misplaced, old quarrels would have been rekindled, wounds reopened, a riot might have broken out. As it was, my uncle Sam, up from Miami Beach, the kindest soul imaginable, grew merry with drink and began banging his silverware on the table, shouting, "more kishka, more kishka," much to the horror of L's genteel German family, who visibly stiffened, averse to the raucous behavior and inelegant diet of Eastern European Jews, the antics of uncivilized Russian peasants. I understood later that my wish for this wedding had less to do with throwing a big party and everything to do with wanting to declare my inchoate love for L by way of Jewish law and tradition, though I was often exasperated by its demands. In two and a half years we'd grown totally entwined with each other, yet I still needed these rituals, these people present, this communal sanction, to tie the knot as my parents and their parents had done.

I didn't learn until years later that my mother, not reconciled to losing her son, had approached L a few days before the wedding urging her to postpone it, on the transparent grounds that I had not gone out with enough women. She must have been fretting for months, then finally grown desperate, for her to make such an outlandish suggestion. Instead of getting angry, L reminded her gently that it would be embarrassing, and far too late, since the arrangements were set and the guests were virtually on their way. My mother accepted this practical response to her last-minute spasm of resistance but once again asked L never to tell me that she had brought this up, and for years she didn't. I don't know whether I would have been diverted or horrified, probably both. It certainly would have been a sour note in my ear, though L, not always so patient, took it all in stride as one last obstacle to our being together.

We had no great honeymoon plans. Living in New Haven, virtually penniless, we plumped for spending a few days in New York, at the slightly shabby Paris Hotel on Ninety-Seventh Street and West End Avenue of all places, where student couples from Columbia and Barnard sometimes shacked up. Perhaps I was catching up with the not-so-wild adventures I'd missed in my college years. Staying on in the city but sequestered from friends and family turned out to be exactly what would most delight us. Perhaps there was a frisson of the illicit about it. We had been together for years yet, to our great surprise, being married felt strangely different. We looked at each other with widened eyes, touched each other's bodies with a novel sense of connection. Once or twice in the next few days we ran into people we knew but we made sure to tell them we weren't there, we were somewhere else, and in truth we were.

Ten

New Beginnings

W HEN WE RETURNED to New Haven in the second week of January, it seemed like the land that time forgot, an insular college town where things changed slowly if at all. Our own lives had taken a serious turn. It felt peculiarly grown-up to be a married man, to keep house and live together openly in our five-room flat on dilapidated Beers Street, on a block rapidly turning black, just down the street from a large Catholic hospital complex. The break between semesters gave us the chance to get used to our new lives together as husband and wife, an acknowledged couple playing at roles we still associated with our parents. L, who took my name, was at first startled to hear herself called Mrs. Dickstein, a title she associated entirely with my mother.

As we settled into our cozy nest, we kept hearing the rumble of distant thunder from the world around us. It was 1965, the turning point of what was fast becoming a tumultuous decade, though we could not yet feel its full impact. Lyndon Johnson was about to be inaugurated for his first full term as president after winning in a reassuring landslide, and this would enable him to push through even more far-reaching social legislation such as Medicare and a voting-rights bill. Yet urban riots in Watts and elsewhere would soon bring racial progress into question. This growing unrest at home echoed the bloody warfare abroad. The public reaction to the escalation of the war was at first limited to the activist Left, the universities, and a handful of journalists and editorial writers. Except for few mavericks like Oregon's Senator Wayne Morse, who had cast one of only two votes against a war resolution the preceding summer, Johnson still had Congress in his hands, a Congress long inured to deferring to the president on foreign and military matters. Yet an escalating sense of dismay, of real horror, spread through our little community as the nation grew violently polarized over the war.

As I took up work for the spring semester, it was hard to imagine how my own life would be entangled in this national trauma. Besides my serendipitous work on German drama and my assistant's duties in Hollander's course on modern poetry, there was the thesis I could not seem to begin. I always had another critical book to read, another poem that demanded close scrutiny. Each day L would set off on her bike to her job at Yale's biology lab, about a mile away, and each day I would hole up at home or in the library putting off the moment of reckoning when I'd actually have to set down the first sentence. This was the bump in the road at which many graduate students crashed and burned, or simply dropped out. It was helpful to have a fat issue of the *New York Times* on hand, or an early number of the *New York Review of Books*, overflowing with long, dense articles by important names, or the flippant countercultural pages of the *Village Voice* reporting on whatever we were missing in New York; all these needed to be read from cover to cover. I had a mild case of grad student paralysis, which demanded that I keep busy all the time, busy with other things. Accustomed to the short haul, the quick turnaround, I had no idea of what it meant to write a thesis, to pull together a shitload of reading and build up an argument at book length. In all my classes I'd never written anything longer than fifteen pages, and even that was a stretch.

Fortunately, the subject I'd chosen absorbed me more and more. Keats was perhaps the most attractive figure in English literature. Though he was damaged by the early death of his parents, by chronic money worries and viciously uncomprehending reviews, his nonpareil letters show him as warm, spontaneous, sharply observant, manly, ambitious for just renown, brimming with quicksilver ideas, drawn to the best models, delighted with his own senses, and touchingly devoted to his orphaned siblings and a small circle of loyal friends. In the face of poor sales and those astonishingly obtuse reviews, they husbanded his letters and drafts and had an unshakable belief in his unrecognized talent. In a period of only four years, from 1816 through 1819, his poetry went through a metamorphosis that would have taken a lifetime for most writers. He had begun writing poetry after years of apprenticeship as a medical student, and this must have contributed to the physicality, the delight in the natural world, that makes his writing feel so palpable and immediate. From year to year it evolved from spontaneous musings and dreamy associations, the mild sensory pleasures of a morning on Hampstead Heath, to the death-haunted themes of his mature work.

Keats's early poems were relaxed and fanciful, sensuous pastoral writing in a minor key, but his later work was charged with erotic longing that deepened as his life turned darker. His greatest poems are enriched by the kind of catharsis we undergo in tragedy, yet also by a ripe sense of natural fruition, his unalloyed pleasure in the ways living things wax and wane. He was a writer immensely alive to fugitive feelings and physical sensations, even as he was enmeshed in more shadowy passages of human experience—weakness and decline, illness and death. As a senior in college I was drawn to him as a conflicted, at times tormented figure whose equilibrium was never given, always hard-won. This was the Keats of the "Ode to a Nightingale," oppressed by the recent death of his beloved younger brother. There we find him in flight from an excess of self-reflection, haunted by a world where "youth grows pale, and spectre-thin, and dies." Once bright and carefree, like the nightingale he overhears in his garden, he's now eager to drown himself in one opiate or another, including the siren-song of "pure" poetry. Like other Romantic poets, he had sought escape, a balm for the brooding mind. But he returns at the end to a chastened sense of his "sole self," free of illusion, and takes leave of this internal drama with large open questions:

> *Was it a vision, or a waking dream?*
> *Fled is that music:—Do I wake or sleep?*

Here and elsewhere Keats compressed his whole poetic journey into the brief compass of a single poem—in self-dedicating sonnets taking off from great works of art (the Elgin Marbles, Chapman's translation of Homer, *King Lear*), in odes addressed to mythical divinities (Psyche), vivid personifications (Melancholy, Indolence), imagined artifacts of an earlier time (the Grecian urn), or in narrative romances and would-be epics about the birth of poetic consciousness. Like Wordsworth revisiting the landscape near Tintern Abbey, Keats could seize on almost anything as a measure of his progress from callow immaturity to more exalted aims as a man and artist, a tragic awareness sometimes glimpsed only from afar. He knew what poetic fame, poetic achievement looked like; he longed for it with every fiber of his being. Yet his quavering sense of destiny was hedged by depressing fears of early death.

I was thrilled by these mingled feelings, his exalted ambitions as well as dismal anxieties; they gave his life and work a tragic cast that always spoke to me. Another subject might easily have gone stale on me, weighing down my days and nights with boredom or resentment—an epic of forced labor. Keats, with his incandescent vitality, never ceased to inspire me even as he could make me feel small and inconsequential, a grateful chorus to his full-throated orisons, a lame witness to his unsparing self-examination. But it always remained a pleasure to attend closely to every note and, where I could, to sing along as best a critic could, enthralled by his staging of the movements of his own mind.

Through the spring of 1965 I was caught up in the scale and drama of my undertaking, without the slightest notion of where to begin. I explained my predicament to John Hollander, who offered me a helpful bit of advice. "Just plunge in, start anywhere," he said, "and you can come back to fix it later." That piece of practical wisdom made all the difference; it implied a series of provisional steps rather than some inevitable opening. If my subject was Keats's amazing poetic development, my way into it was through the ebb and flow of the poet's labile mind, the evasions and recognitions, the pained knowledge, that had first drawn me to the "Ode to a Nightingale." It seemed ideal, not simply expedient, to begin with early poems that reflected the carefree languor of his youth and then the surge of self-awareness that he tried and failed to turn aside.

Having lost his parents at a tender age, then going through the wasting death of his brother Tom, Keats came to see our lives as besieged—yet also exalted—by our subjection to time and change, an apprehension of death. Under the spell of existential themes that meshed with my own temperament, I had always taken these all-too-human concerns as a linchpin of serious writing, my way into a writer's work. Now I lit upon a largely unnoticed winter lyric, "In drear-nighted December," not published till almost a decade after his death, that compares the unconscious flow of nature in its seasonal rounds with the restless mind of man, fretting about loss, never sure of renewal and rebirth. Keats comes up with a striking phrase for this elusive yet desirable forgetting: "The feel of not to feel it, / When there is none to heal it, / Nor numbed sense to steel it, / Was never said in rhyme." With this poem and this passage I was off and running. "The feel of not to feel it," the numb oblivion to what he would later call "this world of pains and troubles," was just what he would work to overcome in the interior dialogues that lend drama to his greatest works.

His advance into this bleak poetic territory was something he predicted and prepared for long before he could manage it in rhyme. It's at the heart of a sonnet written soon afterward when he set about to reread *King Lear.* Who but Keats would write a poem not after reading a great work but about readying himself to read it, steeling himself for the demanding encounter with an almost unendurable vision? He was performing an act of consecration, putting aside the pleasures of "golden-tongued Romance," luxuries that richly appealed to him, to undergo a purgatorial passage through Shakespeare's most painful and profound play. "Let me not wander in a barren dream," the poem concludes:

> But when I am consumèd in the fire,
> Give me new phoenix wings to fly at my desire.

Having just finished a quest romance gleaned from ancient myth, *Endymion,* his longest work, he almost immediately realized its limits. Keats looked anxiously toward the fiery forge of tragedy, which he saw not as destruction but as purgation: a creative, Phoenix-like burning through, a hoped-for rebirth. All through that winter and spring of 1818, in poems addressed to Milton, to Spenser, to Homer, even to the prematurely dead Scotsman Robert Burns, Keats dedicated himself again and again to a higher calling, all the while admitting that it still felt out of reach.

> *But vain is now the burning and the strife,*
> *Pangs are in vain—until I grow high-rife*
> *With old philosophy;*
> *And mad with glimpses at futurity!*

Seeking inspiration he invoked these writers but also took off on a stupendous walking tour in the north of England and Scotland. All the Romantic poets were prodigious walkers, ever in search, often composing as they walked, perhaps swinging the rhythm of their steps into the cadence of their lines. Keats was resolved to seek out inspiring sights, especially those associated with poets he loved; he would walk the ground where Wordsworth and Burns had walked, visit their homes in search of uplifting models. (Burns had been dead for twenty years but Keats wrote several poems in his honor, including a sonnet written in his very cottage. He tried to call on Wordsworth, but much to Keats's disgust he was out electioneering for a conservative candidate, having long since outgrown his revolutionary youth.) In the sonnet "When I have fears that I may cease to be," Keats voices the feeling that his own time might be cut short, that he might not live to emulate these models and fulfill his promise. By the end his hope and courage momentarily fail him:

> *Then on the shore*
> *Of this wide world I stand alone, and think*
> *Till love and fame to nothingness do sink.*

When I ask myself what drew me to Keats, I think of these grandiose aims but also the crushing doubts and fears that accompanied them. In my own small way I too, at exactly the same age, was caught between an ambition to conquer the world, to make my mark, and a fear that I would fall apart, even die, before achieving anything at all. My bouts of psychosomatic symptoms were at bottom fears of early death, a sorry fate (I thought gloomily) that still would take me off the hook, excuse any failure. My parents and teachers had always expected me to perform, to excel, had in fact *insisted* on it, and this propelled me at once to please them and to evade their expectations. Behind an amiable, laid-back façade, a surface that was all smiles and good will, I was a driven creature, fearful of falling short, though success at school had always come with little apparent effort. Instead of seeking out a neglected minor writer for my thesis, I took on a poet who dreamed great dreams, died haplessly young, yet burned brightly before his light was extinguished. Mocked by his contemporaries, he was vindicated by posterity.

Though he made fun in his letters of Wordsworth's "egotistical sublime," Keats appealed to me as a figure of heroic self-scrutiny, which I took to be the North Star for Romantic and modern writers. Their work aspired to the hard-won insight enacted in tragedy even as it foreshadowed the forms of introspection worked out by psychoanalysis. He had his own theory of self-development, which, in one of his most probing letters, he called "Soul making," describing how souls acquire identity "till each one is personally itself." In an earlier letter he had compared human life to a mansion of many rooms in which we gradually proceed from an Eden-like innocence and a languorous passivity to an arduous turn through life's rough passages, a world of pain, heartbreak, sickness, and oppression. His mature poems are dotted with moments of growth or transition, as in his would-be epic, *Hyperion*, when the young Apollo, golden successor to the old Olympians, assumes his godhead in an earthshaking physical transformation:

> *Soon wild commotions shook him, and made flush*
> *All the immortal fairness of his limbs;*
> *Most like the struggle at the gate of death;*
> *Or liker still to one who should take leave*
> *Of pale immortal death, and with a pang*
> *As hot as death's is chill, with fierce convulse*
> *Die into life.*

What young reader has ever been able to resist the clarion call of this verse, the vision of becoming that it conjures up so feverishly? In Keats's last important poem, *The Fall of Hyperion*, an unfinished revision of this incomplete work, the poet himself must undergo this ordeal, a convulsive, deathlike initiation. The poet who once (in *Endymion*) luxuriated in an "ardent listlessness" now must join the ranks of those "to whom the miseries of the world / Are misery, and will not let them rest." Keats didn't live long enough to become this kind of Shakespearean (or Dantesque, or Miltonic) poet, but in a brief span of time he pursued this troubled but triumphant course in the most intense manner imaginable. The six great odes of 1819 show him wrestling with these alternatives: the sensory and the spiritual, the erotic and the tragic, an idle receptivity and a cathartic burst of activity, the unfolding rhythms of nature and the restlessness of human striving. From the outset I was riveted by the drama of his inner life and my fascination with it never let up.

I felt attached to a comet as it burned its way through the atmosphere. The material was so rich that it added another plane—higher, more rarefied—to my banal graduate student existence. I loved it so much that I wondered: would anyone ever pay me for doing this? It was a privilege to be struggling each day with such a gorgeous tapestry of language yet humbling to see it translated into my own more pedestrian terms, the kind that would be accepted as scholarly commentary. Yet I found I had a knack for unpacking the intricacies of literary texts, especially when they tapped into the recesses of my emotional life. If the Keats of heroic aspiration was a tonic for me, the dying Keats was a burden. I came to identify with him, to the point of imagining I would not live much longer than he had, especially since he had fortuitously expired on my birthday.

I could only marvel at his large view of how any human life plays itself out. Always seeing man's progress in stages, Keats compares it sometimes to the seasons, with its spring of promise, its summer of bounty, its fall of melancholy reflection, and finally its winter chill. Of the last of these "human seasons" he writes, "He has his Winter too of pale misfeature, / Or else he would forego his mortal nature." Keats's odes, written just before his mortal illness set in, touch repeatedly on death, always with a different spin. The Nightingale ode reaches its climax with the recognition that mortality separates him from its unearthly and enduring song, that its timeless sound, echoing through the ages, can be treacherous as well as transcendent. "Thou was not born for death, immortal Bird! / No hungry generations tread thee down." By the end he imagines it as a requiem over his earthly remains. In the "Ode on Melancholy" death becomes erotic self-consummation, the culminating peak of sensory pleasure. Most of the odes were written amid the promise of spring, but the last of them, "To Autumn," takes on a different aura. It is in many ways a perfect poem yet I was not ready to respond to its Zen-like acceptance of death as fruition and repletion, the culmination of a natural process. I preferred the odes that were stippled with internal conflict, with desperate foreboding as well as burning desire.

My own life was caught up in a muted struggle. Marriage seemed the most fortunate state imaginable; I could no longer recall why I'd been so reluctant to take it on. I was reasonably content with my work, my friends, yet still felt vulnerable, provisional, insecure. Everyone except L saw me as a happy-go-lucky soul, smiley, effervescent, but the anxieties of my Cambridge year had never been fully dispelled. At times I felt fragile, breakable. The stomach troubles reappeared, stirring up old worries about my health. Mild chest pains would send me into spasms of anxiety that kept me on edge. I was ashamed of this weakness, embarrassed by it, shared it with no one. I saw it as a deep personal flaw, even a moral failing, and so I breathed not a word to friends or family. One day, I knew, I'd have to break its hold over me or perish trying.

Working on a thesis required distractions well beyond the *Times* and the *Village Voice*. After researching a chapter, I would try to write three or four decent pages a day, then break off when L returned from work. Moviegoing helped make life in New Haven tolerable. Every week brought some breakthrough work from France or Italy, Sweden, India or Japan: new films by Truffaut, Godard, Claude Chabrol, Fellini, Antonioni, Visconti, Bergman, Buñuel, Satyajit Ray, or Akira Kurosawa. Performances by Jean-Pierre Léaud in *The 400 Blows*, Jean-Paul Belmondo in *Breathless*, Jeanne Moreau in *Jules and Jim*, Monica Vitti and Anna Karina as frequent muses of Antonioni and Godard, and Marcello Mastroianni as Fellini's alter ego became touchstones of our waking lives. But the leading lights of American genre films, long taken for granted, were also being rediscovered and celebrated, especially Hitchcock, Hawks, and Ford, just as they were putting out their last, autumnal works. The student-run Yale Film Society was putting on retrospectives of these directors, now christened auteurs, in a large classroom in Linsly-Chittenden Hall, where for fifty cents a head we could fill in the gaps in film education. They had the taste of guilty pleasures, wonderfully remote from the books we were laboring over. We lived as much for the next Humphrey Bogart retrospective as for the latest Japanese samurai film. I was already a film buff, thanks to the art cinemas of the Upper West Side, the venerable Thalia, an oddly raked space the size of a shoe box, and the newish New Yorker, where learned film notes added spice to the double features. These had been reinforced by the stupendous film culture that saved me from loneliness and depression in Cambridge. Now back at Yale, seeing eight Hawks or Ford films in a few weeks' time, ranging from westerns and adventure films to screwball comedies, democratized my taste and deepened my superficial knowledge of film history. It was an echo of my unhinged life in Cambridge, where I had gotten up the nerve to start writing about movies.

Teaching modern American poetry preoccupied me as much as discovering these old and new movies. Hollander had asked me to give one lecture on each of the poets in his undergraduate course, and this sometimes proved a challenge. Until then I'd read modern poetry mainly for the language, the unconventional rhythms, the unnerving obscurity, the provocative deviations from traditional rhyme and diction. It mattered little that the "meaning" of the poem often remained hard to grasp, since the gist of it was boldly iconoclastic. I valued it as a special language, mysterious and allusive, at times even gnomic. I could get by on Eliot: his incantatory manner made his language seem inevitable and this had always mesmerized me. But I felt inadequate in teaching really elusive poets like Wallace Stevens or Hart Crane, favorites of Bloom's but dauntingly opaque to me. No serious body of critical interpretation had yet accumulated around them—how different from today! I usually found a key poem or two that did make more sense to me, that was open to the kind of close reading I knew how to do.

One such poem, I thought, was Stevens's late work addressed to George Santayana, "To an Old Philosopher in Rome," written not long before both writers died. Santayana, who had given up teaching philosophy at Harvard forty years earlier, was living ascetically in a convent in Rome, cared for by nuns who treated him as a revered if unbelieving guest. Stevens, something of an amateur philosopher himself, had once submitted a piece to the *Review of Metaphysics*, only to be brusquely rejected by its crusty editor, the Yale professor Paul Weiss. His pride wounded, Stevens left it in his drawer. He must have felt an affinity for Santayana's peculiar Catholic paganism and admired his survival into extreme old age, a man "on the threshold of heaven," as Rome itself is perhaps the threshold of heaven.

But no matter how many times I read it, no matter how much commentary I scrawled in a tiny hand in the poem's margins, it stubbornly refused to yield its secrets. It had a logic, a structure, a tissue of references, an aura of significance, that simply wouldn't come clear for me. Finally, in despair, I called Hollander and without the least pause he gave me a breathless fifty-minute rap about the poem, which I more or less transmitted to the class the following day. It was one of the best critical lessons I ever had, though in a style that was his alone and couldn't be replicated. It reminded me of the nervy brilliance of my best teachers at Columbia, especially Jim Zito and Andrew Chiappe, who had also been John's teacher a decade before me. That lightning flash of insight was exactly what I missed in my classes at Yale; virtually any graduate school in those stodgy days was the wrong place to look for it. All too often the mind-numbing habits of scholarly research outweighed the cultivation of intelligence.

The arrival at Yale of younger scholars like Hollander, Hartman, Bloom, and E. D. Hirsch Jr., with their strong Romantic and modern interests, changed the literary education there, but I arrived too soon to take courses with them. All but Bloom were turned down for tenure, though Hartman and Hollander were eventually called back to pursue stellar academic careers as Yale's leading literary scholars. Luckily, though I had not studied with him, I had the pleasure of working with Harold, very much in his own idiosyncratic fashion. I would submit my work chapter by chapter, then come to his big, rambling house on Linden Street to discuss it. As a voluble and chivalrous admirer of women, he would always insist that I bring along L for company. When we arrived he would invariably pay extravagant compliments to her beauty, her fine character, and lecture me on how unworthy I was to have this woman as my spouse. Charmed to the quick, she loved every minute of this ritual, and so did I, since I warmly agreed with him.

After these ritual exchanges I would retire to his third-floor study to question him about his comments on my chapter, though mostly we talked about everything else you could imagine. In one of his letters Keats described running into Coleridge in one of his walks, Coleridge the polymath who was by then more celebrated for his talk than for his poetry, the best of which lay behind him. Keats, infinitely amused, records a long list of the subjects the older man had touched upon (starting with nightingales!), then adds, "I heard his voice as he came towards me—I heard it as he moved away—I heard it all the interval—if it may be called so." Harold did not quite soliloquize in this fashion but he had his own flow of brilliant talk, often eccentric, always highly opinionated. His was the kind of quicksilver mind that had enraptured me at Columbia, and I was delighted to encounter it again in an unpropitious setting where it was not yet highly valued, a department in which he was very much the interloper. Our talks didn't provide much guidance for my thesis but then, in my youthful confidence, I didn't feel I needed it. When he added subtle qualifications to what I wrote, I was grateful to include them; when he crossed out whole pages with comments like "arrant nonsense," I usually restored them and we went our own way.

He thought my work, inflected (or infected) by Trilling's influence, was too sober and moralistic, too much anchored in the dark, the self-conscious, the quotidian. I thought his inspired readings of the Romantic poets put too much of their weight on the sublime, the apocalyptic. He saw the Romantics as visionaries, always reaching out of the frame of ordinary experiences toward a fuller sense of being; I responded to them most strongly as tragic realists, aspiring to transcendence, as overheard in the nightingale's undying song, but ultimately facing up to the stark limits of human possibility. Had I worked on Blake and Shelley, who ultimately *were* visionaries, we would have been constantly at loggerheads; he acknowledged that Keats was different, closer to Wordsworth, far more earthbound; he seemed perfectly pleased to let me take my own path, and we got along wonderfully. Besides, we shared something deeper: though he was ten years older, we were both brainy Jewish kids from New York, had grown up in modest but aspiring immigrant families, and felt mostly out of place at Yale, which had just begun to take in more than a handful of students like us.

It was surprising that we were so enamored of the Romantics, who mostly hated cities and were drawn powerfully to nature, something for which urban Jews had notoriously little feeling. One day in March, when Harold was graciously showing us out, I spotted the first spring flowers and some lines from Shakespeare sprang to mind: "Harold," I said, " 'daffodils, / That come before the swallow dares, and take / The winds of March with beauty.' Might these be daffodils?" My mentor, as unworldly as I was, looked blank and confessed he had no idea, recalling that one English critic had dubbed him "an armchair Wordsworthian," a label he embraced with pride. Years later, when I found myself teaching Wordsworth's poetry, I would often begin with one of his most beautiful lyrics, "I Wandered Lonely as a Cloud." It took off from an animated sea of daffodils undulating in the wind ("Beside the lake, beneath the trees, / Fluttering and dancing in the breeze"), but its subject, typically, was less the scene itself than its later effect on his mind as he quietly assimilates it to his inmost being. It becomes a cure for loneliness, for depression. ("And then my heart with pleasure fills, / And dances with the daffodils.") It was this achingly modern project of self-scrutiny, not simply natural observation, that excited us in these poets. Their brooding depth of feeling seemed to make them our contemporaries.

New Haven might have been a backwater, self-enclosed and out of touch, yet even there it was hard to focus on poetry as the world around us grew more tense and polarized with each passing week. Thanks to the daily bombing of North Vietnam and the dispatch of more and more troops, the war was fast becoming an American war, including a ground war. This soon set off mass protests. I was aghast not only at the escalating war abroad but at the rising racial bitterness at home. Despite new civil rights laws, the nonviolent marches were giving way to spasms of anger and frustration. By August, riots in the Watts section of Los Angeles would set a pattern for outbreaks of violence in other major cities, including Newark and Detroit, that would leave their inner cities decimated. As if in tandem, popular culture was exploding in its own way that summer of 1965 as the Beatles performed for ecstatic teens at Shea Stadium and Bob Dylan enraged folk music purists by picking up an electric guitar and intruding hard rock into the Newport Folk Festival.

It took us the better part of that year to catch up with these cultural changes, although we were intrigued by the waiflike Dylan and his plaintive country drawl. We got caught up in protest marches and antiwar rallies, one of them on the Green in the tranquil, tony seaside town of Guilford, which had voted overwhelmingly for Goldwater the preceding year. The rhetoric at these demonstrations was at once impassioned, clichéd, and irrefutable. The nation was going down the wrong path, the exact opposite of the one the electorate had just chosen, and we had no choice but to protest. It was not clear whether anyone was listening, but we needed at least to free ourselves of any complicity with a war being prosecuted in our name.

Early in the summer, to get away for a spell, we drove up to Maine and found a guesthouse on the water, only to discover that the Atlantic there was far too cold for swimming; the icy water seemed to cut us off at the ankles. Once we returned we began taking the Bridgeport ferry across the Long Island Sound to spend weekends in Rocky Point, where my aunts, uncles, and older cousins, who had all danced at our wedding, seemed astonished to find me a married man rather than the raw youth, immature for his age, who had left town at fourteen. There we took a special pleasure in sleeping openly in the same bed, in the same cramped room where we had once enjoyed furtive sex while everyone else was off at the beach.

Some of our friends—the McGanns, the Dalsimers, the Johnstons—were already having children as we were enjoying our freedom summer—the last, as it would turn out. Slender, fit, and beautiful, L had brought back a bikini from Europe, with barely a hankie and some strings at the groin. She looked spectacular, and it must have puffed up my male pride to show her off at the beach of my boyhood. Such skimpy garb, so much naked skin, had not yet shown up on most American beaches. My mother and her sisters were duly scandalized, perhaps embarrassed before their blue-collar Italian neighbors. Tante Lily, always tough and outspoken, was their designated emissary. "Somebody, I won't say who, said, *es posst nisht*, it don't seem right, for a professor's wife to go around half-*nakitt*," she said to L, who, assuming that she was channeling my mother, countered that I was still only a graduate student. She couldn't help being amused by their prudish objections. She liked Lily very much but she was at least as stubborn as my aunt could be; no one was going to tell her what to wear.

One weekend we returned from New Haven to find that half the bathing suit, the skimpy bottom, had disappeared from the edge of the tub where she thought she had left it to dry. L searched everywhere, wondering if she'd left it on the clothesline instead, and she finally asked Lily if she had any idea what had become of it. Acting as if accused of petty larceny, the old lady was indignant at the very idea she had anything to do with it, insisting she would never have gone into the house at all, though she had a key. She was so definite, so offended, that L wondered whether *she* had misplaced it, but it never turned up. Twenty years later, at Lily's funeral, her son-in-law Harry, who had more than appreciated the sight of L in her bikini, confessed that Lily had impounded it and tossed it down the outhouse. The family's honor was saved. We were hardly provocateurs yet must have offended middle-class propriety with such a public display of bare young flesh. By now the sixties were in full swing but not here, not yet. Still, our weekends at the beach made it a delectable summer, linking fond recollections of my Long Island past with our New Haven present.

In the fall semester I was set to be a section man for Alvin Kernan's lecture course on Shakespeare, leading a small group of students in weekly discussions. Soon after it began I was dogged once again by vague symptoms—stomach pains, chest pains, gnawing anxiety—and missed one of the first meetings. I found it humiliating that L had to go to class to announce that I couldn't be there that day. It was clear to me that I needed more psychotherapy; it had worked for me in Cambridge, though it had not exactly solved my problems. I was enough on edge that during the huge power blackout that November, when the whole northeastern electric grid crashed—the lights in New Haven only dimmed and flickered—my first thought was that my eyes were giving out.

I found a shrink who seemed sharp enough and I dutifully showed up once a week at his office on Trumbull Street to pick apart what was ailing me. I never missed another class but this therapy was at best a holding action and went nowhere. Sometimes the good doctor treated me as a source of ideas, asking me for references for something I'd mentioned, such as a phrase I quoted from Leavis's essay on Shelley. At other times he appeared bored and disengaged; once he even closed his eyes and dozed off. After a minute or so I stopped speaking and this soon brought him around. "Why did you stop?" he asked. "It seemed you fell asleep." "What made you feel that way?" he countered rather lamely. "Because you *were* asleep," I said, angered at the shrinky move that made it *my* problem yet just as annoyed at myself for failing to interest him. I knew that I needed more serious treatment, though we could scarcely afford it. Instead, as in Cambridge, I kept busy, making sure I left little time for glum introspection.

Assuming my thesis would be done by the following summer, I threw myself into the search for a full-time job. We couldn't know we were living in the waning days of an academic boom; jobs were plentiful for any newly minted Ph.D.—it was simply a matter of choosing one over the other. Department chairs came calling at Yale like major-league scouts checking out the talent. Thanks to the old-boy network, students could be placed in plum jobs with a well-placed phone call, some back-channel commendation. Dwight Culler, one of our resident Victorians, told me of an opening at the Carlyle "factory" at Duke, where the letters of Thomas and Jane Carlyle were being churned out in a multivolume editing project that would go on forever. Not for me, I knew: the irascible Carlyle was indeed my cup of tea, or brew of ale, but textual editing was not. I interviewed for a job at the University of Wisconsin but the interviewer, a fine scholar named Walter Rideout, smiled when he saw that I'd gone to Columbia and already published pieces in *Partisan Review*. He seemed happy to give me an oral workout but guessed he would never lure me to Madison. I felt the same way, a little superior to anything in the boondocks, but years later, while working on the 1930s, I came to appreciate his pioneering book on the radical novel, a most unlikely enthusiasm for the 1950s.

Bloom recommended me for a job at Haverford College, the prestigious Quaker institution just outside Philadelphia. Invited to visit, I was charmed by everything I saw: a small liberal arts college, a hands-on faculty passionately devoted to teaching, a long tradition of moral conscience and social activism, an idyllic campus only a short distance from a major city. The college was located on Philadelphia's Main Line, a gold coast where the price of homes was simply out of reach, so a great deal of faculty housing was provided right on campus. I was shown a handsome if unassuming house that could be rented for ninety dollars a month, cheap even then. It tapped into my cherished fantasies of small-town life and a nurturing community. As part of the interviews, I lectured on Keats to a voluble gathering of faculty from several departments and had a lively audience with the president himself, a model of genial informality. He was so intimate and encouraging I couldn't help being flattered. It was more like being ardently wooed than hunting for a job. Sensing that we might resist relocating to a small college, they encouraged me to return with my new wife to look the place over.

I was brimming with enthusiasm when L met me at the train station in New York. I had lived all my life in the city, and this was the kind of community of scholars in a sylvan setting that, as a city boy, I had often longingly imagined. I painted a picture of the lush green campus, the charming house I had seen, the pleasures of living and working in the same place, where students and colleagues could drop by. Before I knew it L began crying. "I don't want to be a faculty wife, pouring tea for students." She had already left one college town, New Haven, and come back only grudgingly, her "biggest sacrifice," she often joked. She had no intention of becoming the smiling helpmeet of my professional life. I was shaken to realize, as if for the first time, how much marriage involved accommodation, adjusting to the wishes of another person even when they rubbed up against your own. This was hardly more than a bland truism but I needed to experience it on my own. L's independence was instinctive, temperamental. Whatever I myself wanted—and I didn't really know yet—we would need to search out ways to make us both happy.

The urban option, or one of them at least, was represented by my old school, Columbia, which had only recently plucked me out of New Haven and sent me off for that year in England. I had kept in touch with several of my teachers, including Chiappe and Marcus, who must have arranged a formal interview, though I have no memory of it. A teaching job, as I've said, could be handed out more informally then, almost as patronage appointments if someone with influence got behind it. One Sunday morning I got a call from Quentin Anderson, who chaired the college wing of the department, offering me a position for seven thousand dollars a year, not exactly a handsome sum but close enough to the going rate. I thanked him enthusiastically but said I'd promised Haverford I'd make no decision until the middle of the week, by which time I should be hearing from them. Anderson was a man of few words but I could hear the incredulity in his silence, a stunned disbelief that I would seriously consider any other place.

He must have presumed I was shaking them down. "Seventy-five hundred and not a penny more," he said, with a clang of finality. I was grateful for the offer, I said again, but could tell him nothing until midweek. Now he signed off sounding thwarted, vaguely disgruntled. Since I hardly knew him, I guessed it was Columbia's collective arrogance he was voicing, not simply his own. Happily, I'd pocketed a cool five hundred dollars just by keeping my word. It was a haphazard, involuntary form of negotiating, the only kind I knew how to do.

Two days later the offer from Haverford came through. I had already gotten a long letter from an observant Jew on the faculty to assure me that I wouldn't feel uncomfortable there, just in case that might be holding me back. No such misgiving had crossed my mind. I thought about the offer seriously for twenty-four hours before signing on for the Columbia job. L desperately wanted to move back to the city, the urban beehive that had rescued her from the oppression and boredom of life in New Haven. I had happy memories of my Columbia years—the core curriculum that had introduced me to the ample geography of Western culture, the combative forms of intellectual exchange that sparked so many earnest conversations, even the classical grace of the campus and the gritty ethnic mix of a neighborhood that had come to seem like home. So the die was cast and the hunt for a teaching job was over, though most of my thesis was still to be written.

The following month another piece of our future unexpectedly fell into place. L had missed her period once or twice but her cycle had always been erratic. With an innocence that seems astonishing today we thought little of this, but I accompanied her to the gynecologist for a consultation. As I sat in the waiting room surrounded by pregnant women, glancing through a pile of magazines directed at those women, it never crossed my mind that we might be in the same situation. When L emerged from the doctor's office with a broad grin on her face—carrying a pile of baby magazines, no less—I still didn't get it. And when she told me she was almost three months pregnant, so far along that no test was necessary, it seemed like a bolt from the blue. I must have turned several colors out of sheer disbelief but also embarrassment, as if our sex life had been blatantly trumpeted to the world. What could I have been thinking?

A moment later I was thrilled beyond words, awash with wild expectation, determined to shelter L in her delicate condition, though she needed
no coddling: she had never felt better, without a day of morning sickness.
A few months earlier we had visited Betty Johnston, Ken's wife, in the
hospital where she had just given birth to their first child. We were so
taken with this—overjoyed, really—that the thought of having a baby
must have been catching. When initially told they were expecting, I had let
out such a loud whoop on the phone that Ken was taken aback; I sounded
more excited, he said, than his own reserved Swedish parents. Vicariously
enjoying their experience, we were playing with parenthood without taking full responsibility for it.

One fortunate thing about awaiting the birth of a child is the long period
of gestation nature considerately provides to get used to it, though for us
the time was shorter than most. You think ahead, make practical plans,
slowly adjust to a new identity, but—quite deceptively—nothing in your
life seems altered. Having a baby, the sea change it would bring, remained
little more than an abstraction. I continued working on Keats, L continued
going to the lab, though the doctor, fearing a fall, insisted she stop biking.
But just below the surface my own excitement was percolating. It's often
said that some men are turned off by their wives' pregnancy. Unable to see
them as both mothers and lovers, they turn elsewhere or lose interest. That
astonishes me, since everything about the pregnancy turned me on: we had
made a baby together, L's body was blooming with it, she felt good about it,
and I was bursting with peacock pride. I had grown up in a large extended
family, a chaos of aunts, uncles, and cousins. I adored children. But the
oncoming actuality—of bringing another life into the world and nurturing
it—was no more than a distant rumor.

This gradually grew more real during the next few months. My mother
had given birth in 1940 under anesthesia, as many women still did in 1966,
but by then the move to demedicalize childbirth—to experience it more
fully as a natural process, free of deadening drugs—had gained ground.
Yale–New Haven Hospital was sponsoring a natural childbirth class, with
men as fully involved partners, preparing to help their mates time their
contractions and stay on top of their labor with breathing exercises. It meant
that I too could play a role in the birth of our child. This was cutting-edge

stuff but in many ways it seemed like something of a game; we felt like children ourselves, playing at life. When they passed a large doll around to demonstrate how to hold a baby, L grabbed it by one leg; this shocked other soon-to-be mothers, who audibly gasped.

The baby itself was as yet unreal to us. Other concerns loomed large in my life. The therapy I was in had little immediate effect but convinced me I needed to go beyond it. At my grimmest moments I wondered whether I would really take up the new job. When I bought new clothes to teach in, I had flickering doubts I would ever use them, fleeting thoughts of death or of some kind of breakdown. Whatever had held me back from marriage was straining to keep me stuck again. Only a full-scale analysis, then the gold standard of mental health, held out hope of making a difference but it was something I could barely contemplate and ill afford. I applied to the New York Psychoanalytic Institute, the Freudian shul on East Eighty-Second Street, to serve as a control—a guinea pig, in a sense—for some analyst's on-the-job training. The hurdles for admission included a wrenching series of interviews, a gauntlet demanding prodigious bouts of self-exposure. It was said that those who were turned down by the institute were either too well or too sick to profit from it, but you were never told which pool of rejects you landed in. Once you were chosen, though, the cost would be scaled to whatever you could pay.

Attacking two problems at once, whenever I came to town for an interview I put in long hours scouring the Upper West Side for an apartment. The best way to find a flat then was to canvass the building itself, search out the super for an insider tip on a vacancy, even a prospective vacancy, and slip him some money under the table. The West Side was changing then. The elderly tenants with large flats in grand but decaying buildings on West End Avenue and Riverside Drive, many of them German refugees who had arrived in the 1930s, were inexorably dying off. Macabre though it seemed, it paid to scan the death notices in the *Times* for some lead on a spacious apartment in these once luxurious, now badly run-down rental buildings. The canny janitors, who were one step ahead of the obituary listings, held choice information. So I spent those days split between hunting down supers or talkative tenants on West End Avenue and interviewing with shrinks, some of whom still had piquant Viennese accents. After I described some physical symptoms to one of them, he asked, "Und vat about ze intestinal system, ze path of *least* resistance?" I was able to assure him that my stomach too had kicked in with an impressive claim on my free-floating anxieties. Always a good performer, I felt I was saying the right things, putting on a convincing show as a candidate for treatment. My rich larder of symptoms made for choice clinical fodder and, however embarrassing, it was already something of a relief just to talk about them.

In search of further distraction from the thesis, I looked for other writing I could do. Picking up my connection with *Partisan Review*, I offered to review Hartman's long-awaited book on Wordsworth, though they rarely took note of academic works, especially on any literature earlier than the modern era. Reading the book closely heightened my sense of how the shifting layers of interior reflection, the dialogue of the mind with itself, remained at the heart of Romantic poetry. I also did a piece on a new Chekhov production (directed by one of my idols, John Gielgud) that was passing through New Haven and sent it to a new quarterly in the *PR* mold, *Salmagundi*. When the *Times Book Review* printed a PEN talk by Saul Bellow kvetching about how his generation of writers had been unappreciated by obtuse academics, I dashed off a mocking rebuttal using *Herzog*, the first book of his I'd really loved, to make the case against him. Professors were too invested in earlier modern writers, he claimed, and spoiled by their cushy jobs and good medical benefits. Why shouldn't *he* get more of that attention? His little screed sounded exactly like one of Herzog's self-absorbed, slightly unhinged complaints, but here was Bellow publishing it straight, minus even a shred of protective irony.

With a cocksure display of confidence, I mailed it off to the *Book Review*, which bounced it back almost by return mail. That fall it would come out in *Partisan Review*, where some of the quarreling editors, for their own reasons, had the notion of taking down their most prized writer a peg or two. The founding editors, Philip Rahv and William Phillips, had long been locked in a struggle to control the magazine; younger editors were forced to take sides as well. They had already published an ill-conceived blast at *Herzog* by a new editor, Richard Poirier. In the fratricidal world of the New York intellectuals this was a minor episode. But Bellow was bitter, as I later learned, though he undoubtedly blamed the editors more than he blamed me, a young nobody. Thanks to this rancor there was a sharp break; he would not write for *PR* for another three decades.

Most of my writing time was spent on Keats as I raced to finish the thesis before the last week of July when the baby was due. I might have managed it somehow, but five or six weeks before that date we awoke during the night in a soaking bed. I was befuddled, completely at sea, but L grasped immediately that her waters had broken. After she had spent two days in the hospital with only weak contractions, the doctor induced labor and, miraculously, all those breathing exercises kicked in. L was in a terrible sweat, beyond anything I had ever seen, and though I was participating, attentive—timing contractions, holding hands, putting ice on her forehead—I felt intense frustration that I couldn't do more. The pain, when it came, looked excruciating yet I was wide-eyed with wonder, lost in the stars. "Tell me," I asked her, "is it *beautiful* pain?" "Hell, no," she said, "it just *hurts*." So much for the difference between fatherhood and motherhood, a condition I could only idealize.

It was all a perfect cliché, the reinvention of the wheel, yet we were living it to the hilt. When we first saw the baby, scrawny, delicate, barely five pounds, he seemed like a miracle of creation, infinitely vulnerable yet perfect, right down to the tiny fingernails and toes. Like every other first-time parent, we found it hard to imagine we had actually produced this creature, that he sprang out of my seed and L's body. The whole long pregnancy, the months of expectation, her distended belly, had still not prepared us for this new life, separate from us but achingly dependent. We could see just how dependent when our doctor, Morris Wessel, let us take Jeremy home, though he lost a few ounces in those first days. Dr. Wessel, a legendary New Haven pediatrician, was as much an astute psychologist of new parents as a shrewd and intuitive physician to their offspring. He sized us up as a couple who could cope with an underweight baby many weeks premature, and somehow we did, though his stomach was so small, his appetite so sluggish, that he needed to be fed every two or three hours. In line with our natural regimen, L was breast-feeding but had to stop abruptly when the baby's tan, healthy-looking complexion turned out to be a case of jaundice, common in premies. And so my chief responsibility shifted from writing about Keats to spending hours each day at the laundromat, since the baby, in those pre-Pampers times, invariably soaked through everything.

One complication was that he weighed too little to be circumcised on the eighth day, as Jewish law demands; this disturbed L's father no end. Another wrinkle was that New Haven, like the rest of the Northeast, was experiencing one of the hottest summers on record, and on the day Jeremy could finally have his bris, thirty days after his birth, along with his *Pidyan ha-ben* (a ritual "redemption" of the firstborn), the temperature was hovering near a hundred degrees. The air in our ground-floor apartment was suffocating as family and friends descended on us, though my mother, recuperating from gall bladder surgery, delayed far too long, and a life-threatening siege of pancreatitis, had to stay home. The mohel who performed the circumcision was another colorful, ubiquitous New Haven character, Zelly Surasky, L's father's pinochle partner, a gregarious talker whose sideline was selling insurance and mutual funds. Much in demand, he seemed to have snipped the foreskin of every Jewish child in southern Connecticut.

My father, shy as ever, was slated to serve in the honorific role of the sandek, holding the baby on a pillow in his lap during the procedure, but he turned green at the prospect. L's ebullient dad, reliably earthy, not at all squeamish, immediately jumped in to show how it was done. Wisely, his daughter was hustled out into another room, horrified that her baby was being mutilated in a rite that seemed barbaric to her. As if to confirm this, the young tyke, on being cut, let out a fierce shriek, perhaps because he was a month rather than a week old—his nerve endings were more developed, or so we were told. As if we ourselves had been cut to the quick, we were terrifically relieved when the long day ended. Yet I felt swept up in the train of Jewish tradition, the covenant that stretched from father Abraham to my father Abraham, as we brought our tiny son into the fold. Such traditions mattered to me, though I was hard put to explain why. They were woven into the texture of my life; I couldn't imagine setting them aside.

We moved to New York in mid-August, taking only our clothes, some Salvation Army furniture, many cartons of books, along with brick-and-board bookcases—rough wooden boards we had stained light brown and large whitish bricks we had liberated from New Haven construction sites after dark, my heart racing wildly with each foray. The mover we hired complained jokingly: "Whaddya got in these boxes, lady, bricks?" Little did he know. When we got to New York, our apartment on West 105th Street, ten blocks from Columbia, which we found through one of the real estate listings in the *Times*, was anything but ready. The vintage West Side building, dating from 1916, was on the wrong side of Broadway—the Amsterdam Avenue side, not the Riverside Drive side—and the apartment was a wreck, last painted a nauseating green and turquoise sometime around World War II. But the five rooms were spacious, with solid walls, high ceilings, and spectacular views, over the rooftops, in three directions. The once genteel neighborhood was in an advanced state of decay, with neglected apartment houses, shabby storefronts, and an epidemic of petty street crime. Still, that stretch of Broadway was a river of busy street life, twenty-four hours a day, as well as an intimate oasis for small business—a tiny Associated supermarket across the street, a Daitch Dairy a block north, kosher delicatessens that had kept me alive as a student, aging craftsmen who had plied their trade forever.

The building had obviously seen better times. Two old ladies we met in the elevator warned us against moving in. They had lived there since the 1920s and remembered the days when the doormen wore white gloves and the owner lived on the ground floor and kept vigilant watch over the building and its respectable occupants. Now a shady lawyer owned it, did little maintenance, and bled the building dry. He pressured the rent-controlled tenants to move out, sometimes making their lives a misery. In the apartment we took he had refused to replace a large window that had blown out in a winter storm, many months earlier; the stubborn tenant, another old-timer, had simply closed off that room, leaving it open to wind, rain, and snow, damaging the beautiful hardwood floor. The kitchen still had prewar appliances: a refrigerator with the motor on top, a two-tone enamel stove badly corroded around the burners, a porcelain sink on spindly legs. The appliances would be replaced on the cheap, triggering a slight rent increase, but we agreed to take the apartment "as is," as the owner demanded, without even a paint job. This was illegal but we could hardly sue. "You're not a lawyer, are you?" he snarled at me. "We don't want any lawyers in the building." I understood why.

Bill, the amiable super, offered to paint the place for very little money but when we arrived it was nowhere near half done. There was as much paint on the floors as on the ceilings and walls. He had left the kitchen for last, removed the old appliances but had not yet brought in new ones. We discovered that, saint that he was, he had a weakness for the bottle and an ingratiating habit of telling people whatever they wanted to hear. Friends came to visit, to see our new place, to welcome us to town, and we received them sitting in the only habitable spot, the corners of our large bed, the one new piece of furniture we had bought other than the baby's crib. Yet it was festive to be there, reinstalled, if tenuously, on the Upper West Side we had left years earlier, only a few blocks from where we had spent our most carefree romantic days.

We felt that we were coming home yet everything was new; our lives had been hugely transformed. I had a new job in a new city, new yet old. We had a new baby in a new apartment, though it looked as if it had been ravaged by war. I had an unfinished thesis that seemed miles away. Around us the nation itself grew daily more polarized from an unfinished war that turned more intractable from week to week. Living in a mixed neighborhood full of poor people and penniless academics, we could feel the racial tension on the street. I was mugged more than once for the meager contents of my wallet. With parenthood, with teaching, my life, our marriage, entered uncharted ground just as the world at large, riven by bitter divisions, was growing ever more unstable. Rock music would provide the sonic background to this instability, and we soon were listening to more and more of it, Dylan, the Beatles, the Rolling Stones, and half a dozen other performers and bands. The music radiated a charge of sexual energy yet was also infused with a snarl of anger and a loud rhythmic pulse of violence. For a time, many more traditional styles in art, from classical music to Henry James, felt out of synch with our lives, as if they belonged to a slower, quieter, more reflective age. There was acute moral anguish in the air—about the war, about the enveloping racial bitterness—but also a whiff of adventure, the thrill of the untried, the untested. The sixties had really begun, *our* sixties had begun, and it seemed at once a moment of grave peril and a bracing time to be alive.

Eleven

INTO THE FRAY

R ECENT RESEARCHERS have attested that our fullest memories seem to
go back to our twenties, though they can't agree on why those times
remain so vivid to us. Is that when our identity is formed (or hardened into
place) or quite the opposite—those first years of adulthood, when everything seems open to us, every experience new and fresh, since so much of
it is happening for the first time? My life till then had been bounded by
religion, by all-boys schooling and my own fears of breaking out, amplified
by the warnings of danger that issued regularly from my parents' straitened lives. These first grown-up years were far from the happiest time of
my life yet in retrospect that decade, the 1960s, seemed to last half a century, as if time moved more slowly and every day, every year, seemed full
to overflowing. I was coming into my own just at the time when the world
around me was in eruption, breaking loose from its moorings in abrupt,
unimaginable ways.

Coming to teach at Columbia in the fall of 1966 I found myself in
an unfamiliar role in a place I had left behind five years earlier, now just
beginning to reflect the convulsions of the decade. The Sundial at the center of campus was the university's Hyde Park Corner, its Union Square,
the magnet for increasingly frequent protest rallies. The restless energies
that had once propelled late-night panty raids at Barnard were boiling up
into antiwar and civil rights demonstrations. The day before yesterday

hardly a black face had been seen at Columbia, though Harlem was just down the hill. Now a large number of black students had been recruited for the freshman class, which suddenly looked more like New York and less like a New England prep school. Tuition remained low, scholarships were generous, and blacks were taking some of the paths the children of immigrant Jews had traveled decades earlier. The university was still a bastion of privilege, unlike its proletarian neighbor, City College, but it had long been a vehicle for inducting outsiders into a wider culture. Young Jews like me had leaped at the chance to get their rough edges sanded off, to swim toward the mainstream. It was not yet clear whether the new black students, nursing bitter grievances, would take the same bait. Thanks to the rise of black nationalism, they were under pressure to reject integration and carve out a separate world for themselves, a world of racial pride and truculent radical gestures.

I would be teaching two sections of freshman English, the course in which my showy high school prose had first undergone a rude shock. But my main challenge would be the core Humanities course, a signature initiation at Columbia, embracing key figures of Western literature and philosophy from Greek to modern. This storehouse of classic works had once stunned me with the recognition of how little I knew. With minute annual variations the syllabus remained the same but the surrounding world was not. Teaching Homer's *Iliad*, for me, was like reading it for the first time, and this reminded me of how naive and untutored I had been at seventeen. But confronting it as the Vietnam War was heating up made an incalculable difference, sharpening its impact, as it had done for sensitive readers like Simone Weil during World War II. Her urgent existential reading of the poem as an orgy of blood and graphic violence foreshadowed the very ways it would impact receptive students in 1966.

These students were a joy to teach. At Yale, where many of my charges were "legacies," some of them bearing the same family names as the imitation Gothic buildings, an unspoken undergraduate code still made it a breach of tact to raise your hand, draw attention to yourself, or talk in class. As a section man I'd done everything I could to rouse them into speech. Vaguely, I expected the same youthful resistance at Columbia and came in prepared to pummel my students with questions, to prod them with an electrical charge. But at the first query about fourteen hands shot up, reminding me of my own shameless hand in the air in years past. With a sigh of relief I knew I was home free. Not every session was as intense as those on the *Iliad* but nearly all of them were alive, burbling with energy; I needed to redirect or hold back students, not stun them into speaking up. The reading list was massive—after Homer it was a rapid, steady march, a book a week—but staying one or two steps ahead of the class I was enjoying my own general education, grappling with these works as if new to me. With a baby at home and a mountain of class preparation, I found myself taking a crash course in Greek and Roman literature; my rudely interrupted thesis remained safely in the box, unread and untouched.

I was still at heart a student myself, since teaching was above all a learning experience and I was also very close to them in age. All of twenty-six, I looked nineteen, and this led to some awkward moments. My first time in the English department office I was treated brusquely by the young secretary who practically kicked me out, as if I were trespassing. "Oh, we thought you were a student," she said when I explained myself. "Is that how you treat students?" I asked her incredulously. The department itself was oddly fragmented, with separate branches in different schools: Columbia College, where I was appointed; the School of General Studies, aimed at adult undergraduates; and the oversize graduate program, a legacy of Nicholas Murray Butler's vision of Columbia as a German research university. It was easy never to cross paths with colleagues in another wing of the department, especially because the college faculty was snobbish about its exalted status. To them the study of literature was a branch of high culture, part of what Jacques Barzun called the House of Intellect. Their business was interpretation, ideas, not the minutiae of research. They barely took notice of the GS faculty and looked askance at their graduate colleagues as dry-as-dust scholars, technicians of the imagination. Everyone took this anomalous split for granted, though many deeply resented it, as I would later discover.

Having grown up with the college faculty, I shared their prejudice against "mere" scholarship, the kind of busywork I'd tried to avoid at Yale. The whole core curriculum at Columbia was based on the notion that even an adolescent, under the guiding hand of a general intelligence, could rise to a direct encounter with major works of Western art and thought, could vibrate to their impact across a gulf of history, geography, and language. But where would I have been teaching Greek literature without timely help from Cedric Whitman's *Homer and the Heroic Tradition*, H. D. F. Kitto's *Greek Tragedy*, M. I. Finley's *The World of Odysseus*, and E. R. Dodds's *The Greeks and the Irrational*? I approached the *Iliad* and the tragedies of Aeschylus, Sophocles, and Euripides for what they had to say about time-less human concerns, but the class would have gone badly astray had I not boned up on the wider social world and the formal conventions in which they came together. Without that balance between keenly attentive reading and really informed historical understanding, class discussions would have been little better than late-night palaver in the college dorm, mixing blatant ignorance with flashes of intuitive insight.

Even more than in most liberal arts colleges, this department seemed to value brilliance over scholarship, putting an emphasis on undergradu-ate teaching that was rare in a large research university. I had always had friends in school who were smart, funny, and original but my new junior colleagues were an exceptionally brainy and voluble lot. The fourth floor of Hamilton Hall, where we shared offices, was a perpetual scene of high-wire conversation. Whether the subject was the literature we were teaching or reading, the edgy movies and plays that were opening week after week, or the ordeal of our country going up in flames, the intellectual firepower was daunting. Some of this was no doubt showboating. This was an all-male faculty, like the college's student body, and it made the give-and-take that much more competitive; beneath the nervous bonhomie there was all sorts of showing off. No one forgot that as junior members we were all in a fishbowl, on permanent display, competing for the scarce tenured positions that might be open a few years down the line. When some of our elders such as Trilling (dour and diffident) or Anderson (impressive in his silences) joined these conversations the atmosphere was collegial, as if arresting observations were the only thing that mattered, but the under-currents were fierce; we acted as though we had to prove ourselves at every minute. Sarcastic wit and strong opinions were the common currency. L noticed that I would come home limp with exhaustion from these after-hours sessions. I was no longer a student but in this barely disguised hierarchy I still longed for the approval of my elders, some of whom had been role models when I was most impressionable.

Our senior colleagues didn't make things any easier, since they never masked the fact that we were all on probation, always being sized up and judged, and probably just passing through. Not long before I arrived, Anderson, the chair, had casually suggested that a junior professor seek another job as they were standing side by side at the urinals. One incident highlighted the impersonal cruelty of this atmosphere. When the pregnant wife of a young medievalist died horribly of cancer, only one of the older professors—Anderson, in fact—showed up with his wife at the funeral. In this oppressive climate the junior faculty, all rocking in the same boat, bonded tightly. My officemates were both named Paul but they couldn't have been more unlike. Paul Zweig had the dark, compact good looks and velvety voice of a would-be poet and the soul of a French intellectual, both of which he essentially was. He had grown up near the boardwalk in Brighton Beach, graduated from the college a decade earlier, and spent most of the ensuing years in Paris, playing jazz piano in bars to support himself, learning French so well he seemed born to it, dabbling in communism, and completing a doctorate at the Sorbonne on two avatars of the counterculture, the plebeian Whitman and the forerunner of surrealism Lautréamont. Five years older than me, he carried himself with astonishing bravura. Paul Delany was English by birth and temperament but his family had relocated to Canada. He'd done his doctoral work at Berkeley, where he met his wife, the tempestuous Sheila, the daughter of Jewish leftists in New Haven. His wickedly dry wit contrasted with his wife's more provocative style, but also with the other Paul's flowery eloquence, to say nothing of my own bright, perky manner. Amid the high-voltage stress levels in that corner of Hamilton Hall, teeming with untenured instructors and preceptors, all feeling under siege, we became an unlikely but supportive threesome, thriving on each other's stimulating company and nicely contrasting styles.

By late fall I had found the groove of my teaching; I was pleased with my classes, full of smart, chirpy kids, and completely caught up in the great works we were exploring, however naively. On the surface I was cocky, arrogant, full of confidence. But I also felt frazzled by the self-inflicted pressure to prove myself, some need to show I was still the A student, worthy of the faith invested in me. This place had helped form me and I allowed it to judge me, but of course it really *was* judging me. This was hard to set aside. It might have been easier for me in a school where I had no history, where my elders might show more empathy for the soul-rending stresses and outsize ambitions of the young.

At home L and I were settled into the apartment, which had finally gotten painted and equipped; the baby, despite his premature arrival, had at last gained weight, looked buoyantly healthy, and had begun to sleep through the night. For the first time in half a year our lives were proceeding smoothly and I would have to buckle down to work. On the fortunate Friday that followed Thanksgiving I picked up my thesis where I had abruptly left off—somewhere in the middle of a discussion of Keats's ravishing "Ode to Psyche"—and started writing again. I would have to submit it to Yale by April to hold on to my job and get promoted to assistant professor. But my time grew even more scarce as the prospects for an affordable psychoanalysis looked up. I had passed three hurdles, separate interviews with analysts who belonged to the institute, followed by a discomforting appearance before a large panel that would have the final say. At last I got the go-ahead and, in December, was finally assigned to a doctor as part of his training.

My meeting with Dr. R in his office on East Eighty-Ninth Street at first went exactly like the conversations I'd been having with therapists for years: I delivered a deft, oft-rehearsed overview of my problems so far—the recurrent anxieties, nagging physical symptoms, and the hopes I invested in treatment. Dr. R was wiry and sharp-eyed, with a welcoming but detached look, radiating a volatile nervous energy held in reserve. He too, I imagined, would be judging me as I'd be exposing myself. He could not have been much older than I was but I endowed him with grave authority, just as my parents had always done with doctors. I was looking for a makeover that would shore up the functioning parts of my inner life while banishing the near-crippling fears of illness and inadequacy that made me feel at times so undermined. But I also worried that, as I took my feelings apart, the defenses that still worked for me would be broken down, not shored up.

I had read Freud's cultural works like *Civilization and Its Discontents* and *The Future of an Illusion*, his attack on religion, but knew little about the technique of analysis beyond what I had learned from my own therapy. I simply assumed that thanks to the discoveries of Dr. Freud, Dr. R somehow held the key to my ultimate well-being, to the calm and competent person, always in perfect control, that I wanted to become. Still, he seemed to be jumping the gun when he pointed to the dark-leather couch and asked whether I'd like to lie down. Was I so ill that I had to lie down? Was it a gurney on which I would be strapped down and wheeled away? I knew the fabled couch was part of the analytic process but it was still an unexpected thing to be asked to do, as if I would be addressing the ceiling and the walls. It felt like crossing a barrier into unfamiliar territory, and so it was, for the moment I began speaking I could feel the ice beginning to break up. It became clear how much I'd instinctively oriented what I said to his reaction, the look in his eyes, the expression on his face, impassive as it was. I probably did it with everyone I knew. Having him sit behind me—a disembodied voice—out of sight, freed me to soliloquize and then to free-associate, though of course I was still poised for his response, restrained though it was, weighing it with everything I said.

The real analysis did not begin until months later, when my self-analysis ran dry and I reached the limit of my own explanations for the fix I felt I was in, the cycle of anxiety that could throw me off balance. I was seeing him five days a week, the time equivalent of adding two courses to my weekly schedule. This was not therapy as I had known it but rather an additional circuit plugged into my daily life, a running commentary on everything I thought and felt. My exertions in school, the new baby, my daily trek to his East Side office left me tired much of the time, always on the run. So I found an unexpected benefit in lying down on this leather couch, with a fresh serviette under my head, as if stepping outside my own life. It allowed me to relax and clear my head. My fatigue eroded the censorship I might have brought to what I was saying. I could let my mind roam and catch my wayward and fugitive reactions. Curiously, I had no grasp whatever of the "transference" that is crucial to the analytic process, the projection onto the silent analyst of relationships from your own life. Instead, I accused him repeatedly of being more interested in what I said about *him* than about any other subject. Perhaps it was good luck that I was not too wised up and still had a world to learn about how such an analysis might actually work.

Meanwhile, my life itself went on with a sometimes feverish intensity. For the spring semester a new freshman course was introduced, focused on a single work and the dizzyingly different ways it might arguably be read. It was as much a course in critical methodology as in the works themselves. The instructors tended to choose massive, complex books that lined up with their interests, *Moby-Dick* or *Ulysses* or *Tristram Shandy*—the universe in a single work—but I had a thesis to finish and got the green light to take up the poetry of Keats as a coherent body of work. I was teaching his poems for the first time, testing my readings even as I was writing them down.

For all my troubles there, my ties to Yale were still strong and we often went back to New Haven that year. Robert Brustein, whose lectures on modern drama I had audited as an undergraduate, had taken over as dean of the Yale Drama School and director of the Yale Rep, which was doing provocative plays hooked into the national crisis. We would go up to catch topical and explosive plays like Joseph Heller's ingenious *We Bombed in New Haven*, which made its debut right there in New Haven, Megan Terry's antiwar musical *Viet Rock*, and Arnold Weinstein's Brechtian *Dynamite Tonite*. In these absurdist, circuslike works, as unpredictable as the world around them, the theater became an unexpected venue for new forms of social protest, more anarchic than ideological, full of comic outrage and arresting spectacle. Our visits also gave L's folks a chance to see their grandson though they showed little interest in him; meanwhile, I would run my new work on Keats past Harold Bloom. Such a mix of family and professional life, of poetry, antiwar protest, and cultural spectacle, was built into my scattered life in the 1960s, a time when no combination of demands seemed too incongruous.

As I finished the thesis a moment of panic set in. Borrowing a leaf from Hegel, from phenomenology, but even more from the poetry of Wordsworth, his greatest inspiration, I had pivoted my work on Keats's consciousness of self, his attention to the ebb and flow of his own mind— what I myself was now trying to do on the couch. But all at once, as if on cue, I was struck by a flash of doubt. Much of what I had written seemed to turn on my reading of a single poem, that largely unnoticed lyric "In drear-nighted December," and especially on the concluding lines that began with the key phrase "The feel of not to feel it," the feel of absence, insentience, the numbing of one's awareness of time and change, of mortality. Keats was comparing the fretfulness of the human mind to the unconscious flow of nature, which seemed so oblivious to the cycle of creation and destruction. If I had misread this poem, I wondered, was my whole thesis built on sand?

I sat with Bloom in his attic study, laid out the poem on his lap alongside my pages on it, and voiced my concern, trying to damp down the feeling of last-minute panic. Harold was the definition of a luftmensch, eloquently aloft in a cloud of his own knowing, and I felt as though I were tugging him with ropes down to terra firma. "What's the problem?" he said, after scanning what I'd put before him. "Well," I fumbled, "it's my reading, the reference, the 'it'—I thought I might be, well, wrong." A benign but puzzled looked crossed his face. "It's just as plausible as any other reading," he said at last, looking paternally protective. My concern, which was really about the thesis as a whole, quickly dropped away but for years afterward his reaction resonated with me. Caught in some wrinkle of time, I still had the quaint notion there could be a right and a wrong reading, while he was happy to let a hundred flowers bloom, or a hundred Blooms flower. Postmodern relativism was on the horizon, the uncertainty principle was in the air. By this light, every interpretation was constructed, provisional, rooted in the circumstances that gave rise to it. I couldn't wholly disagree; there were no absolute truths to offset the doubts built into the modern mind. The oncoming clash of the theory years lay before us like a fissure in the landscape, an abyss for the interpretive mind—a *mise en abîme*, it would later be called—and he would grow even less happy with it than I would, becoming the most staunch defender of literature itself against the corrosive effects of literary theory.

I tied up the loose ends of the thesis quickly and, as custom demanded it then, handed it over to the typist, who complained grumpily that typing a thesis was harder than writing it, since I only had to write *one* while she had to type many. She certainly had a point. I made the five copies I had to submit and put the finishing touches on them one Saturday morning in mid-April, then headed down to Central Park for a gigantic antiwar rally and march to the UN, led by Martin Luther King Jr. It was the largest demonstration I had ever joined, one of the largest New York had ever witnessed. Whatever the impact, I felt at least that I had taken a stand, separated myself, at least for that moment, from what our government was doing. It was also a bit of reparation for all the time spent on the thesis, the family, the couch while the world around me was in turmoil. When I returned and the Sabbath had safely ended—L's parents would otherwise have disowned us—we took off for New Haven, where I had a full day to check and collate the copies before submitting them. As I glanced through the pages, my eyes lit on a typo, then another and another, as if the typist had been determined to show me just how hard her work had been. Among other mishaps, she had corrected the quirky spellings in many of Keats's letters, one of the marks of their winning spontaneity.

I spread the five copies out on the kitchen table and, as I scanned each page, L and her mother inked in the corrections on each copy, working as if on an assembly line. Her father, retired from the food business, had become a real estate broker and Sunday was his biggest day. Coming home he was at first curious about all the paper laid out in the kitchen, then impatient, then increasingly annoyed, pointing to his watch, muttering, "late . . . my dinner . . . late." L's mother shushed him out of the room, and we could hear him stomping around the apartment. For me, submitting my thesis was a life-changing moment; my job, a dream job, depended on it; as usual, I couldn't imagine anyone wouldn't be overjoyed for me. After all, wasn't I the apple of my mother's eye, destined to conquer the world? Instead, I had merely disrupted a man's iron routine, stoked his hunger pangs. Not so much earlier L's parents had vehemently opposed her marriage *to a student*, someone not yet ready to support her. Six weeks after we tied the knot they came to Beers Street for a rare visit, bringing me an unexpected birthday present, a term life insurance policy—to make sure, as they said, that if something happened to me, she wouldn't "land on our doorstep." I was turning twenty-five and they were insuring my life! Now, in 1967, only two years later, quite irresponsibly, we had a child to boot. I was inches away from receiving my degree and he growled that his dinner was not yet on the table. L was embarrassed and I was bewildered. My own parents would have fasted for a week to see me get through. I was hopelessly spoiled, assuming the world would yield to my needs, would make way for the coronation of the young Jewish prince. Yet somehow the copies were duly corrected, dinner appeared on the kitchen table, and I deposited the thesis the next day.

It was approved by the department with only minor reservations. One of the faculty reporting on it, I learned, was Cleanth Brooks, the distinguished New Critic, whose courses I had managed to pass over. A few stray typos were duly noted, as was some confusion between British and American usage. (Example: the Brits—Keats included—would not have used "casket" as a euphemism for "coffin," as we did.) Brooks characterized the style as "Trillingesque," though it was not clear whether he meant that as a criticism or a compliment. My supervisor, Bloom, then no great fan of Trilling's, was away that term and could not navigate my work through the departmental meeting, but a younger colleague, Michael O'Loughlin, whom I had known as a Danforth fellow, helped steer it through, and he filled me in afterward, blow by blow.

A month and a half later the family gathered at the commencement to see me invested: my parents, taking in the Yale campus for the first time, beaming with visible pride; L's parents, who perhaps had by then forgiven me for their delayed dinner; my sister, Doris, just graduating from Queens College; and Jeremy in his stroller, not quite a year old, unsure of what the fuss was about but enjoying the sunny June day in the radiant surroundings of the Gothic campus. Thus I became a Doctor of Philosophy, a specialist in early nineteenth-century British poetry, at one of the most turbulent moments in American history.

While the university was enacting one of its time-honored rituals on a resplendent campus, the nation's malaise was worsening. You sensed the moral anguish, the pervasive disquiet, all the time, yet tried to keep it from taking over your life. The war was escalating rapidly but so were the protests against it; more Americans and many more Vietnamese were dying, all accompanied by lugubrious speeches by President Johnson. One of the whiz kids who were architects of the war, Secretary of Defense McNamara, had already lost heart without publicly registering his misgivings. The cultural changes of the decade were also making themselves felt. That spring Paul Zweig turned us on to pot in his Columbia apartment high above 125th Street and Riverside Drive. It seemed to slow everything down, at once making us more tuned in to every sensation and more distant from everything—laid back, floating—not my customary state of mind.

We were listening to more and more rock, for Bob Dylan, the Beatles, and the Stones were producing their best albums, along with rock voices as varied as the mellifluous Simon & Garfunkel, evoking the sounds of silence and Scarborough Fair; the Doors, whose organ tones and eerie vocals echoed as through a haunted house; and Big Brother and the Holding Company, featuring an electrifying Janis Joplin, a self-consuming stage presence who would soon go off on her own before dying young. For someone who had grown up on the 1950s *Hit Parade* and the musicals of Rodgers and Hammerstein, rock music burst forth like a demonic display of sexual energy, especially in tracks like the Doors' "Light My Fire." Jim Morrison, the Doors' lead singer, sounded positively sepulchral in the twelve-minute dirge called "The End." Behind the kinetic, pulsing beat, rock could be nasty or tender, baroque or austerely simple, druggy, violent, or apocalyptic, daringly surreal or folky and bluesy, irrepressibly childlike or impossibly jaded. Many people not much older than us found it barbaric. To jazz fans and some classically trained musicians it seemed musically primitive. It would provide a cacophonous but highly expressive sound track for an eruptive decade.

Perhaps the tipping point for us came in June 1967 with the release of *Sgt. Pepper's Lonely Hearts Club Band.* A few years earlier a friend of L's, visiting us in New Haven, had brought us an early Beatles album. The mop tops seemed adorable and harmless then, with their jeering Liverpool accents and knockabout sense of fun that came though infectiously in the romping spirit of their movies, *A Hard Day's Night* and *Help!* At first, like the young Sinatra, they were mobbed by hysterical teenage fans. But as their music grew more sophisticated and their lyrics darkened, they stopped performing live and aimed for effects that could be produced only in the studio, electronically layered sounds that had already made albums like *Rubber Soul* and *Revolver* so original. Their development as artists was as rapid as Keats's at the same age, in some of the same directions. We were hooked as the adolescent longing of "I Wanna Hold Your Hand" gave way to the haunting disappointment of "I'm Looking through You" and "It's Only Love and That Is All," to the dreary lives of "all the lonely people" ("Eleanor Rigby") and the even starker shading of "For No One." There a man looks into a woman's eyes and sees nothing, a frightening emotional blankness, "no sign of love behind the tears shed for no one." In "Tomorrow Never Knows" the listeners were invited to turn off their minds, relax, and float downstream, an appeal echoed in some LSD-induced songs on *Sgt. Pepper* and its successor, later in the year, the more druggy *Magical Mystery Tour.*

In the landscape of my education there was a supposedly unbridgeable gap between the cutting-edge modern arts, often fragmentary and complex, and the easy listening of pop culture. The Beatles, Dylan, and the Stones came as a revelation. The complications of the music and lyrics, the length and intricacy of their songs, shattered the barriers that had defined popular music, especially in the 1950s. The new music was at once playful and deep, accessible yet mildly esoteric. Though John Lennon's infectious wordplay was indebted to Joyce, the Beatles were not modernists, yet the modern arts, innovative and iconoclastic, had prepared us for them. *Sgt. Pepper*, put together over hundreds of hours, overwhelmed us with its rich musical sound, deploying multiple tracks, overdubbing, and unusual instruments, Eastern and classical. They showcased its increasingly surreal lyrics and dark-grained portraits, especially "A Day in the Life" and "She's Leaving Home," about sour relationships and self-destructive people, whose lives tapped into a well of unhappiness far beyond adolescent angst. Yet all this was loosely framed as a series of music-hall routines, as T. S. Eliot had done with the overlay of voices and jagged fragments that made up *The Waste Land*. With exhilarating brio the Beatles had blurred the lines between high and popular culture, buried the clichés of the thirty-two-bar love song, and exploded youthful irreverence and insecurity into a worldview, as Bob Dylan was doing then in albums like *Bringing It All Back Home*, *Highway 61 Revisited*, and *Blonde on Blonde*. As I emerged from the cocoon of completing my thesis, I found myself confronted with a wildly creative yet also deeply agitated cultural scene.

Since I was in analysis we stayed in town for half that summer of '67, then went out to Rocky Point for August. Bringing our one-year-old into the haunts of my childhood revived powerful memories of the old family uproar, the baking sun and salty seaside air, the stony beach and calm, crystalline surf. On the working side I had proposed an ambitious course on William Blake for that fall, something new for the department, without realizing how difficult it would be. Now I was going through his work with the aid of learned commentaries by Northrop Frye, Bloom, and E. D. Hirsch. They all took radically different approaches to it, with Frye reconstructing Blake's "system" as a whole, even filling in the gaps, while Bloom and Hirsch pursued sharply contrasting takes on individual poems. I had suggested the Blake course in all innocence, so to speak, with no special agenda, simply because I was awed by his seemingly childlike lyrics, satanically witty proverbs, and gnomic prophetic books, which I'd barely begun to understand. Their mythic stories and invented characters, like Urizen, Orc, and Los—"giant forms," he called them—had a distant kinship with the fantasy literature of a later day, from Tolkien onward. But it did not take me long to realize that Blake's sexual and political radicalism, powered by language that borrowed from Milton and the Hebrew Bible, formed a quasi-religious vision that linked up uncannily with the social uproar all around me.

Thanks to the waves of millennial hope and revolutionary unrest that rippled across the Channel from France, Blake's England in the 1790s had an eerie resemblance to America in the 1960s. A new historiography, ushered in by E. P. Thompson's *The Making of the English Working Class*, helped me locate Blake in that milieu of radical pamphlets, nascent feminism, and rising class consciousness, along with the repressive treason and conspiracy trials through which the government struck back. Instead of being the odd loner, largely self-invented, as we had long thought, Blake was braided into the counterculture of his day. If his *America* took off from our own political revolution, his *Marriage of Heaven and Hell* wittily proposed a moral and religious revolution, a blow against caution, self-censorship, and repression: "The road of excess leads to the palace of wisdom." "He who desires but acts not, breeds pestilence." "You never know what is enough unless you know what is more than enough." "Exuberance is beauty."

This language of excess, so startlingly phrased, read like an unexpected gospel for the 1960s, a coded message in a bottle. Blake anticipated Nietzsche's motto: "Live dangerously." My students were surprised and excited, since they imagined that sex had just been invented, that *they* had invented it. The nub of Blake's *Visions of the Daughters of Albion* is an injured woman's brief for what we know as sexual liberation and even gender equality, themes not only ahead of their time but well ahead of the

1960s. At the poem's center, lightly garbed in myth, is a fraught triangle: a woman has been taken by force; the man who overpowered her then brutally discards her, and her benighted suitor, distraught, folds into depression because she is now a fallen woman. But the meat of the poem is what comes next. After first blaming herself, she breaks free of conventional guilt feelings and proudly claims her own sexuality. The style was Blake's alone but the theme proved eerily contemporary. Ignored, sometimes seen as mad in his own time, he seemed just the man for our own.

As the French Revolution collapsed into the Terror, Blake grew disenchanted with politics and placed his hopes in the imagination as a renovating force. I hadn't fully grasped the difficulty of his later work, with its elaborate personal mythology. I can still see myself poring over those long books, *The Four Zoas*, *Milton*, and *Jerusalem*, line by line, trying also to decode both the highly original poetry and the strange visual language of Blake's illustrations and designs. By the end I was a passionate Blakean and so were some of my students, who continued to live with his vision for years afterward. One of them, Michael Aeschliman, the gifted son of a stern Swiss-born minister, became a friend as well as a Blake convert, and continued to send me heady bulletins from the Blake front for the next two decades.

That summer after my thesis was done, on the heels of a busy first year of teaching, I promised myself some long-sought freedom to read. I took up big books I had put aside for years, including Joseph Heller's *Catch-22* and Thomas Pynchon's debut novel, *V.* I had shied clear of Heller because my roommate Eli, a chemist, not at all literary, had laughed so uproariously as he was reading it; I got the impression that it was a farcical army joke book like *No Time for Sergeants*. To my surprise I found that the intimate Jewish fiction I had come to love in Malamud and Grace Paley, in Bellow, Henry Roth, and Philip Roth, had morphed in Heller into a Kafkaesque black humor. A similar sea change had overtaken the historical novel in Pynchon's devious, eccentric imagination. The ingredients included some schlemiel humor borrowed from the Jews, the drifters' underground life evoked by the Beats, and large chunks of Conradian historical writing, much of it tongue-in-cheek but cunningly researched. There was a strain of paranoia in both writers—in Heller's sense that your own army was trying to get you killed, in Pynchon's elaboration of intricate plots—that uncannily anticipated the conspiratorial mood, the rampant suspicion, that was beginning to color the whole decade.

These novels weren't told in a linear way and didn't stay confined to domestic relationships like many small-scale postwar novels. Pynchon's elaborate mosaic of contemporary and pseudo-historical episodes matched Heller's ingeniously rearranged time frame, remixing past and present into a kind of paralysis in which their characters are boxed in. An undertow of conspiracy, the imagination of disaster—these were the books' organizing principles. Like Stanley Kubrick's film *Dr. Strangelove* and John Frankenheimer's *The Manchurian Candidate*, which came out at the same time as these novels, they were at once funny and terrifying. Taken unawares by these novels, I read them as straws in the wind, versions of the same book. In their very plotting, hugely overdone, hinting at hidden connections and fearful symmetries, they laid bare an overdetermined world, so intricately designed that I reread the Pynchon novel immediately after finishing it to grasp how it came together. Though set largely in a reimagined past, these two novels had everything to do with the upheavals around us, yet were written and published before our season of discontent really kicked in. They treated what Paul Goodman and other social critics called the "organized society" not as an object of protest but as the jaws of a vise, an iron condition of existence, comically dreadful but ineluctable. I began to see ways in which different strands of the culture of the sixties were interrelated, part of the florid weave of a single fabric. I saw them as cultural barometers that made it perfectly clear, as if we needed another sign, that the climate of the country, the mental weather, had shifted precipitously.

Younger Americans were trying to live in unconventional ways—dropping out, retreating to farms and communes to live a more "natural" life, reclaiming urban ghettos as bohemian enclaves, getting stoned or taking psychedelic trips (sometimes with catastrophic results), embracing nudity and experimenting with sex (sometimes in groups, even in public places), inventing squishy new forms of psychotherapy that held out some promise of personal liberation. Flamboyantly, the Beats had acted out a living critique of the stiff, cautious, get-ahead culture of the 1950s; now it was spreading to the restless young, their cohort enlarged by the baby boom, inflamed by the Vietnam War, charged up by their own hormones and an unprecedented range of choice. Unlike the generations that had lived through the Depression and total war, they seemed to enjoy a freedom from consequence, thanks to the birth control pill and the booming postwar economy.

Along with other sixties rebellions, the counterculture was in part a luxury accrued from the fruits of prosperity. The kid brother of a close friend was moving to Oregon with his girlfriend and I asked him about their plans. "We're not into future-tripping," he said dismissively, as if I were some kind of control freak, obsessively mapping out my life and imposing it on his. Other young people were confident there would always be a job when they wanted one, or an indulgent parent to bail them out. My students were the children of the middle class, or else plucked out for distinction from among the deserving poor. They were already privileged yet also troubled, aroused, angry.

Here I was, a newly minted assistant professor, doing what I had always wanted to do—teaching seminal works that stood the test of time, talking about them with smart colleagues and alert, appreciative students—yet I too was uneasy, unhappy, caught up in the toxic atmosphere of the time. I hated what the country was doing in my name. I was only a few years older than my students yet I envied their freedom. I was lucky in my marriage, delighted to be a father; still, I felt I had missed out on something, perhaps the wilder times my students were just now living out. For them as for me, political protest was also a personal rebellion: a way of breaking out, bearing witness, renouncing collaboration. The countercultural turn found public expression at the Human Be-Ins that spread from Golden Gate Park in San Francisco to the Sheep Meadow in New York's Central Park, gigantic yet surprisingly benign gatherings that radiated good feeling, some of it slightly idiotic, much of it chemically induced. These were occasions for the young to get collectively stoned, to come together happily as a crowd. My friend Marshall loved these events for their sheer numbers, their goofy ambience, and he often pulled us along, though we were skeptical about the pandemic of impersonal love. He saw them as utopian moments of real community, a recoil from a culture tainted by moral hypocrisy, careerism, and war. The New Left kids and these counterculture types were wary of each other but came together that fall in a huge march on the Pentagon.

Early one October morning my wife and I boarded a bus from the Columbia campus to Washington, having deposited our son with my parents in Queens the night before. I was pleased to see some much older faculty on board, glad this would not simply be another youthful cry in the wilderness. We were determined to make a statement and couldn't imagine *not* going. The aim was less to change our government's direction—that seemed impossible—but to demonstrate, through strength of numbers and apt symbolism, that its policies had lost credibility and public sanction. At the same time we looked for a kind of catharsis, purging ourselves of complicity with a war prosecuted against our will by the men we had elected.

The day began with a rally at the Lincoln Memorial, where the speeches were forgettable, as usual. Perhaps this made up for our having missed the epochal civil rights march of four years earlier. We marched the mile or two across the Memorial Bridge, where trench-coated FBI photographers were snapping our pictures, toward a rally at the designated site, a meaningless parking lot some distance from the Pentagon. I was in a panic of anticipation as we broke through the barriers and raced up to the Pentagon itself, ringed by troops. There a group of yippies led by Allen Ginsberg and Abbie Hoffman were trying to levitate the building, to exorcize the malign spirits emanating from it. That was as sound a strategy as any other, and peaceful to boot. Others broke into the building and were quickly arrested. Some of the celebrities at the head of the march, like Norman Mailer, had already surrendered to arrest, as he reported in *The Armies of the Night*, his mock-heroic book about the march. The rest of us did little more than chant our protests against the war, though we could not help noticing the look of terror in the eyes of the young army recruits who guarded the building. Here the war, the antiwar movement, the counterculture, and a raft of ordinary young Americans came together on a symbolic field of battle. In the end it was mainly a media event typical of the sixties, a theatrical attempt to catch the shifting current of public opinion. Yet it made me feel we had done something to impede the war, perhaps to turn it around by taking a strong collective stand.

The tide did not really turn until the shocking days of the Tet offensive, a few months later. This was a world-changing event, the first of a series of cataclysms that transformed the political landscape. Going for broke,

Vietcong threw all their cadres into simultaneous attacks on major cities and American installations throughout South Vietnam, briefly taking over the city of Hue and occupying our embassy in Saigon. After the initial successes, bolstered by surprise, they were beaten back, even decimated, but this was not how the events filtered through to the American public. Their audacious, coordinated offensive sent a shock wave through the home front. It seemed to show that the Vietcong could operate at will, that our whole war effort, though it inflicted immense casualties, had been for naught—the country would never be secured. It was the beginning of a violent year of demonstrations, confrontations, and assassinations— tremors that ripped America apart in ways that are hard to recapture today, yet were painfully commingled with our personal lives, much like the first Kennedy assassination five years earlier.

A watershed moment came at the end of March 1968. Eugene McCarthy had nearly defeated Lyndon Johnson in the New Hampshire primary and Bobby Kennedy, after agonizing too long, jumped into the race. A panel of foreign policy elders, convened by the president, had advised against any further escalation. At the end of a typically glum, poker-faced TV address Johnson announced unexpectedly that he would not run. L and I leapt to our feet in our living room, cheering loudly, as if our protests had taken hold and we had won a personal victory. This was how demoralized and disgusted we had become and how naive we were about what might follow. McCarthy, we thought, was not the answer. For all his wit and intelligence as well as political courage, he seemed like a dilettante to us, not a future president. He was reserved, curiously detached, with a Catholic sense of man as a fallen creature. His ironic mind didn't seem suitable for govern- ing, or even for the long haul of a presidential campaign. Our hope instead was that Kennedy would win the nomination and gradually end the war, though this seemed like a difficult climb.

The conflict that involved me more directly began at Columbia on April 23 (Shakespeare's birthday, as I could not help observing). Only a few weeks earlier, Martin Luther King Jr. had been killed by a sniper in Memphis, sending another shocking jolt through the nation, especially the already restive black community. His faith in integration and nonviolence, rejected by impatient young black nationalists as well as white segregationists, had offered the promise of a peaceful middle way, and his mesmerizing pulpit manner, with its biblical cadence, had made him the most eloquent figure on the political scene. Moreover, he had expanded his protests from race issues to economic concerns—poverty, inequality—and alienated many, but thrilled us, by taking a leading role in opposing the Vietnam War.

The murder of King brought the racial kettle to a full boil. It led to bloody, destructive riots in the black neighborhoods of many cities, including Washington, Baltimore, and Chicago. When Columbia's elegantly attired president, Grayson Kirk, appeared at a memorial service for King in the university chapel a few days later, a group of radical students seized the pulpit, accused the administration of hypocrisy, then marched out. For more than eight years, going back to my undergraduate days, Columbia had been planning a new gym on neglected public park land between Morningside Heights and Harlem, with separate facilities, even separate entrances, for the university and for the Harlem community. If nothing else, the symbolism was dreadful, insensitive. Increasingly, militant black students labeled this "Gym Crow" and were supported by the young white radicals of the Students for a Democratic Society. Despite many delays the building project had recently broken ground. A protest rally at the Sundial turned—spontaneously, it seemed—into a furious dash down to the construction site. After tearing down a fence the students streamed back to campus, took over the college's main classroom and office building, Hamilton Hall, and briefly held the acting dean hostage—the affable and unflappable Henry Coleman, the same man who had smoothed my way into living on campus when I arrived as a freshman eleven years earlier.

Just as the gym issue was tenuously linked to the national struggle over civil rights, the university's participation in an institute for defense research became a stand-in for the war in Vietnam. This is not the place to offer a history of the weeklong uprising or the student strike that followed; it was the most intensely charged political confrontation I had ever witnessed. As a student journalist and editorial writer I'd always deplored the insensitive, tone-deaf way the university was run. Its longtime president, Nicholas Murray Butler, had shaped it as a lofty international institution, with few local moorings. On Morningside Heights it owned so much property that it was like a real estate holding company. With little concern for the surrounding community, it harassed or evicted longtime tenants, trying every which way to gentrify the neighborhood.

The real university, we thought, was in the classroom, in the library, in the dorms, even on the ball field. The Columbia I loved was the intimate undergraduate college, not the outsize graduate and professional complex or the remote and impersonal administration in Low Library. This leadership had virtually no contact with students, sometimes treating the college like an unwanted stepchild, a source of alumni dollars and little more. The college felt like a community; the university was an abstraction, a corporate entity. As an undergraduate *Spectator* editor I had regularly interviewed President Kirk, though I had no luck in penetrating his implacable reserve and paralyzing stammer. Taking a hands-off approach that catered to the barons in the professional schools, he was as invisible to the faculty as he was to the students. He served on the boards of large companies. To the campus at large he materialized only twice a year, to light the Yule Log in one of the dorms each December, and to bring forth a polished commencement address in June. Now he and his vice president, David Truman, the well-liked former dean of the college, faced an unprecedented student rebellion they were ill equipped to handle. No one had written the book for this unfolding scenario.

Within days students seized and occupied five campus buildings. I saw the campus I loved turned into a war zone. Black students held Hamilton Hall, the nerve center of the college, after expelling their white allies. Black nationalism was in the air; the university feared that Harlem would explode in riots that could spill over onto the campus. A radical caucus took possession of the Math building, graduate students took over Fayerweather Hall, architecture students occupied their home base in Avery, while yet another group had seized the president's office in Low Library, as guards rushed in to rescue a valuable painting. Students went through the president's files, drank his sherry, smoked his cigars, and churned out mimeographed revolutionary messages. With a cheeky insouciance typical of the times, they seemed engaged less in politics than in thumbing their nose at authority. They made a picture of flip irreverence as they climbed down from the second-story windows and sat on the ledges of the campus's most iconic neoclassical building.

I fell in with an ad hoc group of liberal faculty meeting day and night in the ground-floor lounge of Philosophy Hall. The immediate aim was to negotiate an end to the occupation and a resolution of the students' grievances, which soon included a "nonnegotiable" demand that they not be punished or disciplined. Our overriding goal was to avoid a violent outcome, and especially to keep the police from being summoned to evacuate the buildings—or, failing that, to interpose ourselves between the police and the students, not a prospect I looked forward to. We feared an irreparable breach in the mutual respect on which the life of the university—the life of the mind—depended. Our meetings turned into an interminable seminar on means and ends, freedom and the use of force, legitimate and illegitimate methods for effecting social change, but also on the nature of the university, its ideals and values, the codes of behavior by which it lived and thrived. For some, the disruption was a necessary act of dissent, at once urgent and unfortunate, a price to be paid in a time of national emergency to keep the university from acquiescing in policies that even Martin Luther King equated with war crimes. For others the occupation, however peaceful, was itself an act of violence, coercive and illiberal, out of keeping with the consensual norms of the university, which lived on the clash of ideas, not force. By shutting down the institution, the protesters imposed their will on the majority, depriving them of the freedom to pursue their own work.

I had grown up in the cold war era when political change was sluggish at best, fearful at worst, intimidated by the scourge of McCarthyism, loyalty oaths, fears of subversion, and insidious blacklists. I had written articles decrying the bland political climate, when the only safety lay in the dead center and each party seemed frozen into an uneasy consensus, stuck in the middle, determined not to offend. Now everything came unstuck, and in this fluid situation we felt on the cusp of radical change. I went through a furiously intense political education in the heady weeks that followed. To the romantic mind, which was mine at the time, this was our version of Paris in 1790, Petersburg in 1917, Madrid in 1937, Havana in 1959, or so I imagined in the heat of the moment. I thought less about what new order, or complete collapse of order, might follow those tumultuous days.

After the first shock of the building occupations the scene turned almost unbelievably idyllic. It was the middle of spring, when the neoclassical campus glowed in the warm sun, with hordes of students gamboling or picnicking on South Field and sunbathing on the steps of Low Library. On a Sunday afternoon, two days after the administration's first call for the police had been rescinded, L and I brought our two-year-old to the campus lawn. The setting was pastoral, the weather was perfect, and the university felt like a liberated zone as everyone enjoyed an unexpected holiday. This was the carnivalesque side of the uprising, a welcome release from the hair-raising tensions of the preceding week.

The standoff came to a violent end two days later, shortly after I'd left the campus following another day and night of marathon debate. By then both sides had rejected the faculty's mediation proposals, hardened their positions, and were veering toward collision. It must have been well past midnight when I turned on the nonstop coverage of WKCR, the student radio station, to hear that the New York City police were descending on the campus to clear the buildings. I couldn't imagine that the students would forcibly resist but L, vibrating to family memories that went back to Nazi Germany, worried that it would turn violent and begged me not to rush back to campus. Reluctantly I gave in and stayed home, glued to the radio, wondering whether it was her anxious plea or an icicle of cold fear that held me back.

The confrontation turned out even worse than she had foreseen. Under the watchful eyes of community leaders like the psychologist Kenneth Clark, who helped negotiate their exit, the black students in Hamilton Hall surrendered for arrest and were escorted out peacefully, their point made, their dignity intact. But occupants of other buildings fell victim to the equivalent of a police riot. Some faculty blocking the entrances were beaten; students who went limp in a gesture of nonviolent resistance were dragged down stairways and carried out. The buildings themselves were shockingly vandalized. To the blue-collar upholders of the law, it seemed, these spoiled kids had squandered precious advantages their own children might never enjoy. Worse still were the mounted police who charged at bystanders on parts of the campus that were closed off, leaving no avenue of escape. Some were beaten with billy clubs while other police on horseback chased students from Broadway down the hill into Riverside Park. The results of this smashup would be felt for years to come, the tidal effects of a breakdown of comity and trust on all sides. A photo of a stunned-looking student with blood streaming down his head and face appeared in that day's *Spectator* and was reproduced everywhere. As a poster it quickly became an iconic image of campus warfare and official brutality. In the next academic year, copycat uprisings would spread to hundreds of colleges across the country. Campus after campus turned into battlefields, inflamed surrogates for an endless war and an angry, divided nation.

At Columbia a great part of the student body was instantly radicalized by the police action, just as the improvisational radicals of SDS may have hoped. Students called for a strike, and many faculty abided by it, meeting classes at home or elsewhere rather than in Columbia buildings. That morning at a mass meeting of the Ad Hoc Faculty Group I made a brief, hotheaded speech, incoherent with outrage, calling for support for the strike, but the meeting was hastily adjourned before anything could come to a vote. Later that day the combined faculties of all the schools met and set up an executive committee, effectively taking power from the discredited administration and investing it in the hands of a few senior professors. The fabric of the university was irrevocably torn but a new cadre of would-be leaders was emerging to pull together the pieces.

Classes resumed soon afterward, in every imaginable space except the usual classrooms. We met in student union offices, cafés, and our own apartments. Columbia was a gritty urban university, not the kind of school where professors usually met with students at home. I had only one such course in college, that eventful senior seminar with Peter Gay, but here we were, sitting around my living room, discussing Fielding's *Tom Jones*, a rowdy but good-humored work strangely suited to the swirling maelstrom we had just gone through; the book's high and low comedy, its pleasure in mischief, felt therapeutic. Something even more strange took place in the Humanities course on the Western tradition. The syllabus had been stable for over thirty years but the wave of democracy swept over us and students demanded to have their say in what books we would read. We decided to do it by popular vote; since they hadn't read them they asked me to describe what each book was all about. I confess that I tilted the playing field toward works I loved—Montaigne's essays, Rabelais's *Gargantua and Pantagruel*, *King Lear*, *Gulliver's Travels*—and they were enthusiastically approved. Each in its own way, they were as slyly subversive as the moment demanded: grossly sexual, hauntingly metaphysical, or chillingly satirical. Even Montaigne, the wisest, most temperate of men, was provocative in his self-absorption, his minute attention to the wayward movements of his own mind. These were the books usually read at this point in the course yet my students felt dimly empowered; they had made their point. For the next few years this elective option would kick in during the last six weeks of the course, as if in homage to the egalitarian mood inspired by the uprising.

I asked them what subjects they really wanted to tackle in the last two weeks of the semester. "Revolution," said some; "sex," said others. They voted to conclude the course with a work that touched on both, Genet's play *The Balcony*, set in a brothel at the time of an obscure uprising, and finally *The Story of O*, a piece of high-toned literary pornography—also French, what else? Falling behind, we never reached *The Story of O* but I gained some notoriety among senior faculty for having allowed that scandalous work into the precincts of the great books. Years later Quentin Anderson taxed me for doing so at a department meeting. Teaching it in this context would have been a genuine sixties moment but it never came off.

I took no part in the 1968 commencement ceremonies, which were moved, for security reasons, from the outdoor campus to the nearby Cathedral of St. John the Divine, a massive, still unfinished structure but no match in size for the open campus, where the graduation usually was held. Hundreds of graduates got up and walked out to join a counter-commencement on the campus itself, an indication of how much the university was fractured by the uprising, the police intervention, and the ensuing strike, which kept Columbia in a permanent state of emergency. The world around us, too, seemed even more in flux. That night, waking us from a sound sleep, Marshall called. "Turn on the TV," he said. Bobby Kennedy had been assassinated after narrowly winning the California Democratic primary. For the whole preceding month of May we had all been following the news from Paris, where similar campus occupations briefly gained enormous labor support and led to a general strike. At its peak some ten million workers walked out or took control of their own factories. No such alliance developed here at home. Especially after the purge of left-wing labor unions in the 1940s, our own workers were more focused on bread-and-butter issues, not ideology, and organized labor largely supported the Vietnam War. Many workers scorned the protesting students as spoiled rich kids who were simply acting out. Still, public support for the war gradually eroded, especially after the Tet offensive. This gave us little satisfaction, for Nixon's appeal to the "silent majority" and the Democrats' bitter divisions helped get him elected by a hair's breadth that year.

That summer, as students prepared to disrupt the national conventions, I was caught up in the aftermath of the Columbia crisis. The new executive committee, dominated by an ambitious law professor, Michael Sovern, created a task force to determine how the university could be restructured, so as to give students and faculty an outlet for grievances, and some kind of role in how it was governed. I was tapped unexpectedly to serve on a commission that would study Columbia's institutional structure and suggest possible reforms. This felt to me like a peaceful continuation of the spring protests, a way of making the uprising matter. I seized on it as a chance to reshape the university, to make it more enlightened, less corporate, more responsive. I wasn't much older than the radical students; like them, I dreamed of making a real difference.

The job offered a modest summer salary, a boon for us since I was pulling in barely nine thousand dollars a year. We ran out of money toward the end of each month, despite our cheap rent-controlled apartment and my cut-rate analysis, keyed to the little we could afford. The project worked out of ground-floor offices on Morningside Drive facing the very park that had ignited the uprising. It was directed by Frank Grad, a canny, portly law professor with a charming German accent and a perpetually amused, gracious manner. A close friend of Mike Sovern's, he had a fund of stories for every occasion. He had arrived as a teenager escaping the Nazis and now specialized in drafting legislative language, which presumably would help us draw up new protocols for governing the university. I helped organize a core of eager, energetic graduate students who studied Columbia's far-flung operations, including its investments and real estate policies, and their impact upon the surrounding community. One of them was Paul Starr, later a distinguished Princeton sociologist. Our mission took me back to my days of investigative reporting and editorial writing for the *Spectator*.

Some of the material we uncovered, especially about the real estate

operations—run by a Robert Moses–like figure from an office downtown—
was dynamite, but it went nowhere. You might have said that the fix was
in. Eventually I realized that the only purpose of our study was to create a
new University Senate, since Columbia had no functioning legislative body
outside the faculty of each school. Every problem we laid out was set aside,
supposedly to be dealt with by the University Senate, and a few of them
actually were. But the overall result, after Kirk and Truman resigned, was
to shift authority to a new, more nimble group of administrators, who soon
became schooled in counterinsurgency, especially through injunctions and
other court orders, but also in tempered liberal solutions to radical problems. The path to reforming the university was strewn with serious obstacles: the trustees were deeply conservative, and many alumni, including
major contributors, were up in arms about the student takeover. There was
some strong law-and-order sentiment within the faculty, especially in the
professional schools. Career-minded professors resented seeing their work
disrupted by callow undergraduates spouting radical slogans. The slow
pace of change would do little to encourage students to work within the
system.

Still, the uprising marked a turning point in the life of the university
and to some extent in my own life as well. Running the gamut from idealistic protest and acute polarization to violence, futility, and conservative
backlash, it was a compressed version of the decade as a whole. I had always
been intrigued by politics but had never seen the university as a political
laboratory, just what it had now become. Though essentially peaceful, the
uprising was at once disruptive and hugely stimulating. Had I been older,
more set in my ways, I too might have found it hard to get down. A scene
of detached intellectual activity, a zone of reflection, had turned into a bat-
tlefield yet also became an unforeseen learning experience for students and
faculty alike. Cut loose from the university as I had known it, watching it
implode, I was irresistibly drawn in. The conflicts of the decade had hit
home, and I would need to find some way to fathom their meaning.

Twelve

MOVING ON

DURING THE SUMMER after the uprising, as I was working quixotically on mending the structure of the university, a group of SDS activists moved in together—on Fraternity Row, of all places—and set up a commune bent on political self-education. A few of them had been in my classes and I knew them well enough. As individuals I found them serious, bright, and open to argument. En masse, though, they could turn into shouting choruses, their faces contorted by rage. In such groups, sometimes even in private, they grew militant and closed-minded. Their language could harden into name-calling, the kind that makes thinking superfluous. The police became "pigs," integrationists were "Uncle Toms," while imperialism and racism became the catchwords of the moment. With such rhetoric they were no longer talking to us, merely talking *at* us.

As the summer ended and the armies of the Warsaw Pact nations converged on Czechoslovakia to abort the Czech Spring, these kids took off for the Democratic National Convention in Chicago, taking part in pitched street battles between protesters and Mayor Daley's police. This bloody crackdown, played out upon a national stage, proved much worse than the Columbia bust. Along with the preordained results of the convention itself, it helped sink the fortunes of the Democratic candidate, Hubert Humphrey, the onetime liberal firebrand whom Johnson had done all he could to emasculate. The bitter uproar in Chicago became a prologue to the most violent

phase of the decade, the crazy years that saw the frustration and disintegra-
tion of the New Left. As handfuls of radicals turned toward smashing store
windows, making bombs, and even robbing banks, I lost all sympathy with
them, though I could begin to understand what drove them to it. Meanwhile, the war went on, along with the war at home.

With the beginning of classes in the fall of 1968 these existential rebels,
who had learned strategy on the wing, emerged as a would-be revolutionary vanguard armed with Maoist slogans and Leninist ideas. Brandishing
Mao's little red book as their new bible, they soon were contemptuous of
the students they had briefly radicalized. Their success in shutting down
the university and attracting national coverage had given them a heady
sense of power. Soon they would break off into the Weatherman faction,
turning their backs on the nonviolent methods that SDS and the civil rights
movement had once espoused. "The war in Vietnam drove us crazy," said
Mark Rudd, the leader of Columbia's SDS chapter, twenty years later.

The mass of students, lacking their total commitment, were falling
back into normal undergraduate lives; I settled back into teaching. The
presidential campaign seemed as chaotic as the trouble in the streets,
with Humphrey wounded by his loyalty to Johnson, Nixon promoting a
"secret plan"—which he refused to divulge—to end the war in Vietnam,
and fringe candidates like the comedian Dick Gregory and Black Panther
Eldridge Cleaver attracting the hard Left and George Wallace, on the
southern flank, gaining unexpected support from blue-collar Democrats.
As far back as the Democratic convention of 1948 when he was the dynamic
young mayor of Minneapolis, Humphrey had been the standard-bearer for
liberal policies, especially on civil rights. He was one of the founders of
Americans for Democratic Action, which had combined an unapologetic
liberalism with a principled anticommunism throughout the 1950s. But the
unstinting support for the war that Johnson demanded had left him badly
tarnished. It was not until the end of September, when he made a speech
offering a halt in the bombing of North Vietnam, that Humphrey's fortunes
began to improve, though not quite enough to overtake Nixon's early lead.
At the last moment L and I decided to vote for him, holding our noses and
gagging as we cast a ballot for the lesser evil.

If the political situation was dispiriting and the university seemed in shell shock, my teaching situation could not have been more satisfying. After the chaos and grand hopes of the spring we returned to classes keyed up, expectant, as if the millennium were just around the corner. In the Humanities course I was again immersed in the Greek classics, discussing warfare in the *Iliad* as if it were unfolding outside our door and reading Thucydides's account of Athens's disastrous Sicilian expedition as a commentary on our own arrogant overreach in Vietnam. I was also teaching Blake for the second go-round, minus the thrilling edge of discovery but still stunned by his lonely genius as a poet, a visual artist, and an original mind. In the light of our local Armageddon, the turbulence of London and Paris in the 1790s seemed all the more contemporary with New York in the 1960s. I was particularly struck by the parallels with Freud in Blake's treatment of sexuality—not Freud the stoic who gauged the renunciations that were the price of culture but Freud the liberator, the scourge of repression. This was sixties Freud, as revisited by Norman O. Brown in books like *Life against Death* and *Love's Body*. The young Blake's own version of this was memorable: "Those who restrain desire, do so because theirs is weak enough to be restrained; and the restrainer or reason usurps its place & governs the unwilling. And being restrained it by degrees becomes passive, till it is only the shadow of desire." But Blake's later disappointment with revolutionary politics also resonated for us, for like him we were seeing utopian hopes sour into frustration and violence.

The highlight of my week was English 65, the course on the Romantic era that had meant much to me as an undergraduate, exposing me to the literature that would attract and uplift me throughout the decade. Trilling had taught the course for years before moving on to tackle the modern writers, and Steven Marcus, a superb and committed teacher, had followed in his wake. It was a vote of confidence to be tapped to teach it but there was a small condition. As Quentin Anderson had first put it to me, in the preceding term they would need a warm body to teach the literature of the eighteenth century. This included mammoth novels I had not yet read, like Fielding's *Tom Jones* and Richardson's *Clarissa*, which proved amazing, each in its own way, but also the genteel, neoclassical poetry that had *least* attracted me, just as it had been spurned by the Romantic poets I loved. Until then I saw Pope's poetry as a confection of upper-class snobbery and sterile formal precision. His perfectly sculpted iambic couplets had been mocked by Keats in an early poem: "They sway'd about upon a rocking horse, / And thought it Pegasus." This raised the hackles of Lord Byron, the only Romantic poet who thought Pope worth the candle. To Keats these social (and sociable) poets were guilty of low ambition, a falling away from the epic and tragic themes of Spenser, Shakespeare, and Milton, those lions of the imagination. But as I prepared the course, what I found instead was exquisite verse that varied musically from line to line, couplet to couplet, supporting strong social satire crafted with a fine moral passion, to say nothing of the cool urbanity that Byron himself emulated. Pope's epigrammatic writing was memorable; his early "Essay on Criticism" is full of verse that (as someone once put it) we confidently attribute to Shakespeare, aphoristic lines like "to err is human; to forgive, divine." Though I never took these (classical) poets to my (romantic) heart, I came to feel enormous respect for what they had achieved. It was peculiar to be teaching works of such civilized wit at a time of chaotic political instability, even revolution, but it strengthened my grasp of the possibilities of English verse.

Now in the fall, teaching the Romantic poets and their contemporaries, including Jane Austen and Walter Scott, alongside the personal essays of William Hazlitt and Charles Lamb, was like a homecoming. But reading literature simply for pleasure and expounding it for students are radically different experiences. Having spent years with these poets, still I wondered whether I could fully express what gave them such significance for me. Wordsworth's Immortality ode, evoking his wild Edenic childhood and receding past, poignant in his fear of declining powers, had always moved me deeply, often to tears. I had read it aloud to L when I was courting her, as if to offer coded insight into who I really was, my emotional landscape. But had I ever unpacked exactly what held it together, something I needed to do to teach it meaningfully? "We murder to dissect," Wordsworth himself had written, striking at the reasoning heart of our efforts to explain what we read and how it touches us. His friend Coleridge had observed that "poetry gives most pleasure when only generally and not perfectly understood," foreshadowing the peculiar power of devilishly elusive modern works like Eliot's *Waste Land*. I soon learned that many Romantic poems, so limpid on the surface, are far harder to understand than we first think. Once I cracked the nut of Wordsworth's ode some of its shimmering mystery was forever lost to me—but (I hoped) more available to my students, whose fresh, open minds readily astonished me. Approaching the poem analytically felt like a loss of innocence, a tumble into reflection that was yet another step in coming of age.

I hoped to turn my thesis on Keats into a book but all that year I went nowhere near it. Perhaps because of living in New York rather than a university town, I was drawn instead to literary journalism. I wanted to reach not just a network of like-minded scholars but the kinds of ordinary intelligent readers I encountered each day in the city. Years earlier at a graduate student conference I had met Neal Kozodoy, who was now an assistant editor of *Commentary*, the magazine I'd been reading avidly since Norman Podhoretz became its editor in 1960. Whereas *Partisan Review* appeared to address readers who were already in the know, *Commentary* put a premium on clarity, accessibility, as if on a mission to educate, to raise the tone of the conversation. I liked its current thoughtful version of left politics, its intelligent but not flippant cultural coverage, and critical handling of Jewish issues. It welcomed controversy, thrived on it, often soliciting letters attacking its own articles. Other Jewish journals, by comparison, read like synagogue newsletters, too boosterish or parochial, terrified of offending anyone. Instead of a Jewish book, Neal asked me to review a posthumous collection by R. P. Blackmur, whose brilliant early essays had helped a whole generation to understand modern poetry. His later criticism had taken on a wider field, especially the European novel, and it had also grown more personal and unpredictable. This gave me a chance to talk about what had happened to criticism since the high noon of close reading. The sixties had happened, everything had opened up, though I did not quite understand it yet.

In the spring of '69 I did three reviews in quick succession for Richard Gilman, the literary editor of the *New Republic*, including the only strongly negative review of Nabokov's overblown novel *Ada*, a book that had been rapturously received as an ambitious masterpiece. I loved the wildly original *Lolita*, his émigré novel, *Pnin*, and his album of autobiographical essays, *Speak, Memory*. In those books his cherished idiosyncrasies made their peace with realistic storytelling, but the success of *Lolita* enabled him to go for broke in *Ada*. The results seemed monstrously self-indulgent. Everything about it felt bloated and fantastic. Eventually most critics would find the book unreadable. That came a few years later; in 1969 they were awed by the author's artistic ambitions, to say nothing of the lofty contempt he radiated in interviews and essays.

I loved serious reviewing, the kind of writing that opened up a large subject, transfigured a writer long in the public eye, punctured an inflated reputation, or brought news of a bold, fresh talent. I had a mind to reach a wider audience, beyond the quarterlies, outside academe, and I was soon hooked on the instant gratification of seeing my name in print. The wheels of professional journals turned too slowly, glacially. I yearned to be part of an ongoing cultural conversation—the issues, the writers, the perfor-mances that were on everyone's tongue right now, not simply in 1798 or 1819. Though I cherished teaching the great writers of the past, especially the Romantic poets who had become my "field," I had no thought of becom-ing any kind of narrow specialist. Still, my love for the Romantic poets gave me some region of genuine mastery, not simply amateur curiosity, and I enjoyed keeping up with the literature in the field. But reviewing allowed me the kind of binocular vision I had admired in Trilling and other New York intellectuals, trained at once on the past and the present, the living past as seen through a contemporary lens.

Like a perfect storm, the political agitation of the sixties unfolded alongside many cultural tremors, shifts in the arts and in people's ordinary lives, but I couldn't yet see how they fit together. There was an altogether different moral terrain that matched the new political landscape. I'd gotten one cue from reading Pynchon and Heller two years earlier; other indica-tions from novels like Roth's *Portnoy's Complaint* and Updike's *Couples*, which had just broken major sexual barriers; still other signs from theat-rical experiments off-off-Broadway, such as Barbara Garson's send-up of LBJ, *MacBird*, mingling Shakespeare with political satire; and the antiwar plays produced by Robert Brustein at the Yale Rep. Irreverence and provo-cation were everywhere, a sense of breakthrough, an impulse to shock and awaken. In the midst of this tumult the radical anarchist troupe the Living Theatre returned from years of exile in Europe and seized the moment. As an undergraduate I'd grown up on Living Theatre productions like *The Connection*, *The Brig*, and *Tonight We Improvise*. They had broken down not only the fourth wall but the very idea of what constituted a play—the range of its subjects, the way of developing an action—but especially the line between the actors and the audience. In this downtown scene the hip, try-anything impulse of the *Evergreen Review*, Grove Press, and the *Village Voice* had been translated onto the stage. In its European exile the company's work had turned even more radical and it returned to the States with four current productions, including reimagined classic tales like *Frankenstein* and *Antigone*, but especially *Paradise Now*, an anarchist missile about personal liberation that was more a "happening" than a play. Along with Richard, who was now working in publishing, and Marshall, who had begun teaching at City College, we secured tickets to three of these productions at the Brooklyn Academy of Music, not yet the avant-garde bastion it later became.

The company had already been touring restive college campuses across the country. Its pièce de résistance, quite literally, was *Paradise Now*, a performance piece that aimed less to pass an evening in the theater than to foment a revolution. Its very title reflected the go-for-broke utopian dreams of the decade. We witnessed barely clad actors sitting or gyrating as they waved their arms in ritual lamentation, keening over the repressions that were said to regiment all our lives. The actors raced up and down the aisles protesting: "You can't live if you don't have money," "I'm not allowed to smoke marijuana," "I'm not allowed to travel without a passport." They sounded like prosaic reductions of Blake's provocative aphorisms. Yet there were built-in contradictions, for what they said and did, though meant to appear spontaneous, was obviously programmed, albeit shapeless. It would be hard to imagine a moment when American culture was less hemmed in by traditional codes of social behavior, when so many constraints were falling by the wayside, beginning with barriers to nudity and sex. As Julian Beck, the company's cofounder, raced by shouting, "I'm not allowed to take my clothes off," my friend Marshall, for whom those years were like a dream come true, stood up and said "Why not?" as he ripped off his shirt. As he puffed out his chest, proclaiming his freedom from bourgeois convention, I saw Richard sink down in his seat as if to say, I do not know this person. L and I were entranced with the whole awkward spectacle of self-exposure, though we had not the least wish to take part in it.

This was well short of a political revolution but it marked a revolution in what ordinary people did in public. Having grown up in a family in which nudity was unthinkable and sex was unmentionable, I took in the theatrical display of bare flesh with a mixture of excitement and embarrassment. Yet there was something raw and altogether absurd about it, a piece of adolescent hijinx, a licensed exhibitionism disguised as a cri de coeur. It seemed uncooked in comparison with real art. L and I didn't join the cast and some of the audience for a love-in onstage, but we were glad we came. It was a daring cultural moment though not much of a play.

For me as an aspiring critic, a whole new literature and its receptive audience was yet another revealing indicator of social change. One moment of truth arrived with the publication of a rich volume of Allen Ginsberg's poems, *Planet News*, collecting much of what he'd been writing throughout the decade. The Beats had been in the vanguard of what was now happening in the sixties, but Ginsberg seemed to have disappeared after the sensation of *Howl* and *Kaddish*. As the notoriety of the Beats gave way to a broader counterculture, he'd spent much of the decade abroad—in India, North Africa, and Western Europe, hanging out with Paul Bowles in Morocco, getting crowned Kral Majales, King of May, in rebellious Communist Czechoslovakia, and so on. I was pleasantly surprised when I heard a reading he gave at Columbia with his old college friend John Hollander. The two of them seemed like contrasting archetypes of the American poet, Hollander best known for his wit, sophistication, and technical bravura, Ginsberg for his prophetic passion, Blakean sublimity, and—unexpectedly—his sly Jewish humor. Hollander had condemned *Howl* when it first appeared. He called it "a dreadful little volume" exhibiting "an utter lack of decorum of any kind." But more recently Hollander's own poetry, in tune with the times, had shifted toward the confessional, including a wonderful poem, "Helicon," that he addressed to Ginsberg himself as he read it that evening. Ginsberg's poems ranged from the comic to the visionary but were rooted in just the Romantic traditions I was studying and teaching, especially the expansive, ecstatic poetry of Blake and Whitman—poets he had taken up at a time when they were neglected or misunderstood. In one flash of revelation, the radical past and the shock of the new came together for me, and I had the shivery feeling I was the only one who could write about it. A bearded, bald, Buddhist Jew, Ginsberg had become a charismatic presence, bringing together every strand of the new culture from drugs and sex to protest politics and outlaw literature, all in shameless self-cele-bration. Reading and hearing his work split open the whole decade for me. I wondered where and when I might get the chance to write about it.

The opportunity would not come till the fall when I'd be off from teaching, a well-earned reward for three consuming years with the core curriculum. My plan was to turn the Keats thesis into a book—without it I'd have little chance of gaining tenure—but I hoped to find time for other writing as well. Once assured of the sabbatical I felt we could take the sum-mer off, having spent the preceding summer on that quixotic mission to make over the university. In the spring we learned unexpectedly that L was pregnant, but soon thereafter—at perhaps six weeks—she miscarried. We felt depressed, disoriented, but it freed us up to plan an ambitious circuit through France that summer, a blowout before we were nailed down by even greater family responsibilities. The trip meant we wouldn't be getting to Rocky Point, so we made plans to go there for the Memorial Day week-end, taking along my aunt Lily, whose house was next door. That was the moment we'd always ushered in summer when I was growing up. I longed for yet another bite of the apple.

As we pulled into the yard something seemed off-kilter about the old house, which sat at the far corner of the lot. The attic window was framed by two narrow slivers of soot. "My God, there's been a fire," I said. In the back-seat Lily looked faint, clutching her chest. "*Vey iz mir.* My heart," she cried out, "my medicine." There had been a huge conflagration, apparently set by kids who had broken in and were playing with matches. The result was much worse than it looked. Seen from the front the house looked intact but that was only a façade; there was nothing behind it except the basement and the cinder-block foundation. No one had been in the surrounding houses, and so it burned to the ground before the volunteer firemen arrived. The house had become a two-dimensional snapshot of itself. A large sliver of the past, a link to the happiest days of my childhood, had gone up in smoke.

When Lily calmed down we decided to stay with her for the weekend, since there was just enough room for us in her place. So we spent some days at the beach, quite as if nothing untoward had taken place. The next day my mischief-loving cousin Avrumi turned up, a rare visitor to those parts. His raspy voice had a raw New York accent, strictly working class, though he had trained in engineering. Orphaned young, he was my dark shadow, only slightly older, and I was shamelessly fond of him since he behaved in ways I couldn't have done. His eyes glimmered with wicked humor but I didn't anticipate his robust laugh and mocking words: "Hello, ex-homeowner!" I suddenly felt a bottomless sense of loss. This was a bit of schadenfreude from someone who had been knocked around, who had never had a real home of his own, the revenge of the outcast, the footloose orphan to whom the gods had dealt a bad hand. Playing the black sheep of the family, he was so transparent that I could never resist forgiving him for anything he said or did. The old bungalow, smaller than a small apartment, had never been very comfortable but I loved it. It would be years before it was rebuilt into a bland and featureless suburban ranch house.

We felt in luck to be headed for France rather than the Long Island shore that summer. France was the ticket because we'd been so happy there five years earlier, where I had proposed to L, but also because friends would be there for the summer. Paul Zweig, returning to his French roots, had bought a rude stone farmhouse in the Dordogne, barely a mile from the Cave of Lascaux. Dick and Judy Klein, good friends from our Yale days, would be sharing a house somewhere in Provence. Marshall, recently married to the volatile Carole, his former student, would also be traveling through France on a delayed honeymoon trip. It looked like a good time to get away, something that could still be done then on a meager budget.

We found the cheapest flight available—a charter to Brussels, not Paris—and leased the cheapest car we could, the modest Renault 4, a hatchback that looked like a shrunken station wagon. The delivery point near the Bois de Boulogne was like a zoo, so disorganized that it took me all day to gain possession of the car and drive it back in blistering summer heat to the Place de la Sorbonne. We were staying again at the Hôtel-Sélect, much disappointed at how it had been gentrified since 1964 but grateful, with a young child, to have a private bath for the first time. Driving in Europe then could be a challenge; the car was tiny, and it was years since I'd driven a stick shift. But we were delighted to be back in the neighborhood I'd first explored in '61 and '64, the very cobblestones now redolent of the pitched battles of the preceding year. The Latin Quarter was teeming with tourists but had not yet become a theme-park version of itself, as it did a few years later, with chic boutiques and the quaint narrow streets turned into pedestrian malls. It was still a mecca of the storefront bookstores, pocket-sized art cinemas, and cheap prix fixe restaurants of my student days. One of my favorites had been the little Crêperie Bretonne on the Rue Monsieur-le-Prince, where I now sat down before an innocuous chicken dinner, the first *treife* meal I had ever knowingly consumed. It was just what L had done near the Sacré-Coeur five years earlier, with Paris itself as a powerful catalyst. For me it was a wrenching moment, fraught with conflict. We had continued to keep a kosher home, as much for our parents as for ourselves. But it had become clear for a while, especially in my analysis, that I clung to my own kosher regimen more out of hardened habit than deeply felt commitment.

My way of being Jewish was too much defined by what was commanded or forbidden, not enough by what I loved—the familiar liturgy, the sacred and secular texts, the self-mocking humor, the warm family bonds and rich communal traditions. I had persisted in keeping kosher, perhaps, out of loyalty to my parents' way of life and idealized memories of my own childhood, though I had already broken with that life in other ways. I must also have cleaved to eating taboos from an underlying fear, a dim sense of physical peril I now dearly wanted to overcome. These warring impulses had found their battleground in my tummy, as the British loved to call it. I would remain true to the Jews in my own fashion—not just in the food I would never eat. Wider horizons, greater freedom at whatever cost, that was what I wanted, that was why we were here. Going abroad, being in Paris, gave me an exit I was ready to take.

After five sentimental days in Paris we got on the road to Burgundy with Marshall and Carole in tow—they too were heading south—and our fidgety three-year-old perched beside them in the backseat. As they jockeyed for space, bickering with him and with each other, it was like having two additional children along. Our destination was less the great vintages of this wine region than the cathedral art of Vézelay and Autun, the Romanesque architecture and the sculpture of Gislebertus and his anonymous contemporaries from the early twelfth century. This was a window into a period of

Western art I knew nothing about. Marshall had audited Meyer Schapiro's Columbia lectures on Romanesque art; the work proved as impressive, even as "modern," as the great man had claimed, beginning with the tympanum of the Autun cathedral and the serpentine and seductive sculpted relief of Eve, the original temptress, the very image of Goethe's *Ewig-Weibliche*. Sinuous and gravely delicate, this piece immediately became one of our touchstones, a breakthrough in subtle and suggestive human representation amid so many stylized medieval images. It was no wonder that the sculptor was one of the few artist-craftsmen of that era who actually signed his work.

We passed through Lyon on the way to Provence, where we planned to stay put for a few weeks, though we'd had no luck in nailing down a house beforehand. Arriving at the *syndicat d'initiative*, the government tourist office in Avignon, we were informed that a place might be available in Gigondas, a wine village, since a prospective tenant had just that day backed out. The owner, Mme Moravec, was told to expect us but it took much longer to get there than we anticipated. Few if any Americans had ever rented there, mostly Belgians. In fact, a Belgian couple had gotten there an hour before we did. Mme Moravec held back in the fading hope we would still show up. "*Je n'aime pas les belges*," she told us, to our good fortune. An air of ineffable sadness hung over her. She had been married to a Czech painter who had died suddenly a year or two earlier, and proudly showed us his studio, where his clothes, brushes, and canvases were laid out untouched, as if he had just stepped out for a walk. There she generously put up our friends for the night before they took off for the Côte d'Azur.

The town itself seemed as bereft as she was. Surrounded by the remnants of an ancient wall, Gigondas was then a depopulated village of stone houses and narrow, irregular pedestrian streets built into the side of a steep hill. It felt like the ruins of a Pueblo village in New Mexico. Atop the hill sat a ruined old church and a tiny plaza, really just a couple of parking spaces, the only point in the village that could be reached by car, by way of a winding peripheral road. Two-thirds of the houses seemed abandoned thanks to a hegira that went back to the nineteenth century, when it had become safe for farmers to live outside walled towns and close to their surrounding vineyards. Our house on a single floor was no larger than a modest apartment and we could hear the scorpions—not fatal ones, we were assured—scratching their way in the dry, baking heat beneath the roof tiles. For this we paid the grand sum of $110 for a stay of three and a half languorous weeks.

We were surprised to have so little problem traveling with a young child. Jeremy wasn't fully toilet trained, unfortunately, and it turned out that French disposable diapers disintegrated on contact with urine, but my mother sent us a CARE package of Pampers, enough to get us through the siege of Stalingrad. Above all, almost as if we were in Italy, children were welcomed in the French provinces as much as they were shunned in most restaurants in Paris, where dogs were well received but not tots. In Gigondas, at last, Jeremy found kids to play with, though they had no common language. By the time we left he was spinning off musical intonations that sounded like French though we recognized only a handful of individual words, *bonjour, merci, bonbon*. A few more weeks and he might have been speaking the language.

Here we passed much of the summer of the first moon landing, the summer of Chappaquiddick, where the last Kennedy brother nearly derailed his political career, and later the summer of the rain- and mud-drenched Woodstock festival, an event that would come to symbolize a whole generation, though not exactly ours. All this seemed to unfold at a great distance. Without radio or television, without even the metropolitan French papers, we got news of home through the local Communist daily, *La Marseillaise*, which regularly denounced American policy while reveling in the brave exploits of America's astronauts. We, on the other hand, were aghast at the thought of planting an American flag on the moon, though moved by Neil Armstrong's first words ("one small step for a man . . ."), which sounded good even in French.

Our landlady's sister was married to a leading local vintner, and they kept inviting us to watch some of the moon landing on TV. Finally we relented and stopped in to see the astronauts splash down on their return to earth. As we entered their home we were taken aback. Our host was so pro-American that he had an American flag pin on each lapel, but the walls of his house told another story: they were covered with Vichy and anti-Gaullist slogans along with a large portrait of Marshal Pétain, a quarter of a century after the end of the war. I was aghast but said nothing to our host.

Did he not realize we were Jewish? Probably we were just garden-variety Americans, an appealing lot as far as he was concerned. As usual I felt more American abroad than I did at home. I wondered what that might mean to a prosperous but provincial Frenchman nostalgic for Vichy, the regime that had collaborated with the Nazis throughout the war and perpetrated outrages of its own. For us the summer in France was a welcome break from the strident conflicts of the late 1960s but I hadn't expected to be transported back to the 1940s.

As avid swimmers and beach bums we had always tried to spend summers near the water; instead we found ourselves traveling from one hot, landlocked Provençal town to another: to Orange for the Roman remains, to the market town of Carpentras, the local capital, to see its small and beautiful synagogue, the oldest in France (though few if any Jews still made use of it), to other dreamy villages baking in the sun of the Midi—Gordes, Roussillon, Cavaillon—until one day I came down with a nasty strep infection that originated with one of Mme Moravec's previous tenants. The first symptom was a draining fatigue that, typically, made me wonder whether I was coming apart. Within a week the infection was cured by a genial young local doctor, who prescribed the right antibiotic but also something then unknown in the States, a helpful probiotic that promised to shield the digestive system with "over a million unkillable microbes" with each dose. And so it did.

Not long after I recovered it was time to move on—to visit the Zweigs in the Dordogne region of southwest France—eager to see as much as we could along the way. We stopped to visit our old Yale friends Dick and Judy Klein, in Saint-Rémy, though I had only the vaguest notion of how to find their house. After searching every road that sounded like theirs, I gave in and asked at the post office where to find "*les Américains*," and they steered us in the general direction. Though we had written ahead, they seemed somewhat nonplussed by our arrival. Could it be that we had invited ourselves, or tactlessly taken up only a general invitation? We had been warm friends at Yale and in 1966 had helped a French professor, Jacques Ehrmann, organize an important conference on critical theory, where some of the movers and shakers like Paul de Man and J. Hillis Miller met for the first time.

I'd always enjoyed Dick's pugnacious intellectuality, but after three years our paths were parting and we were no longer close. Teaching French at Cornell, Dick bought heavily into deconstruction as Jacques Derrida was publishing his early works. I was just as stubbornly resisting this turn of French theory, finding it sterile and abstract, cut off from the reading experience, from literature, and from life itself. I had gravitated instead toward more public forms of criticism—toward literary journalism and cultural commentary—and came to dislike the focus on methodology, the skepticism about our ability, in language, to say anything about anything. I hoped to stay in touch with fundamental human issues in ways that might speak to the concerns of the general reader, if such a creature still existed. Our visit to the Kleins was amicable but strained; the old camaraderie was gone. After a splendid dinner we stayed overnight and went with them the next morning to see Les Baux, a ruined ancient town of black and gray stone nested atop a mountain of bauxite, a mineral first discovered there. The hilltop site was dramatic, unearthly, like a remnant of prehistory. Les Baux was also known for one of France's most celebrated restaurants, Baumanière, but on our mean budget we couldn't afford to eat there.

Our next stop was the spectacular Gorges du Tarn, a long, irregular gorge of rocky cliffs through which the river Tarn wound its way. To reach it we drove across the Cévennes Mountains, an interminable plateau of stone and shale that felt like a lunar landscape, chalky and gray, one of the emptiest, most eerie settings I had ever passed through. It made us feel we'd never been farther from the known world. After our long drive we didn't reach the Gorges du Tarn till late in the day. Our first view of the cliffs and the river was as breathtaking as Michelin's infallible green guide had promised, with rocks jutting out at every angle, offering constantly shifting views of the river as it coursed along below. But the road itself was another matter, a corniche road chiseled precariously into the side of the cliff, now descending close to the river, now rising to an unspeakable height far above, with little or no protective barrier. At each blind curve or hairpin turn my only sense of security was that we were heading west, in the inside lane, hugging the cliff rather than negotiating the edge.

The Michelin writer informed us that there were points in the gorge that could not be properly seen from the road, hence "*la déscente en barque s'impose*." This untranslatable phrase lodged in my memory, though we never took up the incitement, in part because there was a greater challenge: it was rapidly growing dark. Out of plain fear but also because of the awesome views, I wanted to cover this road in broad daylight; the lives we saved would be our own. We had to find somewhere to stop for the night but there was only one significant town along the way. Its main (or only) inn was completely booked. The proprietors kindly placed us in a private home, where we recuperated from the first part of our fearsome journey. The next morning we traversed the remainder of this sublime but terrifying route in brilliant sunshine.

The rest of the trip was less spectacular. The landscape of the Auvergne region, famous for its folk songs, reminded me of the wooded terrain I knew in upstate New York. But the approach to the Zweigs' farmhouse in the Dordogne was anything but familiar. We drove from main road to side road to dirt road to rutted, overgrown path, at the end of which we were shocked to encounter our friend from the Upper West Side, as if at the end of the world, the distant limits of civilization. Here, unexpectedly, was the nice Jewish boy from Brooklyn, who now seemed totally French, and here too was his beautiful young wife, Francine, trying to learn the language, feeling slightly imprisoned by her husband's assumed identity and his exotic, enfolding French world. The house too looked exotic: two stone structures as yet virtually unrenovated, one of them still smelling strongly of the animals that had been quartered there. So as not to impose, but also for comfort's sake, we'd insisted on staying at a modest inn in nearby Montignac rather than with them. Though I had grown up with country outhouses, I was not prepared to deal with their chemical toilet, since they had as yet no modern plumbing.

We spent the next days with them immersed in rural France at its most picturesque, visiting nicely preserved historic towns like Sarlat, the home of Montaigne's great friend, the humanist Étienne de La Boétie, and eating especially well, thanks to the region's illustrious cuisine, best known for its truffles. I recall one exotic meal on the terrace of a rustic inn overlooking the Dordogne River. Its specialty was boar, which I was not prepared to try, though my eating choices had greatly expanded. I ordered quail instead and felt slightly uneasy at being served the whole bird, with its head and beak intact, as if to remind us that the delicate creature had died for my dinner. The French themselves were not a bit sentimental about animals; they preferred to know exactly what they were eating, such as the rabbits displayed in butcher shops, whose freshness could be gauged by the remaining fur on their legs. We couldn't see the main attraction of the region, Lascaux with its prehistoric cave paintings and their celebrated animal images. First discovered in 1940, they had begun to deteriorate after being opened to the public, developing colonies of mold from the moist breath of legions of visitors. Now only a few people, who made their case to the authorities far in advance, could be admitted. But we visited other caves that had no art but intricate formations of stalagmites and stalactites, strangely beautiful structures we knew only from routine school lessons. Though neither art nor craft, they too, like Keats's Grecian urn, seemed born of silence and slow time, not human time.

After the Dordogne we headed back to Paris to return the car, first staying overnight in Bourges to break the journey and see the imposing cathedral. We had made virtually a complete circuit of France, omitting only the Riviera, where we had spent our best time five years before, and the northern regions of Normandy and Brittany, which we kept in mind for some future visit. Arrogant and touchy, sensitive about national pride, the French could be infuriating but at that moment I couldn't have been more in love with the country. I had known Paris well enough; the France of the provinces, *la France profonde*, was completely new to me, and most of the people we met were open and gracious, far easier to take. I could never have *become* French, like Paul—I was Jewish to the core, and I lacked his gift for mimicry, a genius for self-invention—but neither could I ever limit myself to the English literary tradition like some of my colleagues. I had realized this when I first read Balzac and Stendhal, Sartre and Camus, when I saw *Rules of the Game, Children of Paradise, Forbidden Games, Breathless*, and *Jules and Jim*. French art, the French sensibility, would always live with me, no matter which way my interests turned. But I was also growing more directly involved with American culture, something I had scorned or neglected in college.

I had a long-delayed job to complete when we returned to the States. I hadn't touched the thesis in more than two years of furiously intense teaching. The only thing that would set me moving was a publisher's encouragement. My friend Jerry McGann had just brought out his book

on Byron with the University of Chicago Press, and he recommended me
to his editor, Allen Fitchen, a reserved but quietly serious man, whom I
liked immediately. To my surprise he offered to take a look at the thesis itself, even before I undertook any revision. No one had done that;
I hadn't even reread it myself. In an unguarded moment Trilling, my
reluctant critical model, had expressed an interest in reading it—Keats
was perhaps his favorite poet—but year in and year out it sat untouched
on the corner of his uncluttered desk in Hamilton Hall, a nagging barrier between us. Each time our paths crossed he apologized so profusely
that it crowded out every other subject of conversation. Time and again I
offered to unburden him and take it back but he adamantly refused. In an
unguarded moment of my own I'd mentioned that one of my Yale readers
described the style as Trillingesque. Instead of stimulating his curiosity,
as I must have hoped, this helped make it impossible for him to read.
Ambivalence, especially about his own place in the scheme of things, was
part of the grain of the wood, as though he could not join any club that
would have him for a member. "There's nothing I want to read more," he
would say, with immovable resolve, "especially if I'm in it." He was not
one to encourage disciples or to license any particular way of reading. It
was as if he feared being implicated in any reflection—or distortion—of
his own influence.

Luckily Allen Fitchen felt no qualms about reading it, nor did the stal-
wart McGann, to whom he sent the thesis for a preliminary report, seeking
suggestions for revision. With this in hand he staked a tentative claim on
the book and I took heart, reading everything written about Keats in the
last few years, including another major biography, by Robert Gittings, the
last of three that appeared in that decade. Nothing new, I thought, could
be said about his life, but perhaps I had something to say about the shape of
his inner life, the biography of his mind during his brief but astonishingly
rich creative years. At the same time I asked Neal Kozodoy at *Commentary*
if I could write a piece about Allen Ginsberg, who seemed like an island of
calm in a nation shaken with tumultuous conflicts turning more violent by
the week. I hoped to bring together the literary and political strands of the
decade, since they seemed to converge both in his work and in his ubiquitous public presence. A canny editor with a nose for the zeitgeist, Neal took

this up, though the magazine, and especially its chief editor, Podhoretz, had clearly begun to sour on much of what was taking place all around us.

Ginsberg was a perfect icon for this cultural revolution, though I tried to show that his roots went back into the distant past, to Blake, who had appeared to him in a vision, and to Whitman, whose long, ecstatic lines and prophetic voice had strongly influenced him. Ginsberg's poetry broke sharply with the academic modernism and hidebound moral constrictions of the postwar years; it embodied many of the radical shifts we had seen in the course of the decade. This was the most ambitious piece I had yet written. It touched on all the serious reading I'd done since I finished my thesis, ranging from cultural polemics by Irving Howe, Leslie Fiedler, and Susan Sontag and unconventional fiction by Kurt Vonnegut, Joseph Heller, Thomas Pynchon, and Donald Barthelme to the work of newer poets like Robert Bly, James Wright, and Galway Kinnell whom I'd first encountered through Paul Zweig. Their poems, like Ginsberg's, had moved away from the obscure, tightly formal poetry of the preceding decade, including their own, written under the sign of Eliot and Yeats.

In this shifting cultural terrain these poets helped teach me a new language. As the novelists had abjured realism for comic-apocalyptic writing, laced with history, infused with paranoia, the poets had turned away from the kind of postwar modernism that relied heavily on irony and densely packed literary texture. Under the pressure of strong emotions, the poets now looked more to direct statement than to oblique allusion. Their free verse, closer to cadenced prose, looked subjective and autobiographical but also often surreal, the better to reflect the pressure of the times and their own anger. They had also mobilized against the war, though nothing could have been more alien to post-Eliotic modern poets than such anguished protest poetry. I experienced their work as I took in much of the decade— as a way of opening things up but also a conversion, a change of heart as well as style. A momentous new culture had altered the whole landscape.

It was naive of me to think that *Commentary*, moving politically in the opposite direction, would publish such a sympathetic piece, but it did. Neal made some halfhearted attempts to rein me in. When I resisted he let me have my way. "You're trying to save our soul," he said with a wicked laugh, as if acknowledging that at least one of us was on the road to damnation. I didn't know then that Podhoretz was on leave—trying to write a book on the sixties, no less—or that he'd known Ginsberg for a long time and had clashed with him as early as their undergraduate years at Columbia, where Ginsberg had edited the literary magazine. After failing to complete the book, perhaps because his feelings about the subject were shifting to outright hostility, Podhoretz returned to the magazine to launch a culture war against everything the decade represented, setting *Commentary* on a path, if not to damnation, then at least to neoconservatism. Attack, attack, attack became its watchword; the Left was the enemy, the sixties the root of all our social evils. This scorched-earth campaign made my essay one of the last liberal pieces the magazine would publish.

Meanwhile, a young editor at Basic Books, Erwin Glikes, had a similar idea for a book about the revolutionary twists and turns of the decade. He had been an assistant dean at Columbia during the uprising and had been traumatized by it. He soon left academe for publishing. I had known him slightly at Columbia, where he imbibed the reverence for art and ideas that gave the school its identity. Owlish, bespectacled, already balding, Erwin loved the life of the mind with a naive and inspiring passion but, like Neal or any other good editor, he was sensitive to changes in the cultural weather. When he saw the *Commentary* piece he took me to lunch and suggested there was a book in it, an account of the whole range of the culture of the 1960s beginning with Ginsberg and the Beats. With Keats and tenure filling my plate, I promised to think about it.

Though many of us thought the student protests had stood for Columbia's finest hour, a spasm of moral revulsion in a terrible time, the university was no doubt grievously wounded by it. The occupation of campus buildings had been entirely peaceful until the police were called, but it was portrayed in the media as an eruption of anarchy and riot, turning the university into a playground for pampered children of the middle class. For those of us teaching these students the scene was highly instructive— it gave them a political education, taught them to exercise their social conscience—but the administration was in shambles and the alumni, in alarm or disgust, had stopped giving money. A financial crisis followed hard on the heels of the political crisis.

That fall I learned that half a dozen of my junior colleagues were not being put up by the college English faculty for tenure. This included both Pauls, my officemates, who had already published superb first books. Overcome with anger and indignation, I went storming into the office of the affable George Stade, who had taken over from Quentin Anderson, to protest on behalf of these friends. I told him the department was losing its best and brightest, people who had already done exceptional work. Resources were tight, he insisted, and someone had to go to make room for people like me, an ambiguous bit of reassurance I found it difficult to accept. The funnel was narrowing to a pinhole. Did I really want tenure at the expense of all my friends? Or would my head too be on the block? Had our high-minded community of scholars become a Hobbesian war of each against all? George was the tall, rangy, athlete-scholar of the department. He played touch football Saturday mornings with George Plimpton. He was a gentleman, I liked and trusted him, but wondered whether I was simply being disarmed.

The only solution was to pursue my own projects and let the chips fall as they would. Revisiting the Keats book soon turned from an onerous chore to an unalloyed delight, just as it felt when I'd first started out. Since I had tried to steer clear of academic jargon, the writing itself called for little revision, though I wanted it to reflect what I'd learned as a journalist addressing a wider audience. It was not Keats for the millions, no critical writing could pull that off, but neither was it solely directed at the professional knot of literary scholars.

In the spring I got an unexpected break. Richard Locke had left publishing to become an editor at the *Times Book Review*, and he was able to sell me to his boss, Francis Brown, on the strength of my *Commentary* piece and the reviews for the *New Republic*. The juicy assignment was to review *City Life*, a sui generis collection of stories by Barthelme, a fixture at *The New Yorker* for his witty, deadpan, collage-like fictions. To these he added mysterious illustrations, a mix and match I found not merely experimental but plaintively moving. I tried to sort out the fresh and the genuine from the merely novel. I located his work, like Ginsberg's, at the center of a larger cultural swerve, a metafictional turn in the short story going back to Jorge Luis Borges and reflected in a whole new wave of late-sixties writing. Writers like Barthelme, Robert Coover, and John Barth were taking apart the premises of fiction just as our nation was reexamining its own mores and fundamental values. These shifting patterns struck you no matter where you turned. The changes in American life could be understood through literature, through advertising, through fashion, through movies, though each of them would tell a slightly different tale. As I realized this I discovered what amounted to a mission, a method. I was no historian, but the gyrations of the preceding decade were impossible to resist. I felt I could read the cultural signs—the books, the plays, the music—for their social meaning but also for the sheer pleasure they gave me wherever they managed to come off. Their inventive novelty was a tonic to the spirit.

This work of mine coincided with turning thirty, a fraught milestone in those years, when many of us half-seriously believed that you couldn't trust anyone over that enfeebling age. Did that mean we could no longer trust ourselves? L had turned thirty in December 1969. Feeling royally depressed, she initially refused to get out of bed at all. I somehow managed to get her dressed and out for a celebratory dinner that evening. I myself passed that marker seven weeks later and, revealingly, have no recollection of it. After last spring's miscarriage we were expecting a baby again. L's prudish, sarcastic mother, always ready with disapproval, was horrified when we told her. It was our third pregnancy in four years. "That's disgusting," she said. "You're just like rabbits." Her barbs always came when least expected. She had been at best a dutiful mother herself, but she recoiled from parenting as much as from sex. She told stories of her difficult pregnancy—the fetus in utero had leaned on her kidney—and she rarely resisted the chance to cut her daughter down.

I had the opposite reaction. Being a father brought out the child in me, to say nothing of the warm family feeling that enclosed me as I was growing up. I loved doing things with my toddler, taking him up to the part-time nursery school near campus, watching him grow and learn, pick up language, make sense of the world. L was drawing and sculpting, and one day he looked at one of her clay female nudes and kept saying "broken, broken." Gradually we realized it was the missing penis that was upsetting him. I jokingly suggested to L that she could easily add a penis to the figure to quiet him down, which she rightly took as an outrageous idea, as if I too thought women were missing something.

I spent a good part of that sabbatical at the sandbox on Riverside Drive at 105th Street, often the only dad surrounded mostly by young mothers and their children. Otherwise I worked largely at home, trying yet again to outrace the coming arrival. In the spring on an impulse or perhaps out of sheer laziness I stopped shaving, mildly curious about what would come about. I was surprised when a thick, bushy beard insinuated itself onto my cheeks and chin, scarcely imagining that I would keep it for many years to come. My hair was already down on my shoulders, for this was a hirsute moment in American culture and it pulled me along. I was no hippie but I began to look like one, at once more gruffly masculine and more androgynous. Whenever I saw my mother she would urge me wanly to cut my hair and show my face, the boyish face she knew when I was growing up, and I would laugh it off. It was no longer the face I wanted to present to the world.

In the heated atmosphere of 1970, others besides L's censorious mother felt free to comment on her pregnancy. Feminism was coming in, and motherhood was seen by some as a biological trap that would keep women from realizing their potential. L herself found inspiration in the women's movement and joined a consciousness-raising group, but at one conference she became the butt of critical comments. "What have you done to your body?" a woman stupidly asked her, as if she were doing something unnatural or, worse still, consorting with the enemy. As an only child, stifled by overbearing parents who were appalled by her tomboy ways and high spirits, L was determined not to inflict that exposed condition on our son. Once again she never felt healthier, and I was enchanted by her blossoming sense of well-being. In mid-May, halfway through her eighth month, she asked her doctor whether she should be worried about delivering prematurely again. He reassured her that it was not at all likely but the next day she was in the hospital, giving birth, while I was a few blocks away dropping Jeremy off at nursery school. The baby was a girl, Rachel, weighing slightly under five pounds, looking thin and wizened but healthy. This time, however, thanks to my leave, I'd managed to finish the book. We could spend the next few months focused on family and on a baby who had haphazardly arrived too soon.

At first Rachel failed to gain weight, and our cautious New York doctor refused to release her from the hospital. Taking full responsibility, we signed a release and soon after we took her home she began to thrive. By the end of the summer I was able to go off to my first international conference, a largely Leavisite gathering in the Dutch seaside resort where Thomas Mann had written much of *The Magic Mountain*. Unwisely, L took the children to stay with her parents in New Haven. This interlude was a bolt of recognition for me, one of the few younger critics invited, but an unhappy experience for her. Making her feel unwelcome, as if she had truly landed on their doorstep, her folks merely tolerated her presence but, typically, refused to help with the kids in any way.

Returning to school I knew that my endgame at Columbia was not far away. I was teaching with terrific zest: a new course embracing English, French, and German Romantic writers, a freshman seminar on *Hamlet* and the many conflicting ways it had been interpreted, serving as a test case for every critical method imaginable. Earlier in the year Haverford College had come calling again. I'd found the place attractive yet had turned them down four years earlier; knowing the tenure clock, they now inquired once more. So I came down for a visit and gave another talk, this time on Blake, but also told Columbia I had been approached, which led to additional vague reassurances from my department. But in the fall, on Bloom's recommendation, I got a serious feeler from Queens College, a position with special appeal since it would not force us to move out of the city.

Queens, where my sister had gone to school, had by then replaced City College as the academic jewel of the City University. The whole university was just then engaged in a huge social experiment called Open Enrollment, throwing it open to every high school graduate in the city. Every branch was expanding rapidly. I felt an initial shock when I first visited the Queens campus; it looked like the furthest thing from an Ivy League setting. The English department was stationed in "temporary" Quonset huts that went back decades, with an overflow into a windowless science building of painted cinder blocks. The interview, unlike anything that could happen at Columbia, took place in the most proletarian setting imaginable, over sandwiches at a bowling alley a few blocks from the campus. In the background we could hear the balls rumbling down the lanes and the pins flying. But I really liked the people I met, especially the chair, Bob Towers, a courtly, gray-haired novelist, with the musical lilt of his Virginia background in his soft voice, and Bob Greenberg, a Victorian scholar who still had some Brooklyn in *his* voice.

I must have bowled a strike in the interview; it went well enough for them to offer me a position at a higher rank and much higher salary than what I was making at Columbia. I had mixed feelings about taking a job less than a mile from where I'd grown up, where my parents still lived and kept their store, the fading business that sometimes seemed to have swallowed up their lives. Had I left home and come a long way just to circle back to where I began? Wasn't Columbia my real home, the place that had first burst open my mind as a voluble but troubled freshman straight out of yeshiva? I should stay, I thought, if they wanted me, but I simply had to know. So I brought in the offer, precipitating an early tenure vote, though I knew how badly my buddies had fared a year earlier.

I passed the first hurdle: the college English faculty voted to put me up for tenure. Before the uprising, before the money ran out, this would have been rubber-stamped by the department as a whole, but now the different wings of the department, so long mismatched, were embattled, each fighting for its own turf. Yet the reckoning could not have come at a more favorable moment. I'd just received the page proofs of my Keats book; it would be out in a few months. It was the second week of January. Two weeks earlier, on Bloom's invitation, I'd spoken alongside John Hollander at the MLA convention. There I gave a well-attended paper on Coleridge's early Conversation Poems, such as "The Eolian Harp" and the magical "Frost at Midnight," showing how these relaxed, self-questioning internal dialogues, built up around the ebb and flow of the speaker's mind, had helped inspire his friend Wordsworth's greatest poems, beginning with "Tintern Abbey." By pure chance, the very week of the meeting I had a long front-page review of Mailer's big book about the moon landing in the *Times Book Review*. My academic and public credentials were in pretty good order but, as it turned out, this carried no weight. For all I know these were held against me, as if I were showing off or, worse still, presuming to represent the department, which was so splintered that I'd never met most of my colleagues in the graduate program.

Late one evening, as the decisive meeting ended, George Stade and

Leo Braudy walked down Broadway to tell me in person that I'd been voted down by a narrow margin. I heard little about the meeting itself except that my colleagues from the college, though outnumbered, had made their case and spoken up for me. Trilling, as usual in such meetings, had proved well-meaning but ineffectual. As George described it, he kept repeating that I'd been one of their "best students," until he was quietly told that this might not be the best way to advance someone who had already been teaching and publishing for years. My thesis on Keats still lay on Trilling's desk, gathering dust, soon to be replaced by the book itself, also unread.

I thought I was prepared for anything, but the fortuitous appearance of the featured *Times* piece must have buoyed my confidence, for the shock was jarring. I could have stayed another year, appealed the decision, urged my students to protest, but the whole business revolted me. Instead I quickly accepted the Queens job, a move I would never regret, but also went into a predictable funk. My parents had doted on me, my teachers had encouraged me. Academically, I had lived a charmed life with little visible effort. I had the second-generation hunger to succeed, actually worked hard but loved what I did; a string of scholarships and fellowships had smoothed my way. I had warm friends, a wonderfully supportive yet independent-minded wife, two beautiful children who gave me joy. For all the bouts of insecurity that had propelled me into analysis, I had never experienced any serious rejection. Without wholly burying those fears, the analysis enabled me to understand where they came from and how I might outflank them. Woven into my daily routine, this lengthening thread of self-examination helped keep me on an even keel. Now, it appeared, my life had unaccountably taken a dark turn. Somehow, I hadn't measured up. The very place where I had come of age, where my life had taken shape, was turning me out. For the first time I glimpsed what others described as depression, an affectless sense of sheer void. Whatever moments of gloom I'd known earlier seemed paltry by comparison. The world around me, the dreams I'd invested in it, appeared altogether pointless, without real meaning.

It took years for that blow to heal completely but only a few days for it to be covered over. A burst of confidence, laced with anger and bravado, welled up from some unknown inner core. I sat down at my desk, a hollow pine door on metal legs, stared at my green Royal portable typewriter and started writing, something. I no longer remember what but I can vividly recall the surge of feeling: I'll show those fuckers what I can do, I'll prove how wrong they were. It was a childish notion, an obscene gesture in the face of a whirlwind, but it was healthy, I suppose, and altogether instinctive and life-giving—like the despairing moment I'd floated up, as if involuntarily, from the depths of the Yale pool. For once I knew my own worth and wouldn't let anyone tell me otherwise.

I had one semester left at Columbia, and instead of hanging back I threw myself into it as if I'd just been hired. Teaching a new course on the Victorian social critics—Carlyle, Mill, Ruskin, Arnold, William Morris—I was making good on the thesis that Yale, perhaps wisely, had not allowed me to write. I spoke up forcefully at every department meeting like someone in for the duration. My favorite elder, Fred Dupee, was retiring, and we organized a festive dinner at Lüchow's, the venerable German restaurant off Union Square that had been one of H. L. Mencken's old haunts. With mixed emotions I could feel myself marking my own departure as well.

Carl Woodring, a fine man and a great Romantic scholar, one of the few people I knew in the graduate ranks, asked me to take part in his doctoral seminar on the nineteenth century, and I joined the discussion with zest each week. For the first time, as if I had just arrived, I served as a reader on several dissertations. Perhaps I was trying to show the department what it was losing, but there was no way I could resist getting deeply enmeshed, caught up in the literature that trumped any institution. Meanwhile, I was getting to know some of the people at Queens. Bob Towers, a man of winning grace and charm, invited us to an A-list party without mentioning that it was in my honor; once there I learned that his notion was to introduce us to everyone he knew. Still licking my wounds, feeling a little sorry for myself, I basked in the glow of being wanted and warmly treated.

Other good things soon came my way. Though it came from a university press and was full of close readings of poems known and unknown, my Keats book got a surprising number of reviews. One remarkable weekend in April it was reviewed twice in the *Times*, on Saturday quite effusively by the daily reviewer, Thomas Lask, on Sunday by the already redoubtable Helen Vendler, who took a slightly more jaundiced view, with an agenda I could not follow. I had been writing shorter pieces for *Partisan Review* for the better part of a decade. Now they asked me for a big essay on the torrent of new black writers of the late sixties. This required some catching up, not only on emerging young writers like Toni Morrison, James Alan McPherson, and Ishmael Reed, who had just published their first books, but also on the work of Richard Wright, Ralph Ellison, and James Baldwin, the embattled godfathers of the new generation. Doing this piece, amounting to a self-education, gave me tremendous satisfaction and it caught a wave of current discussion. Reed sent a funny, blustering letter to *PR* attacking me, and John Leonard, the fresh young editor of the *Times Book Review*, picked up with gusto on the essay in a lively article in the *Times*, broadcasting it to a much wider audience. This elicited a blast from one of his own black contributors, who angrily swore off ever writing for the *Times* again. The unstated premise of these salvos was that only blacks should be writing about black writers. In this separatist climate, some black writers, protective of their own terrain, were putting up "No Trespassing" signs targeted at white critics.

Soon afterward *PR* asked me to join the editorial board as a contributing editor. The magazine was no longer at the red-hot center of the literary world but it still had some very good years left, and I would enjoy them to the fullest. I had grown up on the magazine. Many of its fractious contributors, though dangerous to imitate, had become models of how to think and how to cobble together a critical argument. Their quick-witted, combative style was hard to resist; its visceral bite helped inoculate me against the opaque theoretical jargon that had broken out among too many fashion-conscious academics.

Under William Phillips, who had won the struggle for control, the magazine had shifted left in the 1960s; my first task was to help organize a symposium on cultural conservatism, the angry backlash against all the recent radical currents. Some prime targets of the *PR* symposium turned out to be Saul Bellow, who had just published a venomous but brilliant polemical novel, *Mr. Sammler's Planet*, which seemed to indict blacks, women, and disrespectful students as the new barbarians, and Philip Rahv, Phillips's longtime coeditor, who had started a new journal, *Modern Occasions*, devoted to denouncing everyone whose work he disliked, including me. For him my briefs for writers like Ginsberg and Barthelme made me a "swinger," this curmudgeon's all-purpose word for a creature of cultural fashion. Rahv's nay-saying doomed the magazine to a brief life but I couldn't have been more pleased to be singled out.

Above all, working on the black essay convinced me I really did have a book. I quickly outlined nine chapters beginning with Ginsberg and including the Barthelme essay and the piece on black writing and black nationalism. Richard Locke suggested Georges Borchardt as an agent at a time when few academics *had* agents, and so I met one of the most cultivated men in publishing, wry, witty, and ironic, a French Jew who had somehow survived the German occupation. He quickly came to a happy arrangement with Erwin Glikes, whose first offer had been very modest. It gave me an overflowing agenda for the next few years, and Erwin was so pleased he hired me as a consultant to bring new authors to Basic Books.

Soon all my friends—the whole Columbia diaspora, including the two Pauls—were publishing books with him, very good ones, since he was a brilliant, intuitive editor who asked the right questions and could spot the possibilities even in an inchoate idea. He had uncovered some neglected publishing territory between scholarly and trade books, a niche where my own book would fit in nicely. The book would eventually be called *Gates of Eden*, after one of Dylan's most surreal and hypnotically evocative songs. The title said everything about the utopian strain in the sixties yet remained gnomic, ambiguous, for the subject, anything but clear-cut, evoked complicated feelings. I threw myself into the project, perhaps galvanized by Columbia's rejection but mainly inspired by all I had read and witnessed in the decade just past, since it had enriched my life in untold ways. Most of all, I tried to bring some of my own story into it, stimulated by the sixties itself to set down personal testimony.

At twenty, when the decade began, I was a raw, untested youth, less mature than my years, the product of that strict yeshiva education, though I had rebelled against it, and of sheltering parents, ever cautious in their ways, mistrustful of anything new. Like so many Depression couples they were allergic to risk; only an earthquake could provoke them to change jobs or move from where they lived. I myself lived mostly in my mind, often oblivious to what my body told me unless the news seemed alarming. Soon, though, my world was opening up in directions I could not have foreseen.

I'd come to college with some facility in speaking and writing but few practical goals, expecting someday to earn my keep as a lawyer or journalist. But I fell in love with the books I was reading and discovered a happy bent for talking about them, for trusting my impressions and turning them into argument. I found I loved the play of ideas and was surprised to learn that one could make a career of it—in some university, I thought, and also in the highbrow magazines I had begun reading, perhaps even in literate newspapers that kept a broader public informed.

Coming to Yale, I'd become more aware that the *forms* of art, the sheer mastery of technique and language, the dance of conventions and influences, could be as vital as the ideas it put into play. Studying there with scholars rather than general critics, I had to acknowledge that rigor and precision were as essential as passion. I wanted to teach, to inspire, not in order to clone myself in the young but to show them ways of becoming themselves, wherever that might lead. Inevitably, I came to see myself as an intellectual, not simply an academic; I wanted to become a genuine critic, not merely an expositor of texts. "I'm interested in everything," Alfred Kazin once told me, succinctly defining his calling.

By the end of the decade I felt like another person entirely. My parents, as I've said here, were hardworking but ascetic, devoted to family but suspicious of pleasure, averse to any form of self-indulgence. They mocked people who took vacations, who bitched about their troubles, or spent rather than saved what they earned. Meeting L transformed me, for she had already taken in and roundly rejected just such a message, so common among the immigrant generation. She helped awaken my senses, not just in obvious and intimate ways but in experiences ranging from painting and sculpture to the food on the table. Such were my twenties, the 1960s—the very years the whole culture was opening up.

The liberating changes in my own world were modest—after all, I was married, had children, had a job—but our lives unfolded in tune with the times: occasionally getting high, marching against the war, going to deafening rock concerts at the Fillmore East, the temple of rock on the Lower East Side, and letting my hair grow and grow. Some of my elders at Columbia never forgave my sympathy for the student movement, for it had shaken the university as they knew it. Ten years earlier I'd been writing unsigned editorials for the *Columbia Spectator* and term papers for my teachers. Now I was writing for both the happy few in the quarterlies and the hoi polloi who read the *Times* but still teaching under the gaze of my own teachers, being judged by them, wondering whether I would ever be accepted as a peer.

I would always be grateful to Columbia for all it gave me, an education of the spirit in the best humanist tradition, but that was over now. I would remain emotionally connected to it, for it had led me to the life of the mind, the wealth of Western culture; it had shaped my vocation and helped determine the course of my life. But ultimately I would miss only the students, so eager and open-faced that they reminded me of my hungry younger self. I would always feel a slight rush when I stepped onto the campus, just as I had at the close of my freshman year. But leaving the university would be a way of graduating at last, striking out on my own for almost the first time. Amid mixed emotions I could taste an underlying exhilaration, a heady whiff of maturity. My salad days, my apprentice years, had run their course, and I whispered silent words of thanks to the god of new beginnings.

Acknowledgments

This book as a whole is an acknowledgment of many people who played a major role in my life. Here I mention only a few who contributed to the book itself. I'm deeply grateful to my irrepressible editor, Bob Weil, and his assistant, Will Menaker, a keen editor in his own right, for their encouragement, moral support, and close reading of the manuscript. Their many suggestions made it a better book. Georges Borchardt has been my wise and graciously witty agent for more than forty years. His discriminating response to this book was particularly valuable to me. Richard Locke, a loyal friend for half a century, offered me excellent advice as I was working on the book and later went through several chapters with unerring editorial acumen. Anne Roiphe provided both early encouragement and thoughtful comments on the opening chapter. Sam Cherniak gave a helpful reading to a later chapter, and Arnold Goldberg jogged my memories of our school years. Another old friend, Marshall Berman, confirmed the details of some shared experiences shortly before his untimely death on September 11, 2013. I miss our lifelong conversation, so rich in overlapping history that we could finish each other's sentences. At the CUNY Graduate Center, President Bill Kelly made it possible for me to teach and write under ideal conditions. My sister and brother-in-law, Doris and Sam Feinberg, helped me find some family pictures. Lore Dickstein, to whom this book is dedicated, has been my wonderful companion, prime reader, and best friend. She shared much of the journey and many of the memories recorded here. Her unstinting love and support have made everything possible.

ABOUT THE AUTHOR

Morris Dickstein's books include a cultural history of the 1960s—*Gates of Eden*, just reissued by Liveright—and one of the Depression years, *Dancing in the Dark*. Both were nominated for the National Book Critics Circle Award. His reviews and essays have appeared in the *Times Literary Supplement*, the *New York Times Book Review*, *Bookforum*, the *Threepenny Review*, and other journals. He is Distinguished Professor Emeritus of English and Theatre at the CUNY Graduate Center.